POETICA 17

POEMS OF JULES LAFORGUE

D1557329

Poems of Jules Laforgue

TRANSLATED AND INTRODUCED BY

PETER DALE

ANVIL PRESS POETRY

Revised edition published in 2001
by Anvil Press Poetry Ltd
Neptune House 70 Royal Hill London SE10 8RF
First published in 1986

ISBN 0 85646 322 1

This book is published
with financial assistance from
The Arts Council of England

A catalogue record for this book
is available from the British Library

Designed and set in Monotype Ehrhardt by Anvil
Printed and bound in England
by Cromwell Press, Trowbridge, Wiltshire

ACKNOWLEDGEMENTS

Versions of translations in the section 'Other Poems'
originally appeared in *Narrow Straits* published by
Hippopotamus Press; others first appeared in
In Other Words and *The Swansea Review*

Contents

Introduction

THE LIFE OF JULES LAFORGUE

Jules Laforgue was born in Montevideo in 1860, the second son of a family of eleven.[1] In 1866 the family returned to Tarbes in France, though in 1867 his father went back to Montevideo with his wife and the younger children while Jules and his elder brother Émile – later to make his way as a sculptor and artist – stayed in the care of his father's cousin, Pascal Darré, not one of Laforgue's favourite relatives. In 1869 they both began their studies at the *lycée* in Tarbes where Jules was a more or less disaffected mischief. He won a prize only for religious studies. In 1875 the family resettled in France and in 1876 moved to 66, rue des Moines, Paris. Jules studied at what is now the *lycée* Condorcet, then a fairly easy-going establishment.

In 1877 his mother died of pneumonia, three months after a miscarriage – a shock that seems to underlie much of his work. He gave up all thought of the *baccalauréat*. One of his sisters records that he took it three times but was too shy to have his wits about him in the oral, much to his father's disgust. In 1879 the family moved to 5, rue Berthollet, from where several of the earlier poems are addressed. His father, now ill, returned to Tarbes with the family, leaving Jules and his eldest daughter in the apartment. Jules, it seems, studied at art school with his brother for a time. His first poems began to appear during this year in small Toulouse-based magazines. In 1880 he made his first literary friends at evenings organised by the Hydropaths: Goudeau, Charles Cros, Rollinat, Gustave Kahn – who introduced him to Charles Henry, a polymath – and possibly Paul Bourget, a member of the group. Paul Bourget and Henry were probably instrumental in accelerating Laforgue's loss of faith in Catholicism and Christianity in general. In this year

---

[1] The fact that Laforgue was born abroad may have had some influence towards his less than metropolitan or academic approach to French. In 'Autobiographical Preludes' he jokingly calls himself a good Breton. He was amused when French reader to the court of the Empress Augusta to think of himself correcting the pronunciation of French there. These things may well have affected his approach to rhyme and metric.

Laforgue published a prose piece 'The Fiancés of Christmas' in *La Vie Moderne*.

In 1881 Laforgue's interest in art made rapid developments: he attended a course of Taine's lectures; Charles Ephruzzi, a rich collector (one of the first) of impressionists, took him on as his secretary to help with a book on the topic.[2] Laforgue also wrote a novel *Stéphane Vassiliew*, and prepared a selection of poems called *The Sobs of the Earth*, which he later abandoned, though some pieces were altered for *The Complaints*.

His sister left Paris to tend her father, now seriously ill in Tarbes. Laforgue was leading a fairly frugal bohemian existence while educating himself intensively in libraries. Paul Bourget, with Ephruzzi's help, arranged for him to be offered the post of reader in French to the Empress Augusta. Laforgue accepted it, and the frequent reference to exile enters his work. The job was easy and well paid, and for five years his life follows her itinerary through Germany on her regular progresses. He tried to arrange his annual leave to coincide with the sojourn in Baden which he disliked.

In 1883 he had a tempestuous affair with a woman known only as R from notes written in his agenda. (David Arkell seems to have identified her in his 'informal biography' of Laforgue; see bibliography.) The affair was over by July but seems to have triggered several things in *The Complaints*.

In 1884 Charles Henry undertook to handle the arrangements for publishing *The Complaints* in Paris. Vanier, a small literary publisher of growing reputation, accepted the book at the poet's expense. The proofs arrived in dribs and drabs with many delays by February 1885. No adept at proofreading or printing problems, Laforgue made numerous alterations and missed many slips and printer's dodges. As late as March he sent a fiftieth poem to be included. This year he also composed *The Imitation of Our Lady the Moon* and several of the *Legendary Moralities*. *The Complaints* was finally published about 25th July.

In 1886 Laforgue visited Denmark, a pilgrimage to the Hamlet country. He wrote *Flowers of Good Will*, the title a glance at Baudelaire's *The Flowers of Evil*. He spatchcocked the dialogue of

---

[2] In the introduction to his edition of *Les Complaintes*, Michael Collie sees a more or less conscious attempt on Laforgue's part to produce a literary equivalent of impressionism.

The Fairy Council from it, and later, cannibalised much of it for the free-verse poems that appeared as *Last Poems*. He had begun to learn English seriously in Berlin from a redheaded English girl, Leah Lee. Much in these poems concerns their relationship. He grew tired of the Empress's court, excellent as the salary was, determined to return to Paris and make his way as a writer. He had hoped to arrive with a cushion of two thousand francs. This, however, dwindled to twenty. On 6th September he at last proposed to Miss Lee. They were married in a protestant church, St Barnabas, in South Kensington, on 31st December, and returned to France on 3rd January. T. S. Eliot later married Valerie in the same church.

But for the first three months of 1887, and earlier according to some evidence, Laforgue was troubled with a cough, though he had no patience with his doctor whom he dismissed. Bourget obtained the best then possible, Robin, who realising that Laforgue was dying prescribed opium tablets. Ephruzzi provided for his daily needs; he required a fire even in July. He hoped to move to Algiers for the winter and in the meantime planned a change of air in Versailles. Sadly he died on 20th August of tuberculosis, of which his wife also died in June of the following year.

Fortunately, however, on the 6th December Leah Lee, passing through Paris for Menton, had handed over to Teodor Wyzewa, a good friend to Laforgue, particularly in his illness, a case crammed with Laforgue's papers and manuscripts.

THE WORK AND INFLUENCE OF LAFORGUE

Jules Laforgue – like Villon, or in reverse direction, Poe – is one of those poets whose reputation is higher abroad than it is at home. For one thing, Eliot and Pound used him as part of their foundations for the modern movement in English. Secondly, it is clear that the French found, and still find to some extent, an unFrenchness in his work, which reveals the poet as an anglophile with annoying habits like quoting from *Hamlet*, and like Shakespeare using nouns for verbs and what have you.

These circumstances have somewhat obscured Laforgue's own qualities as a poet; nevertheless they make a useful departure area for those who know him as influence first and as poet second. If one starts with the influence he has had it becomes clearer what other qualities may have been overlooked in his work. Not least some of the detail in his original handling of free verse.

It is still in dispute with some as to who was the actual French originator of *vers libre*. If the award must go to a genuine poet who knew exactly what he was doing rather than a haphazard versifier then Laforgue has to be accepted as the originator of the form – and one who was never followed all his own way. Few have used what might be termed ironic rhyme which occurs medially, finally, and apparently at random, to comment on and distance the text. (Pound, Eliot, Charles Williams use rhyme occasionally in mid-line but never quite in this ironic, subverting way.) It is curious that Eliot and Pound found free verse abroad when Tennyson, Arnold and Whitman had already used it in English.

But as with all poets, Laforgue must be judged for his skill with words and here his own qualities are clear: he was first a master of form from pantoum ('Complaint of the Woman Good and Dead', p. 57) through ballad ('Complaint of the Outraged Husband', p. 151), street-song ('Complaint of Forgetting the Dead', p. 145) to complex intercut stanzas, midget sonnet and free verse. He also delighted in forms that echo and repeat such as in 'Complaint of the Incurable Angel', p. 83. Startling with all sorts of rhyme techniques, he is master of the memorable line.

Along with skill one must acknowledge his zest and daring. He starts as a deliberately atrocious punster on the first page of *The Complaints* and goes on refining his approach throughout. Equally, no Academy will stop him using crazy mongrel rhymes such as *s'enfichent* with *sandwiche* (p. 94). Nor could it inhibit him from inventing verbs such as *feu-d'artificeront* (p. 92). And with metaphor it is the same: he wants Europe scalped from his head; he has pockets full of consolations.

One area in which his originality must be undisputed is that of rhyme and sound. He is the inventor of pararhyme in French, as can be seen from 'Lunes en Détresse' (p. 234) and 'Air de Biniou' (p. 382)[3]. In the first he has a running rhyme in *-in*, separated by a rhyme dependent on different vowels followed by *-che*.

---

[3] Pararhyme can operate on a different principle in French because the muted final *-e* can be used to emphasise its preceding consonant which in turn emphasises the vowel difference before it.

Adieu, petits cœurs benjamins
Choyés comme Jésus en crèche,
Qui vous vantiez d'être orphelins
Pour avoir toute la brioche!

In the second he uses a similar device on all rhymes:

Non, non, ma pauvre cornemuse,
Ta complainte est pas si oiseuse;
Et Tout est bien une méprise,
Et l'on peut la trouver mauvaise . . .

In *Derniers Vers* he moves towards even more remote and subtle rhymes such as (both examples are from 'Dimanches'. p. 400):

Les remue à la *pelle*! . . .

Vivent l'Amour et les feux de *paille*! . . .

or:

Dont les chimériques *cloches*
Du joli joli di*manche* . . .

I find it curious that Pound and Eliot showed so little interest in such developments but perhaps it is lucky for Wilfred Owen that they did not follow Laforgue closely here.

Yet no matter how fine the means of expression a poet worthy of attention must have something to say to us. Laforgue certainly has. Far from being the nihilist pure and simple, he was a man desperate for reform. The chief areas in which he hoped against hope for change were in sexual relationships and in our attitude to the earth.

He was in his finest moments one of the first men to be in favour of the liberation of women. Throughout his work there is a fury and despair that so many women were content to regard themselves as breeding machines – perhaps in both senses – and to see themselves as the reflection of some male. He longed for a relationship of equality which had no necessary connection with generation. In his best moments he deplores that women are made slavish, but is too intelligent to see that many are happy enough to play the system:

O historic slaves!
Oh, their little room!
How they can be brought down soon
Towards other floors,

> Towards the most sophisticated caves,
> Towards the least guardian-angel household chores!
> > ['Petition', p. 407]

One of the issues that underlie some of his wilder poems is that of abortion. He saw that no woman could be sexually liberated in the mores of that period without a fairly relaxed attitude to it as a form of contraception and reputation protection. Most of the reforms he wanted would depend on the development of contraception and the economic liberation of women.

These convictions lead him to a major difference from Pound and Eliot, for he uses a consistent approach to imagery: the sun and its setting represent mindless generation, the inevitable result of evolution, and its inexorable corollary of death. Cathedrals and rosace windows frequently stand in for the sun as do girls' eyes. The moon is used to represent the detached attitude of mind of those who escape the sun's influence; the wind represents the need for love, particularly when thwarted; the sea, especially in its submarine aspects, represents the lapsing back and allowing oneself to be swept along by the movement of the universe.

This brings us to a second part of his theme: that universes evolve just as do species, and death is a mere recycling of the unique to make another. Thus since there can be no afterlife we must live a more fulfilled life on our own little stewpot, the earth, in our own little corner of the heavens. We must console one another.[4] (He is closer to Hardy than to Pound and Eliot in this and several other respects.)

In his own right then, Laforgue is important; perhaps more so today in bearing witness to the historical development of the idea of women's liberation – not to mention the illustrating of how easy it was to slip back into outdated attitudes. Secondly, in his resolute, unwilling acceptance that it is to life on earth that we must look for our only happiness and fulfilment, a timely reminder when all sorts of fringe, revivalist religions are trying to bind the mind again. Let

---

[4] For the stewpot image see the last verse of 'Open Sea' (p. 197) and verse 4 of 'Petty Miseries of August' (p. 325). The reference to 'our corner' occurs in the penultimate verse of 'The Good Apostle' (p. 307). The reference to consoling each other may best be seen in 'Complaint of a Certain Sunday' (p. 65). Laforgue is often close to Hardy in wanting Someone to blame.

Pound have the last word here, the final remark on the poet in his 1918 selection: 'Laforgue is incontrovertible.' (*The Little Review*, February 1918.)

Lastly one reads Laforgue with a sense of tragic loss, as one reads Owen and Keats, for he died young and with much promise unfulfilled. But he needs no pathos from me: in the *Last Poems* he is a master of a Heinian pathos:

> It's so fresh here, so fresh the air;
> Oh, and if at this very time,
> She, too, is strolling by the woods somewhere
> To drown her plight
> In the wedding of the lunar light! . . .
> (She so likes a late stroll!)
> She'll have forgotten her stole;
> She'll take sick, seeing the beauty of the time!
> Oh, I don't want to hear that cough from you!
> Oh! I beg you, take care of yourself, please!
> ['Moon Solo', pp. 419–21]

His influence on Pound and Eliot can be seen in several clear areas, though it would take much more than an introduction to determine how superficial or essential that influence was. First, he had developed some of the finest *vers libre* just prior to the times when Pound and Eliot wished to break the hold of the Miltonic pentameter. Secondly, his dominant mode of expression was ironic. Thirdly, he was a master technician, trying to extend his means of expression to include, through his technique of intercutting, the contemporary idiom, science, the city, and multiple ambivalences of feeling. (A technique now so widespread his originality is obscured.) Fourthly, there was simply much in his material that would have attracted the American pair at this time. He was anti-church – Pound, amusingly, shares his distaste for church bells.[5] He was also against the hard-dying cult of the woman-goddess. His mental furniture included evolution and physiology as Wordsworth's included idealism, daffodils and images of mountains. He was, in sum, a poet of the city.

---

[5] Oddly enough, however, Pound cuts a reference to church bells from his version of 'Pierrots' (*Scène courte mais typique*), p. 214.

This last point made him seem the prophet of the meaningless-ness of modern city life[6] to Pound, Eliot and others but much of his reaction was a response to the old order, the Hapsburg court. He was of Paris parishy, a vibrant developing Paris. He hoped things were on the way to improvement and in poems like 'Simple Death-Pangs', in *Last Poems*, could write, albeit finally with irony, like a revolutionary thwarted idealist.

Eliot first came across Laforgue while still in America. Writing to Robert Nichols in August 1917, he remarked: 'I remember getting hold of Laforgue years ago at Harvard, purely through read-ing Symons, and then sending to Paris for texts.' He goes on to say: 'I do feel more grateful to him than to anyone else, and I do not think that I have come across *any other writer since who has meant so much to me* [my italics] as he did at that particular moment, or that particular year.' (*The Letters of T. S. Eliot*, vol. 1, 1908–1922, ed. Valerie Eliot, Faber.) His French friend Jean Verdenal appears well read in Laforgue, able to quote from his letters.

It is instructive to see how Laforgue's influence actually appears in the work of Eliot and Pound. It is a strange feeling to come back to 'The Love Song of J. Alfred Prufrock' and 'Portrait of a Lady' after a long immersion in Laforgue, as opposed to the other way round which must be more usual for English speakers. Everywhere one sees echoes and influence but nothing can be felt as a straight 'lift'. The effect of the irony is also ultimately very different. But to deal with the simplest part first, the form.

Eliot's form in these poems is closely reminiscent of Laforguian methods and yet it is quite distinctive.[7] Eliot's free verse is always conscious of metre and iambic pentameter as is Laforgue's, a little more daringly, of the hexameter or alexandrine. Both poets like banal chorus and banal rhyme, both use ironic foreshortening and lengthening of lines, both intercut with little narrative explanation:

---

[6] Curiously, the city and much of the irony could have been taken from Baudelaire and Rimbaud. Eliot indeed shows this in 'The Waste Land'. But neither of these seems to have attracted Pound much. He preferred Laforgue's intellectual doubt and free verse to Rimbaud's sensuous certainty and prose poems. (He did admit at one time that there had been no advance in poetic technique since Rimbaud.) Laforgue was also a better, more unknown stick with which to 'épater les bourgeois'.

> Among the windings of the violins
> And the ariettes
> Of cracked cornets
> Inside my brain a dull tom-tom begins
> Absurdly hammering a prelude of its own,
> Capricious monotone
> That is at least one definite 'false note.'
> – Let us take the air, in a tobacco trance,
> Admire the monuments,
> Discuss the late events,
> Correct our watches by the public clocks.
> Then sit for half an hour and drink our bocks.
>
> ['Portrait of a Lady']

The *technique* of this is clearly reminiscent of movements such as:

> – «C'est touchant (pauvre fille)
> Et puis après?
> Oh! regardez, là-bas, cet épilogue sous couleur de couchant!
> Et puis, vrai,
> Remarquez que dès l'automne, l'automne!
> Les casinos,
> Qu'on abandonne
> Remisent leur piano;
> Hier l'orchestre attaqua
> Sa dernière polka,
> Hier, la dernière fanfare
> Sanglotait vers les gares . . .»
>
> ['Légende', p. 422]

The only slight technical difference is Laforgue's use of medial rhyme in the opening line to match the end of line three and others with 'hier / dernière'. One might think Eliot's 'take / late' a match for 'regardez / remarquez' but Laforgue's assonance is more highlighted. Though Eliot used a similar sort of random medial rhyme in his minor poems he never used it to send up the material he

---

[7] Eliot said in 1928 of his early free verse: 'The form in which I began to write, in 1908 or 1909, was directly drawn from the study of Laforgue together with the later Elizabethan drama; and I do not know anyone who started from exactly that point . . .' (Introduction to *Ezra Pound: Selected Poems*).

appeared to be conveying as Laforgue often does. The rhymes and near rhymes indicated next show him using this device:

> Mon Dieu, que l'Idéal
> La dépouillât de ce rôle d'ange!
> Qu'elle adoptât l'Homme comme égal!
> Oh, que ses yeux ne *parl*ent plus d'Idéal,
> Mais *sim*plement d'hum*ains* échanges!
> En frère et *sœur* par le *cœur*,
> Et fiancés *par le* passé,
> Et puis unis *par l'In*fini!
> Oh, *sim*plement d'*in*finis échanges
> À la *fin* de journées
> À quatre bras moissonnées,
> Quand les tambours, quand les trompettes,
> Ils s'en vont sonnant la retraite,
> Et qu'on prend le frais sur le pas des portes,
> En vidant les pots de grès
> À la santé des années mortes
> Qui n'ont pas laissé de regrets,
> Au su de tout le canton
> Que depuis toujours nous habitons,
> **Ton ton, ton** taine, **ton ton**.
>
> ['Pétition', pp. 406–8]

There are too many other sound links to be marked clearly.

It is likely, however, that the direct influence of Laforgue is felt in Eliot's use of the ironic line which seems to be based on suggesting some abstract principle severely limited by the contingent and commonplace:

> I have measured out my life with coffee spoons . . .
>
> And time for all the works and days of hands
> That lift and drop a question on your plate . . .
> And have seen the eternal Footman hold my coat and snicker . . .
>
> ['The Love Song of J. Alfred Prufrock']

Such lines owe a debt to Laforgue's:

> et dont la guimpe
> A bien quelque âme pour doublure . . .
>
> ['Maniaque', p. 268]

> whose chemisette
> Has for the lining quite some soul . . .

or:

> Moi, je suis le Grand Chancelier de l'Analyse . . .
> > [*Derniers Vers* IV, 'Dimanches', p. 400]

> Me, I'm the Lord Chancellor of the Analysis . . .

or:

> J'aurai passé ma vie le long des quais
> À faillir m'embarquer . . .
> > [*Derniers Vers* X, p. 430]

> I shall have passed my life, daylight and dark,
> On platforms failing to embark . . .

or:

> Oh, qu'ils sont pittoresques les trains manqués! . . .
> > [*Derniers Vers* X, p. 430]

> Oh, how picturesque the missed trains look! . . .

It is perhaps in his technique of intercutting subjective and objective, city and nature, pipe-dream and reality, romantic and ironic, poetic diction, jargons, and slang that he had most influence on Eliot and Pound, as late as *The Waste Land* and *The Cantos*. It is easiest to demonstrate the technique at its simplest from one of his early poems in set forms, 'Complainte des pianos qu'on entend dans les quartiers aisés' (pp. 52–4):[8]

> Jolie ou vague? triste ou sage? encore pure?
> Ô jours, tout m'est égal? ou, monde, moi je veux?
> Et si vierge, du moins, de la bonne blessure
> Sachant quels gras couchants ont les plus blancs aveux?

---

[8] Eliot also makes reference to pianos but they are not for him so ubiquitous, nor do they represent as for Laforgue the adolescent girl's unwitting assumption into the generation game:

> I remain self-possessed
> Except when a street piano, mechanical and tired
> Reiterates some worn-out common song . . .
> > ['Portrait of a Lady']

> Mon Dieu, à quoi donc rêvent-elles?
> À des Roland, à des dentelles?
>
> – «Cœurs en prison,
> Lentes saisons!

Later, Laforgue's intercuttings became much more cryptic and less narrative.

These techniques are clearly used by Eliot and Pound in the juxtapostions in *The Waste Land* and layering techniques in *The Cantos*. (And, of course, Laforgue predates its use in film and television. It is now ubiquitous.)

The last influence on Eliot is the most difficult to trace: it is in the area of subject-matter. Two things make it hard to pinpoint. The first is that Eliot does not use a fixed value for his references to sun, moon, the sea and so on, whereas in Laforgue they come to be an emotional shorthand. Secondly, Eliot's use of a persona renders his relationship to these things distant and ambivalent. Laforgue's self-mocking is genuine to a greater degree than Eliot's which is aimed more directly at a persona. An example may make this clearer.

> Last, if she dies, one evening, quiet, in my books,
> Feigning I don't yet trust my eyes, I'll try:
> 'Oh, that! but we'd the Wherewithal. It looks
>   It was straight, then – as a die?'
>   ['Another Complaint of Lord Pierrot', p. 115]

Something of this lies at the back of Eliot's:

> Well! and what if she should die some afternoon,
> Afternoon grey and smoky, evening yellow and rose;
> Should die and leave me sitting pen in hand
> With the smoke coming down above the housetops;
> Doubtful, for a while
> Not knowing what to feel or if I understand
> Or whether wise or foolish, tardy or too soon . . .
>   ['Portrait of a Lady']

Laforgue's irony is crisper, younger, much more destructive; Eliot's is more world-weary, less interested in a response, more moral; in fact, it is his own.

The direct borrowings are nearly always made over into his own sensibility; his borrowings are almost a case of a shared modernistic poetic diction, or 'keepings' as Hopkins usefully called such things. (The most baffling to me is the one left in French in 'Rhapsody on a Windy Night':

> The lamp hummed:
> 'Regard the moon,
> La lune ne garde aucune rancune . . .'

where it seems mainly a trick of memory for a very slight poem of Laforgue's.)

With Eliot then, it is difficult not to agree with Kenner where he quotes from Arthur Symons' *The Symbolist Movement in Literature* this description of Laforgue: 'Strictly correct in manner, top-hatted, soberly cravatted, given to English jackets and clerical overcoats, and in case of necessity an invariable umbrella carried under his arm.' Kenner remarks: 'That is the Possum; Laforgue was first of all a *role*.'[9] Eliot took on the role of Laforgue as Laforgue took on the role of the clown.

In a letter to Mary Hutchinson on possibly 11th July 1919 he included Laforgue as the last item in making a list of what he thought comprised modern culture, remarking: 'Laforgue (really inferior to Corbière at his best).' (*The Letters of T. S. Eliot*, vol. 1, 1908–1922, ed. Valerie Eliot, Faber.) A sentiment I would agree with now. Eliot also quotes from X and 'On a Dead Woman', from *Last Poems*, in his essay 'The Metaphysical Poets' of 1921.

Yet, as more biographical details emerge, it may perhaps be seen that another of Eliot's fascinations with Laforgue was not chiefly poetic but with Laforgue's sexual confusions over women – an area in which Eliot had problems of his own and, perhaps, needed some company.

Laforgue's influence on Pound was twofold and much more difficult to delineate. The first is in the matter of technique, diction and theme, parallel with much already said above; the second mentioned in the later *Cantos*, seems to be an influence on thought and feeling.

Laforgue's cryptic stanzas and clipped expression pervade 'Hugh Selwyn Mauberley' but we might more clearly see what Pound was after in considering a translation he did of a Laforgue

---

[9] See Hugh Kenner, *The Pound Era* (Faber), 134.

poem, 'Pierrots' (*Scène courte mais typique*, p. 214).[10] Impatient as
ever, Pound merely omits the things that do not attract his interest.
First of all he pays scant respect to the form of rhyming triplets,
particularly with their quality; secondly, he omits the last three stanzas
stanzas which put the love relationship in all its confusions. He
omits some of the finest ironic touches:

> Et je vais en plein air sans peur et sans reproche,
> Sans jamais me sourire en un miroir de poche.

> Without reproach or fear I walk abroad in style;
> Nor ever give myself a pocket mirror smile.

Nor is he over-concerned with verbal precision, translating
'querelle' as the rather dated 'affray'. The quiddity of Laforgue did
not then attract him. He ignores completely one of Laforgue's
habitual references to 'mourning purple' as his local colour.
(Curiously, and unlike Eliot, he nearly always cites from Laforgue's
poems in regular stanzas.)

It seems that what interested him was the vigour and thrust of
the irony and movement, the unpoetic and modern reference, more
than the actual subtleties of Laforgue's poem – an interest he
labelled 'good verbalism' or 'logopoeia'.

In later life he treated Laforgue with more respect. In Canto
LXXIV, opening *The Pisan Cantos*, comes a cryptic reference to the
Laforguian tag *Væ Soli* (Death to the Lonely Man). It suggests the
fellow-feeling of the prisoner for the man trapped in his own
personality and philosophy, as was Laforgue. In *Drafts and
Fragments*, Canto CXIV, he has a most oblique reference to one of
the less successful poems in Laforgue's first book *The Complaints*:

> But these had thrones,
> and in my mind were still, uncontending –
> not to possession, in hypostasis
> Some hall of mirrors.

---

[10] Pound's version is in *Poem into Poem* edited by George Steiner (Penguin).
In *Translations of Ezra Pound* edited by Kenner (Faber) a complete version
occurs. The pocket mirror image is restored but the image of violet mourn-
ing is confined to a footnote. Omitted verses are restored but the form
treated cursorily.

> Quelque toile
> 'au Louvre en quelque toile'
> to reign, to dance in a maze
> To live a thousand years in a wink.

This is a reference to 'Complaint of Consolations' (p. 106), originally cited by Pound as early as 1918 in an anthology of French poets in *The Little Review*. The fleeting nature of the reference and the lack of close attention to precise context show that Laforgue's work had lived in Pound's mind for all those troubled years. He acknowledges that debt in Canto CXVI:

> and Laforgue more than they thought in him,
> . . .
> And I have learnt more from Jules
> (Jules Laforgue) since then
> deeps in him . . .

These are cryptic remarks but in 1918 Pound said of Laforgue: 'he is an exquisite poet, a deliverer of nations . . . a father of light'!

These men were and are great witnesses to the quality of Laforgue. Yet whatever they took from him – chiefly his irony and his urge to make it new – they left much behind.

Another poet influenced by Laforgue early on – if only it had been later, too – was Hart Crane. His 'Chaplinesque' has an almost straight lift of Laforgue's line referred to above concerning pockets and consolations – and many other near Laforguianisms. 'Pastorale' also has reminiscences of Laforguian themes and resonances. More directly, he prepared versions of the first three poems of the 'Asides of Pierrots' – as they are called in this version.

A NOTE ON THE TRANSLATION

Laforgue is known for vigorous quirkiness in his French and obviously longed for the licence traditionally accorded to English poets. I have tried to give the flavour of all this, though the English language is less outraged by the liberties that are taken with it. The freshness of his rhyming is difficult to indicate as most of his innovations are known to us through imitation rather than the original. The same is true of his prosody which can never look as innovative in English as it did then to the French with their more circumscribed tradition. His experiments with whole poems in feminine rhymes cannot be done in English with their more noisy counterparts.

Suggestions and flavours, then, as with the form which I have tried to parallel. The long line in French may be reduced in English to a pentameter because the muted final -*e* cannot be recognised by our system; unfortunately in some of Laforgue's short lines the brevity of French colloquialisms has necessitated some expansion at various points.

As for the rapidity of his thoughts and the bewildering changes of speaker and mood, the translator is as much at sea as the reader and the only hope is to read in hope.

A NOTE ON THE SECOND EDITION

I am now embarrassed by the liberties I took in the previous versions of these translations – probably under the combined influence of Pound and of the 'creative translation' poets are supposed to do. While retaining a formal parallel, I have moved this revision towards the more literal wherever it could be done without offence to the spirit in areas such as the play on words and ideas.

A NOTE ON THE FRENCH TEXT

I sometimes think that a jinx has presided over all editions of Laforgue. Certainly three things contribute to the textual difficulties of *Les Complaintes*. The first is that it was printed by a man who knew all the tricks of the trade such as how to make a little type go a long way and to keep the customer sweet by sending the odd signature for proofing while generally delaying because of over-commitment of time and equipment. (Arkell's book is very apposite on these points.) Secondly, Laforgue was most inexperienced when it came to printers and proofs – and a very long way off. Thirdly, he wanted some extraordinary things printed. And, as always, there are real misprints.

Only a rule of thumb based on wide reading of Laforgue could possibly be applied to solve some of these problems created by such variables. I have tried to indicate where my rule of thumb deviates from the more scholarly texts. I have aimed to make no silent corrections.

In the later works the problems are perhaps simpler. Laforgue was a prolific writer and makes the odd slip due to creative pressure; his punctuation is thus not always consistently thought through. Again, I have tried to make no silent changes, but a few, noted, to help the reader. Laforgue was always over-fond of exclamation marks and omission marks.

I have everywhere simplified the punctuation of speech, discarding the speech marks at the opening of successive lines. I have noted the major examples but not all. The guiding principle has been to make the reader's task a little easier without smoothing away the quiddity and exuberance of Laforgue's way with words.

ACKNOWLEDGEMENTS

I should like to thank William Cookson, Peter Jay and David McDuff for invaluable criticism and advice. Martin Sorrell has also made comments useful for this revision. The translation would have been a much more cumbersome task were it not for the devoted work of those listed in the bibliography. My debt to such scholars is incalculable, as probably are the slips of my own inadequacy in their fields. Finally I would like to thank Kit Yee Wong of Anvil Press for her care in proofreading the French text.

PETER DALE

Les Complaintes

The Complaints

Au petit bonheur de la fatalité
MUCH ADO ABOUT NOTHING
Shakespeare

At the whim of fate

À PAUL BOURGET

En deuil d'un Moi-le-Magnifique
Lançant de front les cent pur-sang
De ses vingt ans tout hennissants,
Je vague, à jamais Innocent,
Par les blancs parcs ésotériques
De l'Armide Métaphysique.

Un brave bouddhiste en sa châsse,
Albe, oxydé, sans but, pervers,
Qui, du chalumeau de ses nerfs,
Se souffle gravement des vers,
En astres riches, dont la trace
Ne trouble le Temps ni l'Espace.

C'est tout. À mon temple d'ascète
Votre Nom de Lac est piqué:
Puissent mes feuilleteurs du quai,
En rentrant, se r'intoxiquer
De vos AVEUX, *ô pur poëte!*
C'est la grâce que je m'souhaite.

TO PAUL BOURGET

In a Me-the-Magnificent's mourning suit,
The hundred pure-bred blazed on the brow
Of my twenty years' all hinnying row,
Forever Innocent, I wander now
White esoteric parks en route
To Armida's Metaphysics tute.

Fine Buddhist in his holy place,
Wan, rusty, counter, otiose,
Who, with his neural reed-pipe blows
Gravely to himself some verse which glows
In precious stars of which the trace
Unsettles neither Time nor Space.

That's all. In my ascetic shrine
Your name, a lake's, is spouted out.
May my bookstall browsers in their drought
Get drunk back home upon a bout
Of your VOWS, *pure poet and fine!*
That is the favour I wish were mine.

PRÉLUDES AUTOBIOGRAPHIQUES

Soif d'infini martyre? Extase en théorèmes
Que la création est belle, tout de même!

En voulant mettre un peu d'ordre dans ce tiroir,
Je me suis perdu par mes grands vingt ans, ce soir
De Noël gras.   Ah! dérisoire créature!
Fleuve à reflets, où les deuils d'Unique ne durent
Pas plus que d'autres! L'ai-je rêvé, ce Noël
Où je brûlais de pleurs noirs un mouchoir réel,
Parce que, débordant des chagrins de la Terre
Et des frères Soleils, et ne pouvant me faire
Aux monstruosités sans but et sans témoin
Du cher Tout, et bien las de me meurtrir les poings
Aux steppes du cobalt sourd, ivre-mort de doute,
Je vivotais, altéré de *Nihil* de toutes
Les citernes de mon Amour?
                    Seul, pur, songeur,
Me croyant hypertrophique! comme un plongeur
Aux mouvants bosquets des savanes sous-marines,
J'avais roulé par les livres, bon misogyne.

Cathédrale anonyme! en ce Paris, jardin
Obtus et chic, avec son bourgeois de Jourdain
À rêveurs; ses vitraux fardés, ses vieux dimanches
Dans les quartiers tannés où regardent des branches
Par dessus les murs des pensionnats, et ses
Ciels trop poignants à qui l'Angélus fait: assez!

Paris qui, du plus bon bébé de la Nature,
Instaure un lexicon mal cousu de ratures.

Bon breton né sous les Tropiques, chaque soir
J'allais le long d'un quai bien nommé *mon rêvoir*,
Et buvant les étoiles à même: «ô Mystère!
Quel calme chez les astres! ce train-train sur terre!
Est-il Quelqu'un, vers quand, à travers l'infini,
Clamer l'universel *lamasabaktani*?

AUTOBIOGRAPHICAL PRELUDES

Thirst for infinite martyrdom? Ecstasy in theorems
That the creation's beautiful all the same!

Wishing to bring a little order to this drawer,
I've lost myself amid my years, my great big score,
This lardy Yule.
                A derisory creature, this!
River reflections where Mourning for Uniqueness is
No lengthier than for others. Did I dream it this Yule,
Burning an actual handkerchief with black tears' fuel,
Because, bursting in flood with sorrows of the Earth
And brother Suns, unable to adapt my worth
To the monstrosities, unwitnessed, pointless grists,
Of the dear Whole, too indolent to bruise my fists
Against the deaf steppes of cobalt, dead drunk with doubt,
I soldiered on, made thirsty by the Nil poured out
From all the cisterns of my Love?
                          Alone, pure, and dreaming,
Thinking I'm hypertrophic!, like a diver, in streaming
Thickets of submarine savannahs, aquarist,
I've scuttled through the books, a fine misogynist.

Cathedral of anon! In this Paris, chic and dull
Garden with its bourgeois Jourdain of dreamers, null
And dolled-up window displays, its old Sundays in browned-off
Districts where branches gawp over walls of digs they bound off,
And all its skies, in poignancy well over the top,
To whom the Angelus declares: Enough now. Stop!

Paris that, from being the bonniest baby of Nature's,
Now founds a lexicon tacked together with erasures.

Good Breton, born in the tropics, I would go each night
Along a quayside aptly called *my so-long-dream-site*,
And swig the stars right in! 'What calm amid those stars!
O Mystery! On earth these humdrum jolts and jars!
Is Someone there, for when, across infinity,
To shriek the universal *lamasabachthani*?

Voyons; les cercles du Cercle, en effets et causes,
Dans leurs incessants vortex de métamorphoses,
Sentent pourtant, abstrait, ou, ma foi, quelque part,
Battre un cœur! un cœur simple; ou veiller un Regard!
Oh! qu'il n'y ait personne et que Tout continue!
Alors géhenne à fous, sans raison, sans issue!
Et depuis les Toujours, et vers l'Éternité!
Comment donc quleque chose a-t-il jamais été!
Que Tout se sache seul au moins, pour qu'il se tue!
Draguant les chantiers d'étoiles, qu'un Cri se rue,
Mort! emballant en ses linceuls aux clapotis
Irrévocables, ces sols d'impôts abrutis!
Que l'Espace ait un bon haut-le-cœur et vomisse
Le temps nul, et ce Vin aux geysers de justice!
Lyres des nerfs, filles des Harpes d'Idéal
Qui vibriez, aux soirs d'exil, sans songer à mal,
Redevenez plasma! Ni Témoin, ni spectacle!
Chut, ultime vibration de la Débâcle,
Et que Jamais soit Tout, bien intrinsèquement,
Très hermétiquement, primordialement!»

Ah! Le long des calvaires de la Conscience,
La Passion des mondes studieux t'encense,
Aux Orgues des Résignations, Idéal,
Ô Galathée aux pommiers de l'Éden-Natal!

Martyres, croix de l'Art, formules, fugues douces,
Babels d'or où le vent soigne de bonnes mousses;
Mondes vivotant, vaguement étiquetés
De livres, sous la céleste Éternullité:
Vanité, vanité, vous dis-je! – Oh! moi, j'existe,
Mais où sont, maintenant, les nerfs de ce Psalmiste?
Minuit un quart; quels bords te voient passer, aux nuits
Anonymes, ô Nébuleuse-Mère? Et puis,
Qu'il doit agoniser d'étoiles éprouvées,
À cette heure où Christ naît, sans feu pour leurs couvées,
Mais clamant: ô mon Dieu! tant que, vers leur ciel mort,
Une flèche de cathédrale pointe encor
Des polaires surplis! – Ces Terres se sont tues,
Et la création fonctionne têtue!

Let's see; the Circle's circles, in effect and cause,
By raying metamorphoses down without a pause
Feel abstract enough, however, or, my word, somewhere's
A heart that beats! A simple heart; or Look that cares!
But if there should be no one and the Whole should breeze on!
And thus a fools' gehenna, lacking outcome, reason!
And from the Day-after-Day, and to Eternity!
However has anything ever managed to be!
The Whole should know it is alone and thus should die!
Trailing the building-yards of stars, a Shriek should fly:
Death! wrapping in its shrouds with irrevocable rippling
These soiled groats of imposts brutalised and crippling.
Let Space lift up a mighty retch and let it vomit
Time void, and this Wine with geysers of justice from it.
Let lyres of nerves – daughters of the Ideal's Harp-string –
That thrilled on evenings of exile, no ill imagining,
Revert to plasma! No Spectacle, and Witness nil!
Hush, ultimate vibration of the Downfall, be still,
And let Forever be intrinsically All,
Primordially so and most hermetical.'

Ah, along the calvaries of Consciousness gone,
The Passion of worlds of study flatters you on,
Towards the Organ-chords of Resignations, Ideal,
Galatea, to apple trees of Natal-Eden's be-all.

Martyrdoms, the Art Cross, formulas, sweet fugues, blaze
Of gold Babels where the wind tends some fine sprays;
Worlds making do, and docketed haphazardly
With books, beneath the heaven's Eternullity.
Vanity, vanity, I say unto you! – Me, still around,
But where now are that Psalmist's nerve-strings to be found?
Midnight and quarter gone; what banks watch you go past
On these anonymous nights, O Nebulous Mother? And last,
How it must be to die with proven stars, at this same hour
When Christ was born, their broods without a fire or bower,
But shrieking: O my God; while still to their dead skies
A cathedral spire from polar surplices appears to rise!
– Those Earths maintain their silences, they are mute,
And still creation functions, pigheaded, stubborn brute.

Sans issue, elle est Tout; et nulle autre, elle est Tout.
X en soi? Soif à trucs! Songe d'une nuit d'août?
Sans le mot, nous serrons revannés, ô ma Terre!
Puis tes sœurs. *Et nunc et semper, Amen.* Se taire.

Je veux parler au Temps! criais-je. Oh! quelque engrais
Anonyme! Moi! mon Sacré-Cœur! – J'espérais
Qu'à ma mort, tout frémirait, du cèdre à l'hysope;
Que ce Temps, déraillant, tomberait en syncope,
Que, pour venir jeter sur mes lèvres des fleurs,
Les Soleils très navrés détraqueraient leurs chœurs;
Qu'un soir, du moins, mon Cri me jaillissant des moelles,
On verrait, mon Dieu, des signaux dans les étoiles?

Puis, fou devant ce ciel qui toujours nous bouda,
Je rêvais de prêcher la fin, nom d'un Bouddha!
Oh! pâle, mutilé, d'un: «qui m'aime me suive!»
Faisant de leurs cités une unique Ninive,
Mener ces chers bourgeois, fouettés d'alléluias,
Au Saint-Sépulchre maternel du Nirvâna!

Maintenant, je m'en lave les mains (concurrence
Vitale, l'argent, l'art, puis les lois de la France . . .)

Vermis sum, pulvis es! où sont mes nerfs d'hier?
Mes muscles de demain? Et le terreau si fier
De Mon âme, où donc était-il, il y a mille
Siècles! et comme, incessamment, il file, file! . . .
Anonyme! et pour Quoi? – Pardon, Quelconque Loi!
L'être est forme, Brahma seul est Tout-Un en soi.

Ô Robe aux cannelures à jamais doriques
Où grimpent les Passions des grappes cosmiques;
Ô Robe de Maïa, ô Jupe de Maman,
Je baise vos ourlets tombals éperdûment!
Je sais! la vie outrecuidante est une trêve
D'un jour au Bon-Repos qui pas plus ne s'achève
Qu'il n'a commencé. Moi, ma trêve, confiant,
Je la veux cuver au sein de l'INCONSCIENT.

No exit, she's the Whole; none other; the Whole is she.
X in itself? Thirst for gewgaws! August night's reverie?
Without a word, we'll be retired out, O Earth of mine!
Your sisters, too. *Et nunc et semper. Amen.* Cease this whine.

It's Time I want a word with, I cried. What crap by anon.
Me! my Saviour's-Heart! – What I'd been banking on
Was, cedar to the hyssop, all would feel my death;
And that this Time, derailed, would faint from lack of breath;
That Suns would disarrange their choirs to come and toss
Their flowers on my lips, quite woebegone with loss;
One night at least, my Cry flushing me from my bones,
My God, you'd see some signs up in the starry zones?

Then, mad before this sky that sulked at us I would, ah,
Dream that I preached the end in the name of some Buddha!
Oh, pale and maimed, with a 'who loves me, follow me!'
Making their cities a single Nineveh, I'd be
Leading these dear bourgeois, with alleluias pressed,
To Nirvana of the Holy Tomb's maternal breast.

But now I wash my hands of it – the vital cause,
The need for cash, the pull of art, and the French laws . . .

Vermis sum, pulvis es. Where nerves of yesterday?
My muscles of tomorrow? Where was it heaped away
The proud mulch of my soul a thousand centuries past
And how incessantly it scarpers and scarpers fast! . . .
Anon! For What? Pardon, Whatever Law may be!
Being's form, Brahma the All-in-One, self-entity.

O Robe of flutings that are Doric for ever more
Where Passions of the cosmic clusters climb and soar;
O Robe of Maya, O Mummy's apron-strings,
I kiss your graveyard hems, utterly lost in the things.
I know! This overweening life is just a break
In a day of Good Repose – you've scarce had chance to take
It when it's over. Myself, my break, in full trust,
I want to sleep it off on the INCONSCIENT's bust.

Dernière crise. Deux semaines errabundes,
En tout, sans que mon Ange Gardien me réponde.
Dilemme à deux sentiers vers l'Éden des Élus:
Me laisser éponger mon Moi par l'Absolu?
Ou bien, élixirer l'Absolu en moi-même?
C'est passé. J'aime tout, aimant mieux que Tout m'aime.
Donc Je m'en vais flottant aux orgues sous-marins,
Par les coraux, les œufs, les bras verts, les écrins,
Dans la tourbillonnante éternelle agonie
D'un Nirvâna des Danaïdes du génie!
Lacs de syncopes esthétiques! Tunnels d'or!
Pastel défunt! fondant sur une langue! Mort
Mourante ivre-morte! Et la conscience unique
Que c'est dans la Sainte Piscine ésotérique
D'un *lucus* à huis-clos, sans pape et sans laquais,
Que J'ouvre ainsi mes riches veines à Jamais.

En attendant la mort mortelle, sans mystère,
Lors quoi l'usage veut qu'on nous cache sous terre.

Maintenant, tu n'as pas cru devoir rester coi;
Eh bien, un cri humain! s'il en reste un pour toi.

The last crisis. Two weeks of errabundancy
In all, without my Guardian-Angel's answering me.
Dilemma: to the Eden of the Elect, which route:
Either to wipe my Self out in the Absolute?
Or elixirate in me the Absolute, hand in glove?
It's passed. I love all, more than All returns my love.
So I will go away, to sunken tubs I'll drift,
Past corals, eggs, green feelers, tresses that shift
In the eternal whirling of the dying throes
Of a Nirvana of the Danaids of genius. Those
Lakes of aesthetic swoons! Those tunnels made of gold!
Dead pastel, melting on a tongue! Death, out cold,
Dying dead drunk. And, unique as it is,
The consciousness within a private *lucus*'s
Esoteric Holy Piscina without lackeys or pope,
Where I open thus my rich veins to Forever's scope.

Awaiting death everlasting, no mystery in store,
When custom hides us under earth once more.

Well now, you never thought you'd have to stay quite mum;
Oh well, a human cry for you! if one's left to come.

COMPLAINTE PROPITIATOIRE
À L'INCONSCIENT

Aditi

Ô Loi, qui êtes parce que Vous Êtes,
Que Votre Nom soit la Retraite!

— Elles! ramper vers elles d'adoration?
Ou que sur leur misère humaine je me vautre?
Elle m'aime, *infiniment*! Non, d'occasion!
Si non *moi*, ce serait *infiniment* un autre!

    Que votre inconsciente Volonté
    Soit faite dans l'Éternité!

— Dans l'orgue qui par déchirements se châtie,
Croupir, des étés, sous les vitraux, en langueur;
Mourir d'un attouchement de l'Eucharistie,
S'entrer un crucifix maigre et nu dans le cœur?

    Que de votre communion, nous vienne
    Notre sagesse quotidienne!

— Ô croisés de mon sang! transporter les cités!
Bénir la Pâque universelle, sans salaires!
Mourir sur la Montagne, et que l'Humanité,
Aux âges d'or sans fin, me porte en scapulaires?

    Pardonnez-nous nos offences, nos cris,
    Comme étant d'à jamais écrits!

— Crucifier l'infini dans des toiles comme
Un mouchoir, et qu'on dise: «Oh! l'Idéal s'est tu!»
Formuler Tout! En fugues sans fin dire l'Homme!
Être l'âme des arts à zones que veux-tu?

PROPITIATORY COMPLAINT
TO THE INCONSCIENT

Aditi

O Law, which art because Thou Art,
Thy name be Refuge on our part.

– Shes! should I grovel to them worshipping?
Or revel in their human misery for fun?
She loves me, *infinitely*! No, secondhand's the thing!
If not *me*, it would *infinitely* be another one.

May thy inconscient Will then be
Done in all Eternity!

– To wallow, summers, languidly beneath stained glass,
Hearing the organ torture and tear itself apart;
To die from just a touch of Eucharist, and pass
A mean and naked crucifix into the heart.

And from communion with you may
Our wisdom come to us each day.

– Oh, crossed with my blood! to transport cities there!
To bless the universal Easter, without wages!
To die upon the Hill, and Humanity to wear
Me on the scapulars for endless golden ages?

Forgive us our wails and trespasses
Being written from always as what is.

– To crucify in handkerchief-size canvas the infinite,
So it be said: 'Oh, the Ideal stays mute!' The Whole
To formulate! Speak Man in fugues of endless flight!
To be the soul of marginal arts, is that your goal?

Non, rien; délivrez-nous de la Pensée,
Lèpre originelle, ivresse insensée,

Radeau du Mal et de l'Exil;
Ainsi soit-il.

COMPLAINTE-PLACET DE FAUST FILS

Si tu savais, maman Nature,
Comme Je m'aime en tes ennuis,
Tu m'enverrais une enfant pure,
Chaste aux «*et puis?*»

Si tu savais quelles boulettes,
Tes soleils de Panurge! dis,
Tu mettrais le nôtre en miettes,
En plein midi.

Si tu savais, comme la *Table
De tes Matières* est mon fort!
Tu me prendrais comme comptable,
Comptable à mort!

Si tu savais! les fantaisies!
Dont Je puis être le ferment!
Tu ferais de moi ton Sosie,
Tout simplement.

None of it; deliver us from Thinking,
First leper, long, senseless drinking,

Raft of Evil and Banishment;
So be it anent.

PETITIONARY COMPLAINT OF FAUST JUNIOR

Ma Nature, if you knew just how
I love myself in your tedious pen
You'd send me a pure girl child now,
Chaste down to '*and then?*'

And if you knew what utter hashes,
Your suns of Panurge, I say
You'd turn ours into dust and ashes,
In the broad light of day.

If you knew your *Contents Page*
Was my strength in depth and breadth,
Of some account you'd gauge
Me – accountable to the death.

If only you knew! the fantasies!
– That I am able to ferment.
You'd make of me your Double, as is,
Quite simply equivalent.

COMPLAINTE À NOTRE-DAME DES SOIRS

L'Extase du soleil, peuh! La Nature, fade
Usine de sève aux lymphatiques parfums.
Mais les lacs éperdus des longs couchants défunts
Dorlotent mon voilier dans leurs plus riches rades,
   Comme un ange malade . . .
    Ô Notre-Dame des Soirs,
    Que Je vous aime sans espoir!

Lampes des mers! blancs bizarrants! mots à vertiges!
Axiomes *in articulo mortis* déduits!
Ciels vrais! Lune aux échos dont communient les puits!
Yeux des portraits! Soleil qui, saignant son quadrige,
   Cabré, s'y crucifige!
    Ô Notre-Dame des Soirs,
    Certe, ils vont haut vos encensoirs!

Eux sucent des plis dont le frou-frou les suffoque;
Pour un regard, ils battraient du front les pavés;
Puis s'affligent sur maint sein creux, mal abreuvés;
Puis retournent à ces vendanges sexciproques.
   Et moi, moi Je m'en moque!
    Oui, Notre-Dame des Soirs,
    J'en fais, paraît-il, peine à voir.

En voyage, sur les fugitives prairies,
Vous me fuyez; ou du ciel des eaux m'invitez;
Ou m'agacez au tournant d'une vérité;
Or vous ai-je encor dit votre fait, je vous prie?
   Ah! coquette Marie,
    Ah! Notre-Dame des Soirs,
    C'est trop pour vos seuls Reposoirs!

Vos Rites, jalonnés de sales bibliothèques,
Ont voûté mes vingt ans, m'ont tari de chers goûts.
Verrai-je l'oasis fondant au rendez-vous,

COMPLAINT TO OUR LADY OF EVENTIDE

The Ecstasy of the sun! Pooh! Nature's a dull
Factory of saps with those lymphatic aromas.
But lakes, crazed with the sunset's long and dying comas,
Dandle in their richest roads my sail-boat's hull,
   Like a sick angel's skull . . .
   O Lady of Eventide,
   I love you, hope denied.

Sea-lights, bizarrant whites, words' dizzy reels,
Axioms, *in articulo mortis*, deduced and found!
Real skies! Ah, moon of echoes that the wells resound!
Portrait eyes! Sun, bleeding its quadriga, wheels,
   Rears and crucigeals!
   O Lady of Eventide,
   Your censers are well skied.

They suck pleats whose frou-frou stifles them in skirt;
For just a look, they'll beat their heads on paving stones;
Then grieve, ill-quenched, on many a breast all bones;
Then to resexprocated vintages revert.
   A laugh, that, f'r a dead cert.
   O Lady of the Eventide,
   I've made it hard to abide.

In travelling over fleeting prairie after prairie,
You flee from me; or from reflected skies invite me;
Or to the turning of a home-truth you incite me;
So, have I told you what your game is, fair and squarely?
   Ah, coquettish Mary,
   Ah, Lady of Eventide,
   'S too much, your Stations decide.

Your Rites, that dirty libraries stake out to protect,
Have bowed my twenty years, dried me with dear tastes, too.
So shall I see the melting oasis at our rendezvous

Où . . . vos lèvres (dit-on!) à jamais nous dissèquent?
Ô Lune sur La Mecque!
Notre-Dame, Notre-Dame des Soirs,
De *vrais* yeux m'ont dit: au revoir!

COMPLAINTE DES VOIX
SOUS LE FIGUIER BOUDDHIQUE

LES COMMUNIANTES

Ah! ah!
Il neige des hosties
De soie, anéanties!
Ah! ah!
Alléluia!

LES VOLUPTANTES

La lune en son halo ravagé n'est qu'un œil
Mangé de mouches, tout rayonnant des grands deuils.

Vitraux mûrs, déshérités, flagellés d'aurores,
Les Yeux Promis sont plus dans les grands deuils encore.

LES PARANYMPHES

Les *concetti* du crépuscule
Frisaient les bouquets de nos seins;
Son haleine encore y circule,
Et, leur félinant le satin
Fait s'y pâmer deux renoncules.

Devant ce Maître Hypnotiseur,
Expirent leurs frou-frou poseurs;
Elles crispent leurs étamines,

At which . . . your lips (I say!) forever dissect?
    O Moon to Mecca trekked!
    O Lady, Lady of Eventide,
    Eyes *real* to me've goodbyed!

COMPLAINT OF VOICES
UNDER THE BUDDHIST FIG TREE

THE COMMUNICANTS

    Ah! Ah!
It snows with hosts
Of silks, oblivion's ghosts!
    Ah! Ah!
    Alleluia!

THE VOLUPTRESSES

The moon within its ravaged halo's just an eye
Beaming in full mourning, fly-bitten in the sky.

Stained glass, ripe, dispossessed, that dawns flagellate,
The Promised Eyes, in even greater mourning state.

THE BRIDESMAIDS

    The *conceits* of dusk were inclining
    To touch on posies of our breast;
    Its breath still circles and, felining
    The satin for them, has possessed
    Two buttercups with rapt supining.

    Before this Master Hypnotist
    Their poser rustling expires – hist;
    They wilt their muslin stamina; their

   Et se rinfiltrent leurs parfums
    Avec des mines
    D'œillets défunts.

  LES JEUNES GENS

Des rêves engrappés se roulaient aux collines,
Feuilles mortes portant du sang des mousselines,

Cumulus, indolents roulis, qu'un vent tremblé
Vint carder un beau soir des soifs de s'en aller!

  LES COMMUNIANTES

   Ah! ah!
  Il neige des cœurs
  Noués de faveurs,
   Ah! ah!
  Alléluia!

  LES VOLUPTANTES

Reviens, vagir parmi mes cheveux, mes cheveux
Tièdes, je t'y ferai des bracelets d'aveux!

Entends partout les Encensoirs les plus célestes,
L'univers te garde une note unique! reste . . .

  LES PARANYMPHES

  C'est le nid meublé
  Par l'homme idolâtre;
  Les vents déclassés
  Des mois près de l'âtre;
  Rien de passager,
  Presque pas de scènes;
  La vie est si saine,
Quand on sait s'arranger.

Fragrance they infiltrate and scent
    With the air
    Of pinks, spent.

THE YOUNG PEOPLE

And clustered dreams were rolling to the hills,
Dead leaves that bear the blood of muslin spills,

Cumulus, indolent rollings, a shaky wind came on,
To tease out a fine night with thirst for getting gone.

THE COMMUNICANTS

    Ah! Ah!
With hearts it snows,
Knotted with bows,
    Ah! Ah!
    Alleluia!

THE VOLUPTRESSES

Return and wawl amid my hair, my warm hair,
I'll make you there bracelets of vows to wear.

Hear everywhere the heavenliest Censers' say,
The universe keeps for you a unique note! Stay . . .

THE BRIDESMAIDS

    Man, idol-fast,
    This nest provided;
    The winds outclassed
    By months fire-sided;
    No one visiting,
    Hardly ever a row,
    Life is so sane now,
Knowing how to arrange the thing.

Ô fiancé probe,
Commandons ma robe!
Hélas! le bonheur est là, mais lui se dérobe . . .

LES JEUNES GENS

Bestiole à chignon, Nécessaire divin,
Os de chatte, corps de lierre, chef-d'œuvre vain!

Ô femme, mammifère à chignon, ô fétiche,
On t'absout; c'est un Dieu qui par tes yeux nous triche.

Beau commis voyageur, d'une Maison là-haut,
Tes yeux mentent! ils ne nous diront pas le Mot!

Et tes pudeurs ne sont que des passes réflexes
Dont joue un Dieu très fort (Ministère des sexes).

Tu peux donc nous mener au Mirage béant,
Feu-follet connu, vertugadin du Néant;

Mais, fausse sœur, fausse humaine, fausse mortelle,
Nous t'écartèlerons de hontes sangsuelles!

Et si ta dignité se cabre? à deux genoux,
Nous te fermerons la bouche avec des bijoux.

– Vie ou Néant! choisir. Ah! quelle discipline!
Que n'est-il un Éden entre ces deux usines?

Bon; que tes doigts sentimentals
Aient pour nos fronts au teint d'épave
Des condoléances qui lavent
Et des trouvailles d'animal.

Et qu'à jamais ainsi tu ailles
Le long des étouffants dortoirs,
Égrenant les bonnes semailles,
En inclinant ta chaste taille
Sur les sujets de tes devoirs.

Oh, honest, fiancé,
Order my gown today!
So sad! that's happiness but he's off, away . . .

THE YOUNG PEOPLE

Beastlet with a bun, Necessity divine,
Cat-boned, vain masterpiece, sister Ivy Twine!

Woman, mammalian with a bun, oh fetish-prize,
You are absolved; some God hoodwinks us through your eyes.

Commercial-traveller from a Trading-House on high,
Your eyes tell lies! they'll not give us the Word; they lie.

Your modesties are only ploys sprung by reflexes
Some God plays strongly with (Minister of the Sexes).

So to the gaping Mirage you could make us press,
Known jill-o'-the-wisp, farthingale of Nothingness.

Traitor sister, human, mortal, traitor all through,
With sensual shames we'll draw and quarter you!

And if your dignity rebels? Kneeling down we'll settle
And shut your mouth with jewels in precious metal.

– Life or Oblivion! Choosing! What a scourge it is!
Is Eden only in one of these two factories!

Good; may your sentimental fingers
Have for our brows of waif-like hue
Condolences that cleanse us through,
Of lucky animal finds the bringers.

And may you always be a goer
Down dormitories of stifling air,
Shucking for the goodly sower,
In bending your chaste form lower
Over the subjects of your care.

Ah! pour une âme trop tanguée,
Tes baisers sont des potions
Qui la laissent là, bien droguée,
Et s'oubliant à te voir gaie,
Accomplissant tes fonctions
En point narquoise Déléguée.

LES COMMUNIANTES

Des ramiers
Familiers
Sous nos jupes palpitent!
Doux Çakya, venez vite
Les faire prisonniers!

LE FIGUIER

Défaillantes, les Étoiles que la lumière
Épuise, battent plus faiblement des paupières.

Le ver-luisant s'éteint à bout, l'Être pâmé
Agonise à tâtons et se meurt à jamais.

Et l'Idéal égrène en ses mains fugitives
L'éternel chapelet des planètes plaintives.

Pauvres fous, vraiment pauvres fous!
Puis, quand on a fait la crapule
On revient geindre au crépuscule,
Roulant son front dans les genoux
Des Saintes bouddhiques Nounous.

Ah, for a soul too tossed and tugged,
Your close embraces are the unction
That leave him there, so drugged
Your cheeriness from mind is shrugged
Away, when you've performed your function
As mocking Delegate well plugged.

THE COMMUNICANTS

    Ring-doves that are
    Quite familiar,
Under our skirts palpitate!
Sweet Çakya, hurry straight
    To take them prisoner.

THE FIG TREE

And, failing now, the Stars, that light drains dry,
Ever more feebly blink their eyelids as they die.

The glow-worm peters out, Being, faint, at death's door,
Is groping out and kills itself for ever more.

And the Ideal counts off in flying fugitive hands
The eternal rosary of plaintive planet-bands.

    Poor fools, poor fools indeed, all these!
    Since, when one's had a good debauch,
    Half-light, one groans home from the nautch,
    Rolling one's head between the knees
    Of saintly nans in Buddhist nurseries.

COMPLAINTE DE CETTE BONNE LUNE

On entend les Étoiles:

> Dans l'giron
> Du Patron,
> On y danse, on y danse,
> Dans l'giron
> Du Patron,
> On y danse tous en rond.

– Là, voyons, mam'zell' la Lune,
Ne gardons pas ainsi rancune;
Entrez en danse, et vous aurez
Un collier de soleils dorés.

> – Mon Dieu, c'est à vous bien honnête,
> Pour une pauvre Cendrillon;
> Mais, me suffit le médaillon
> Que m'a donné ma sœur planète.

– Fi! votre Terre est un suppôt
De la Pensée! Entrez en fête;
Pour sûr, vous tournerez la tête
Aux astres les plus comme il faut.

> – Merci, merci, je n'ai que ma mie,
> Juste que je l'entends gémir!

– Vous vous trompez, c'est le soupir
Des universelles chimies!

> – Mauvaises langues, taisez-vous!
> Je dois veiller. Tas de traînées,
> Allez courir vos guilledous!

– Va donc, rosière enfarinée!
Hé! Notre-Dame des gens soûls,

COMPLAINT OF THIS GOOD MOON

The Stars are heard:

> In his bounds,
>   Boss's grounds,
> There we dance, there we dance,
> In his bounds,
>   Boss's grounds,
> There we dance on our rounds.

– There, let's see, mad'moiselle Moon,
Let's not be bitter, out of tune;
Join in the dance and you can deck
Golden suns around your neck.

> – My God, it's proper enough for you,
> For Cinderella, poor rapscallion;
> But for me, though, the medallion
> My sister planet gave will do.

– Stuff. Your Earth's the axle-tree
Of Thought. Now come and be the toast!
You'll turn the heads of stars that most
Appear to be as they should be.

> – Thank you, thank you, but I've my dear
> Only while I hear him groan!

– You kid yourself, it's just the moan
Of universal chemistry you hear.

> – You wicked tongues, shut up and stew!
> I must keep watch. You, mob on tow,
> Run and find your night-haunts, do!

– Split, clownish queen of the village show,
Our Lady of the drunken crew,

Des filous et des loups-garous!
Metteuse en rut des vieux matous!
                    Coucou!

Exeunt les Étoiles. Silence et Lune. On entend:

            Sous l'plafond
            Sans fond,
        On y danse, on y danse,
            Sous l'plafond
            Sans fond,
        On y danse tous en rond.

COMPLAINTE DES PIANOS QU'ON ENTEND DANS LES QUARTIERS AISÉS

Menez l'âme que les Lettres ont bien nourrie,
Les pianos, les pianos, dans les quartiers aisés!
Premiers soirs, sans pardessus, chaste flânerie,
Aux complaintes des nerfs incompris ou brisés.

        Ces enfants, à quoi rêvent-elles,
        Dans les ennuis des ritournelles?

            – «Préaux des soirs,
            Christs des dortoirs!

        «Tu t'en vas et tu nous laisses,
        Tu nous laiss's et tu t'en vas,
        Défaire et refaire ses tresses,
        Broder d'éternels canevas.»

Jolie ou vague? triste ou sage? encore pure?
Ô jours, tout m'est égal? ou, monde, moi je veux?
Et si vierge, du moins, de la bonne blessure
Sachant quels gras couchants ont les plus blancs aveux?

Of card-sharps and curmudgeons! You,
Stirrer of tom-cats' hullabaloo!
                    Cuckoo!

Exeunt the Stars. One hears:

                    Roof surround
                        Without bound,
            There we dance, there we dance,
                    Roof surround
                        Without bound,
            There we dance in a round.

COMPLAINT OF PIANOS HEARD IN THE PLUSHY QUARTERS

Oh, draw the soul that Letters have given so much taste,
Pianos, you pianos of the plushy quarter,
These first evenings, coatless, in loafing that is chaste,
With complaints of nerves misunderstood or in disorder.

            These girls, on what dreams do they dwell,
            During the tediums of the ritournelle?

                – 'The evening quads,
                Dorm Christ-Gods!

            'You will go, and us you're leaving,
            Us you're leaving, and you go,
            To weave her tresses, then unweaving,
            Embroider endless canvas, sew.'

Pretty or nondescript, sad or wise, still pure?
O days, not bothered? or me, world, I want it now?
If still virgin, at least, of the good wound, immature,
Knowing what gross settings have the whitest vow?

Mon Dieu, à quoi donc rêvent-elles?
À des Roland, à des dentelles?

      – «Cœurs en prison,
      Lentes saisons!

«Tu t'en vas et tu nous quittes,
Tu nous quitt's et tu t'en vas!
Couvent gris, chœurs de Sulamites,
Sur nos seins nuls croisons nos bras.»

Fatales clés de l'être un beau jour apparues;
Psitt! aux hérédités en ponctuels ferments,
Dans le bal incessant de nos étranges rues;
Ah! pensionnats, théâtres, journaux, romans!

      Allez, stériles ritournelles,
      La vie est vraie et criminelle.

        – «Rideaux tirés,
        Peut-on entrer?

«Tu t'en vas et tu nous laisses,
Tu nous laiss's et tu t'en vas,
La source des frais rosiers baisse,
Vraiment! Et lui qui ne vient pas . . .»

Il viendra! Vous serez les pauvres cœurs en faute,
Fiancés au remords comme aux essais sans fond,
Et les suffisants cœurs cossus, n'ayant d'autre hôte
Qu'un train-train pavoisé d'estime et de chiffons.

      Mourir? peut-être brodent-elles,
      Pour un oncle à dot, des bretelles?

        – «Jamais! Jamais!
        Si tu savais!

«Tu t'en vas et tu nous quittes,
Tu nous quitt's et tu t'en vas,

My God, on what dreams do they dwell?
Of Rolands, lace-work, who can tell?

> – 'With hearts in jail
> The seasons trail!

> 'You will go and leave us be,
> Leave us be, and you will go!
> Shulamite choirs, grey nunnery,
> Let's cross our arms on null breasts, so.'

Then fatal keys to being one fine day appeared;
Psst! with heredities in punctual ferments' vapours,
In the unceasing ball of our strange streets so weird;
Ah, boarding schools, theatres, novels, papers.

> Come off it, barren ritournelle,
> Life's real and criminal, a sell.

> – 'Curtains drawn centre,
> May one enter?

> 'You will go, and us you're leaving,
> Us you leave and you will go,
> The rose-blooms' source there's no retrieving,
> Indeed! And he won't ever show . . . .'

Oh, he will come. And you the wretched hearts to blame,
Engaged to regret like essays on an endless theme,
Cosseted, smug hearts, having no other guest but same
Old humdrum days decked out with fashions and esteem.

> So die? Or braces embroider well
> To make an uncle's dowry swell?

> – 'No, never, no!
> If you could know!

> 'You will go and leave us be,
> Leave us be, and you will go,

Mais tu nous reviendras bien vite
Guérir mon beau mal, n'est-ce pas?»

Et c'est vrai! l'Idéal les fait divaguer toutes,
Vigne bohême, même en ces quartiers aisés.
La vie est là; le pur flacon des vives gouttes
Sera, *comme il convient*, d'eau propre baptisé.

Aussi, bientôt, se joueront-elles
De plus exactes ritournelles.

– «Seul oreiller!
Mur familier!

«Tu t'en vas et tu nous laisses,
Tu nous laiss's et tu t'en vas.
Que ne suis-je morte à la messe!
Ô mois, ô linges, ô repas!»

COMPLAINTE DE LA BONNE DÉFUNTE

Elle fuyait par l'avenue,
Je la suivais illuminé,
Ses yeux disaient: «J'ai deviné
Hélas! que tu m'as reconnue!»

Je la suivis illuminé!
Yeux désolés, bouche ingénue,
Pourquoi l'avais-je reconnue,
Elle, loyal rêve mort-né?

Yeux trop mûrs, mais bouche ingénue;
Œillet blanc, d'azur trop veiné;
Oh! oui, rien qu'un rêve mort-né,
Car, défunte elle est devenue.

But you'll come back speedily
To cure my fine malaise – that so?'

And it's true! The Ideal will drive them all to stray,
Bohemian vine, even in this plushy quarter.
That's life; the pure decanter of lively drams one day
Will be, *as right and proper*, baptised in straight water.

Soon, also they'll make bagatelles
Of much more regular ritournelles.

– 'One pillow all!
Familiar wall!

'You will go and leave us be,
Leave us be and you will go.
If mass isn't the death of me!
Oh months, oh linen, cook and sew.'

COMPLAINT OF THE WOMAN GOOD AND DEAD

She fled along the avenue,
And, holy fool, I followed her,
Her eyes were saying: 'I infer,
Alas, you've recognised me too.'

And, holy fool, I followed her!
That callow mouth, those eyes that rue,
Why had I recognised just who,
She, still-born dream, none loyaler.

Blank carnation, too veiny blue;
Eyes too mature, mouth callower,
Oh yes, a still-born dream, that's her,
For she's become a corpse all through.

Gis, œillet, d'azur trop veiné,
La vie humaine continue
Sans toi, défunte devenue.
– Oh! je rentrerai sans dîner!

Vrai, je ne l'ai jamais connue.

COMPLAINTE DE L'ORGUE DE BARBARIE

Orgue, orgue de Barbarie,
Don Quichotte, Souffre-Douleur,
Vidasse, vidasse ton cœur,
Ma pauvre rosse endolorie.

Hein, étés idiots,
Octobres malades,
Printemps, purges fades,
Hivers tout vieillots?

– «Quel silence, dans la forêt d'automne,
Quand le soleil en son sang s'abandonne!»

Gaz, haillons d'affiches,
Feu les casinos,
Cercueils des pianos,
Ah, mortels postiches.

– «Déjà la nuit, qu'on surveille à peine
Le frou-frou de sa titubante traîne.»

Romans pour les quais,
Photos élégiaques,
Escarpins, vieux claques,
D'un coup de balai.

Carnation, too veiny blue you were,
Lie here; life flows on through,
Successful corpse, not missing you.
– Oh, I'll go home, dinner defer.

True, I never did know who.

COMPLAINT OF THE BARREL-ORGAN

Organ, barrel-organ, jack,
Don Quixote and Laughing-Stock,
Void your heart out, void, old crock,
My poor old broken-hearted hack.

What? Summer's fool gold;
Octobers all groggy;
Spring, purging soggy;
Winters so old?

– 'What silence in the autumn woods hangs still
When sun in gore surrenders to the kill!'

Late casinos' bier,
Gas, ad-rag medley,
Piano coffins, deadly
Hair-pieces, oh dear!

– 'It's night already; how you have to strain
To catch the frou-frou of her drunken train.'

Novels turned out,
Elegiac snaps,
Pumps, old hats, caps,
From a cleaning bout.

– «Oh! j'ai peur, nous avons perdu la route;
Paul, ce bois est mal famé! chut, écoute . . .»

       Végétal fidèle,
       Ève aime toujours
       LUI! jamais pour
       Nous, jamais pour elle.

– «Ô ballets corrosifs! réel, le crime?
La lune me pardonnait dans les cimes.»

       Vêpres, Ostensoirs,
       Couchants! Sulamites
       De province aux rites
       Exilants des soirs!

– «Ils m'ont brûlée; et depuis, vagabonde
Au fond des bois frais, j'implore le monde.»

       Et les vents s'engueulent,
       Tout le long des nuits!
       Qu'est-c'que moi j'y puis,
       Qu'est-ce donc qu'ils veulent?

– «Je vais guérir, voyez la cicatrice,
Oh! je ne veux pas aller à l'hospice!»

       Des berceaux fienteux
       Aux bières de même,
       Bons couples sans gêne,
       Tournez deux à deux.

Orgue, Orgue de Barbarie!
Scie autant que Souffre-Douleur,
Vidasse, vidasse ton cœur,
Ma pauvre rosse endolorie.

– 'Oh, I'm afraid; we've lost our way in the dark;
This wood's notorious, Paul. Hush, hark!'

> Faithful, vegetal,
> Eve loves for ever
> HIM! for her, never,
> For us, not at all.

– 'Corrosive ballets! Is it actually a crime?
The moon has pardoned me on peaks sublime.'

> Monstrance, Evensong,
> Sunsets, Shulamites,
> Provincials with rites
> Exilent at evening. So long!

– 'They've burnt me: and after that, left a vagabond
Deep in fresh woods, I implore the world beyond.'

> The winds kick up a row
> The whole night through!
> What 'm I able to do?
> What 're they after now?

– 'I'm going to recover; this scar, look at it.
I don't want to go to hospital, not a bit!'

> From dung-warm cot,
> To piss-warm bier,
> Two by two here,
> Unruffled trot.

> Organ, barrel-Organ, jack,
> Bore on as much as Laughing-Stock,
> Void, void your heart, old crock,
> My poor old broken-hearted hack.

COMPLAINTE D'UN CERTAIN DIMANCHE

Elle ne concevait pas qu'aimer fût l'ennemi d'aimer.

SAINTE-BEUVE: VOLUPTÉ

L'homme n'est pas méchant, ni la femme éphémère.
Ah! fous dont au casino battent les talons,
Tout homme pleure un jour et toute femme est mère
      Nous sommes tous filials, allons!
Mais quoi! les Destins ont des partis-pris si tristes,
Qui font que, les uns loin des autres, l'on s'exile,
Qu'on se traite à tort et à travers d'égoïstes,
Et qu'on s'use à trouver quelque unique Évangile.
Ah! jusqu'à ce que la nature soit bien bonne,
      Moi je veux vivre monotone.

Dans ce village en falaises, loin, vers les cloches,
Je redescends dévisagé par les enfants
Qui s'en vont faire bénir de tièdes brioches;
      Et rentré, mon sacré-cœur se fend!
Les moineaux des vieux toits pépient à ma fenêtre,
Ils me regardent dîner, sans faim, à la carte,
Des âmes d'amis morts les habitent, peut-être?
Je leur jette du pain: comme blessés, ils partent!
Ah! jusqu'à ce que la nature soit bien bonne,
      Moi je veux vivre monotone.

Elle est partie hier. Suis-je pas triste d'elle?
Mais c'est vrai! Voilà donc le fond de mon chagrin!
Oh! ma vie est aux plis de ta jupe fidèle!
      Son mouchoir me flottait sur le Rhin . . .
Seul. — Le Couchant retient un moment son Quadrige
En rayons où le ballet des moucherons danse,
Puis, vers les toits fumants de la soupe, il s'afflige . . .
Et c'est le Soir, l'insaisissable confidence . . .
Ah! jusqu'à ce que la nature soit bien bonne,
      Faudra-t-il vivre monotone?

Que d'yeux, en éventail, en ogive, ou d'inceste,
Depuis que l'Être espère, ont réclamé leur droits!

COMPLAINT OF A CERTAIN SUNDAY

She did not understand that loving had been inimical to love.

SAINTE-BEUVE: VOLUPTÉ

Man isn't bad nor woman just a passing thing.
Ah, fools whose heels in the casino stamp the leather,
All men will weep some day, all women be mothering;
    Come on, we're all filial together!
Then what! The Fates are still so sadly prejudiced
They make one, far from others, in self-exile live;
Some treat each other randomly as the egotist;
Others routinely find some unique Gospel give.
Ah, until nature shows a nice and kind concern,
    The humdrum life'll serve my turn.

In this village in the cliffs, far off, I head
Back down towards the bells stared at by children taking
Warm loaves to go and get a blessing on the bread;
    Back in, my sacred heart is breaking!
The sparrows on the ancient roofs chirp at the pane.
They watch me dining, without hunger, *à la carte*;
Perhaps the souls of dead friends live in them again?
I throw them crumbs and, as if hurt, they fly apart!
Ah, until nature shows a nice and kind concern
    The humdrum life'll serve my turn.

She left here yesterday. Is that why I'm so down?
Yes, true! So that's the basis of this pique of mine!
Oh, my life is faithful to the pleating of your gown!
    Her handkerchief floated to me on the Rhine . . .
Alone. – The sunset reins in its chariot and four,
A moment, with rays that light a ballet-dance of flies,
Then, over roofs that steam from supper, grieves once more.
And now it's Evening, the unseizable secret of skies . . .
Ah, until nature shows a nice and kind concern
    Must living be this humdrum turn?

How many eyes, in fan, in arch, or from incest,
Since this Being hopes, have claimed once more their hold.

Ô ciels, les yeux pourrissent-ils comme le reste?
   Oh! qu'il fait seul! oh! fait-il froid!
Oh! que d'après-midi d'automne à vivre encore!
Le Spleen, eunuque à froid, sur nos rêves se vautre!
Or, ne pouvant redevenir des madrépores,
Ô mes humains, consolons-nous les uns les autres.
Et jusqu'à ce que la nature soit bien bonne,
   Tâchons de vivre monotone.

COMPLAINTE D'UN AUTRE DIMANCHE

C'était un très-au vent d'octobre paysage,
Que découpe, aujourd'hui dimanche, la fenêtre,
Avec sa jalousie en travers, hors d'usage,
Où sèche, depuis quand! une paire de guêtres
Tachant de deux mals blancs ce glabre paysage.

Un couchant mal bâti suppurant du livide;
Le coin d'une buanderie aux tuiles sales;
En plein, le Val-de-Grâce, comme un qui préside;
Cinq arbres en proie à de mesquines rafales
Qui marbrent ce ciel crû de bandages livides.

Puis les squelettes de glycines aux ficelles,
En proie à des rafales encor plus mesquines!
Ô lendemains de noce! ô bribes de dentelles!
Montrent-elles assez la corde, ces glycines
Recroquevillant leur agonie aux ficelles!

Ah! qu'est-ce que je fais, ici, dans cette chambre!
Des vers. Et puis, après? ô sordide limace!
Quoi! la vie est unique, et toi, sous ce scaphandre,
Tu te racontes sans fin, et tu te ressasses!
Seras-tu donc toujours un qui garde la chambre?

Ce fut un bien au vent d'octobre paysage . . .

Oh heavens, do eyes decay the same as all the rest?
    Oh, how lone it turns! Oh, getting cold!
Oh, yet to live in the autumn afternoon still!
That Spleen, chill eunuch, pounds our dreams into a slough!
Yet since we can't be madrepores again at will,
O fellow beings, let's console each other now.
And until nature shows a nice and kind concern
    Attempt to live the humdrum turn.

COMPLAINT OF ANOTHER SUNDAY

It was a most in-wind-of-October countryside,
Today, Sunday, cut out by the window-pane,
Its blind uncustomarily across, where, dried
Since whenever it was! a pair of gaiters stain
With two festerings the clean-shaven countryside.

A sunset, of poor build, suppurates from the wan;
The corner of a laundry, tile on dirty tile;
Full view, the Val-de-Grâce like someone watching on;
Five trees, a prey to shabby gusts of shoddy bile,
Veining this sky swollen in dressings pale and wan.

And next wisteria skeletons with all the strings,
A prey to gusts of even yet more shabby stuff!
O wedding day-afters, oh lacy bits of things!
And these wisterias, they're threadbare enough,
Shrivelling out their deaths with all the strings.

Ah, what am I doing sticking around indoors!
Verse. And then what after that? You sordid slug!
What! Life's unique, and you, in this diving-gear of yours,
Assess, reassess yourself, yarn in your own lug!
So will you always be the one sticking in doors?

It'd been quite an in wind of October countryside . . .

COMPLAINTE DU FŒTUS DE POÈTE

Blasé dis-je! En avant,
Déchirer la nuit gluante des racines,
À travers maman, amour tout d'albumine,
Vers le plus clair! vers l'alme et riche étamine
        D'un soleil levant!

– Chacun son tour, il est temps que je m'émancipe,
Irradiant des Limbes mon inédit type!

            En avant!
Sauvé des steppes du mucus, à la nage
Téter soleil! et soûl de lait d'or, bavant,
Dodo à les seins dorloteurs des nuages,
        Voyageurs savants!

– À rêve que veux-tu, là-bas, je vivrai dupe
D'une âme en coup de vent dans la fraîcheur des jupes!

            En avant!
Dodo sur le lait caillé des bons nuages
Dans la main de Dieu, bleue, aux mille yeux vivants
Aux pays du vin viril faire naufrage!
            Courage,
        Là, là, je me dégage . . .

– Et je communierai, le front vers l'Orient,
Sous les espèces des baisers inconscients!

            En avant!
Cogne, glas des nuits! filtre, soleil solide!
Adieu, forêts d'aquarium qui, me couvant,
Avez mis ce levain dans ma chrysalide!
        Mais j'ai froid? En avant!
        Ah! maman . . .

Vous, Madame, allaitez le plus longtemps possible
Et du plus Seul de vous ce pauvre enfant-terrible.

COMPLAINT OF THE POET'S FOETUS

Cloyed, say I! Advance
And shear a way through the sticky night of roots
Through mum, a love of albumen absolutes,
Towards the clearest, the bountiful, and rich shoots
        Of a rising sun. My chance!

– To each his turn, I must set free, now the time is ripe,
Radiant from Limbo, my strange unpublished type!

        Advance! Advance!
Rescued from steppes of mucus, then, in swimming,
Suckle sun, and with gold milk in a drunk trance,
Dribbling, go bye-byes on dandler clouds skimming,
        Seasoned travellers of France.

– To dream that you wish, down there, I'll live the dupe
Of a soul, in flurryings of freshness that skirts scoop!

        Advance! Advance!
On the clotted milk of good clouds, go bye-byes
In God's hand, blue, in the thousand eyes' bright glance
In the regions of the manly wine capsize!
        Cheer up, thighs.
        There, I break the ties.

– And with brow towards the East I will commune
Under the species of inconscient kisses soon!

        Advance! Advance!
Beat, knell of nights! real sun filter through all this!
Farewell now, you forests of aquarium plants
That, brooding me, have put this yeast in my chrysalis!
        But am I cold? Advance!
        Oh, mum, glance . . .

You, Madam, suckle as long as you can do
This wretched *enfant terrible*, the Loneliest for you.

COMPLAINTE DES PUBERTÉS DIFFICILES

Un éléphant de Jade, œil mi-clos souriant,
Méditait sous la riche éternelle pendule,
Bon bouddha d'exilé qui trouve ridicule
Qu'on pleure vers les Nils des couchants d'Orient,
Quand bave notre crépuscule.

Mais, sot Éden de Florian,
En un vase de Sèvre ou de fins bergers fades
S'offrent des bouquets bleus et des moutons frisés,
Un œillet expirait ses pubères baisers
Sous la trompe sans flair de l'éléphant de Jade.

À ces bergers peints de pommade
Dans le lait, à ce couple impuissant d'opéra
Transi jusqu'au trépas en la pâte de Sèvres,
Un gros petit dieu Pan venu de Tanagra
Tendait ses bras tout inconscients et ses lèvres.

Sourds aux vanités de Paris,
Les lauriers fanés des tentures,
Les mascarons d'or des lambris,
Les bouquins aux pâles reliures
Tournoyaient par la pièce obscure,
Chantant, sans orgueil, sans mépris:
«Tout est frais dès qu'on veut comprendre la Nature.»

Mais lui, cabré devant ces soirs accoutumés,
Où montait la gaîté des enfants de son age,
Seul au balcon, disait, les yeux brûlés de rages:
«J'ai du génie, enfin: nulle ne veut m'aimer!»

COMPLAINT OF DIFFICULT PUBERTIES

An elephant of Jade, eye half-closed, a smile,
Meditated under the rich eternal pendulum,
Fine buddha of an exile who ridicules how some
Could weep for Oriental sunsets of the Nile
      When our drivelling twilights come.

    But, soppy Eden in Florian's style,
In a Sèvres vase where shepherds, fine junk, parade
Offerings of curly sheep and posies of blue flowers
A carnation eye sighed its pubescent kiss all hours
Under the unsmelling trunk of the elephant of Jade.

    To these shepherds painted with pomade
In milk, to this impotent pair from opera,
Faint on the point of dying in the Sèvres slips,
A plump little Pan-god, come over from Tanagra,
Was proffering his quite inconscient arms and lips.

      To vanities of Paris blind,
      The faded hangings, laurel-wound,
      Panels with golden masks lined,
      The old books in pale spines bound,
      In the gloomy room all spinning round,
      Sang with no scorn or pride of mind:
'Once you want to understand Nature, all's fresh and sound.'

But hamstrung, facing these routine evenings, he,
As rose the gaiety of children of his own age,
Alone on the balcony, exclaimed, eyes fired with rage:
'A genius me, then: no girl's ever keen on me.'

COMPLAINTE DE LA FIN DES JOURNÉES

Vous qui passez, oyez donc un pauvre être,
Chassé des *Simples* qu'on peut reconnaître
Soignant, las, quelque œillet à leur fenêtre!
      Passants, hâtifs passants,
Oh! qui veut visiter les palais de mes sens?

            Maints ciboires
            De déboires,
            Un encor!

Ah! l'enfant qui vit de ce nom, poète!
Il se rêvait, seul, pansant Philoctète
Aux nuits de Lemnos; ou, loin, grêle ascète.
      Et des vers aux moineaux,
Par le lycée en vacances, sous les préaux!

            Offertoire,
            En mémoire
            D'un consort.

Mon Dieu, que tout fait signe de se taire!
Mon Dieu, qu'on est follement solitaire!
Où sont tes yeux, premier dieu de la Terre
            Qui ravala ce cri:
«Têtue Éternité! je m'en vais incompris . . .»?

            Pauvre histoire!
            Transitoire?
            Passe-port?

J'ai dit: mon Dieu. La terre est orpheline
Aux ciels, parmi les séminaires des Routines.
Va, suis quelque robe de mousseline . . .
            – Inconsciente Loi,
Faites que ce crachoir s'éloigne un peu de moi!

COMPLAINT OF THE END OF DAYS

You passers-by, now heed a wretched mortal guy,
Driven from the Simple you can identify
Caring, fagged, some pink in their window! Passers-by,
      Hasty passers hence,
Oh, who's for touring the palaces of my senses?

          Of pyx, a power
          Tasting sour.
          One more, one more.

Ah, this kid who's living off this poet title!
He dreamed, alone, tending Philoctetes by night
On Lemnos; or, far off, an ascetic, slight.
      And, in school's covered ways,
Of die-verse worms for sparrows in the holidays.

          Offertory hour,
          In memory now: a
          Consort no more.

My God, how everything signals keeping silent!
My God, how each one is a madly lonely island!
Premier god of Earth where is your eye leant,
      Who swallowed up this cry:
'Eternity, mule-head, I'm going off, misjudged. 'Bye . . .'?

          Tale such a shower!
          In transit? Our
          Passport for . . . ?

I've said it now: My God! The earth is comfortless
In seminaries of Routines, the heavens' orphaness.
So, go, and follow whatever muslin dress . . .
      – Inconscient Decree,
Make this spittoon pass away a bit from me!

Vomitoire
De la Foire,
C'est la mort.

COMPLAINTE DE LA VIGIE
AUX MINUITS POLAIRES

Le Globe, vers l'aimant,
Chemine exactement,
Teinté de mers si bleues,
De cités tout en toits,
De réseaux de convois
Qui grignottent des lieues.

Ô ma côte en sanglots!
Pas loin de Saint-Malo,
Un bourg fumeux vivotte,
Qui tient sous son clocher,
Où grince un coq perché,
L'Ex-Voto d'un pilote!

Aux cierges, au vitrail,
D'un autel en corail,
Une jeune Madone
Tend, d'un air ébaubi,
Un beau cœur de rubis
Qui se meurt et rayonne!

Un gros cœur tout en sang,
Un bon cœur ruisselant,
Qui, du soir à l'aurore,
Et de l'aurore au soir,
Se meurt, de ne pouvoir
Saigner, ah! saigner plus encore!

Puke-dish glower,
Of Fairground hour,
It's death's door.

COMPLAINT OF THE LOOK-OUT
AT POLAR MIDNIGHTS

Towards the lover the Globe
Directly heads, her robe
Tinted with seas so blue,
With cities, roofs all shown,
With convoy networks thrown,
More treaties to accrue.

Oh, my coast is sobbing so!
Not far from St Malo
A foggy town makes shift
And keeps, beneath its peal
And the weathercock's odd squeal,
A pilot's Votive Gift.

Madonna, young, dumbfound,
To stained glass and candles round
A coral altar, holds out
A fine gem-crusted heart
Killing itself to dart
And spread its beams about.

A heavy heart in its blood,
A kind heart in full flood,
That, sunrise till the set,
From set till rising hour,
Is dying from lack of power
To bleed, ah, bleed even more yet!

COMPLAINTE DE LA LUNE EN PROVINCE

Ah! la belle pleine Lune,
Grosse comme une fortune!

La retraite sonne au loin,
Un passant, monsieur l'adjoint;

Un clavecin joue en face,
Un chat traverse la place:

La province qui s'endort!
Plaquant un dernier accord,

Le piano clôt sa fenêtre.
Quelle heure peut-il bien être?

Calme Lune, quel exil!
Faut-il dire: ainsi soit-il?

Lune, ô dilettante Lune,
À tous les climats commune,

Tu vis hier le Missouri,
Et les remparts de Paris,

Les fiords bleus de la Norwège,
Les pôles, les mers, que sais-je?

Lune heureuse! ainsi tu vois,
À cette heure, le convoi

De son voyage de noce!
Ils sont partis pour l'Écosse.

Quel panneau, si, cet hiver,
Elle eût pris au mot mes vers!

COMPLAINT OF THE MOON IN THE PROVINCES

Ah, moon the fine, full Moon,
Large as a fortune calls the tune!

Far off the sounds of last post die.
Someone, deputy mayor, walks by;

Harpsichord, opposite, plays an air;
A cat is coming across the square:

The province sleeping like a board!
Thumping out a final chord,

The piano shuts its window tight.
What exactly is the time of night?

Calm moon, this exile's hell to me.
But must one say: so let it be?

Moon, Moon, you dilettante, you,
Common to all climates; your view

Was the Missouri yesterday;
The Paris ramparts came your way,

The blue Norwegian fjords, snow
Of poles, seas – and what I don't know.

Oh happy Moon, thus you perceive,
This very moment, her train leave,

Her honeymoon she's going on.
To Scotland, that's where they have gone.

Some trap this winter if she'd read
My verse as meaning what it said!

Lune, vagabonde Lune,
Faisons cause et mœurs communes?

Ô riches nuits! je me meurs,
La province dans le cœur!

Et la lune a, bonne vieille,
Du coton dans les oreilles.

COMPLAINTE DES PRINTEMPS

Permettez, ô sirène,
Voici que votre haleine
Embaume la verveine;
C'est l'printemps qui s'amène!

– Ce système, en effet, ramène le printemps,
Avec son impudent cortège d'excitants.

Ôtez donc ces mitaines;
Et n'ayez, inhumaine,
Que mes soupirs pour traîne:
Ous' qu'il y a de la gêne . . .

– Ah! yeux bleus méditant sur l'ennui de leur art!
Et vous, jeunes divins, aux soirs crus de hasard!

Du géant à la naine,
Vois, tout bon sire entraîne
Quelque contemporaine,
Prendre l'air, par hygiène . . .

– Mais vous saignez ainsi pour l'amour de l'exil!
Pour l'amour de l'Amour! D'ailleurs, ainsi soit-il . . .

Moon, vagabond moon, shall we make
A common cause, one manner take?

Nights, oh rich. I'm a dead duck,
The province in my heart stuck!

And the moon has, the good old dear,
Cotton-wool stuffed in each ear.

COMPLAINT OF SPRINGS

Excuse me, siren-jane,
Here comes your breath again
Scented with the vervain.
The spring's arrived, that's plain.

– The system, in effect, puts spring in circulation
With all its impudent cortège of excitation.

Off with those gloves again;
Fair cruelty, retain
Only my sighs for train:
There's an embarrassing vein . . .

– Ah, blue eyes meditating the tedium of their art!
And you, young gods, on brutish evenings chance the heart!

From giant to dwarfish swain,
Watch every jerk obtain
Some contemporary jane
For health walks down the lane . . .

– You bleed your heart out for the love of banishment,
For love of Love. Okay, so be it. Give it vent . . .

T'ai-je fait de la peine?
Oh! viens vers les fontaines
Où tournent les phalènes
Des Nuits Élyséennes!

– Pimbèche aux yeux vaincus, bellâtre aux beaux jarrets,
Donnez votre fumier à la fleur du Regret.

Voilà que son haleine
N'embaum' plus la verveine!
Drôle de phénomène . . .
Hein, à l'année prochaine?

– Vierges d'hier, ce soir traîneuses de fœtus,
À genoux! voici l'heure où se plaint l'Angélus.

Nous n'irons plus aux bois,
Les pins sont éternels,
Les cors ont des appels! . . .

Neiges des pâles mois,
Vous serez mon missel!
– Jusqu'au jour de dégel.

COMPLAINTE DE L'AUTOMNE MONOTONE

Automne, automne, adieux de l'Adieu!
La tisane bout, noyant mon feu;
Le vent s'époumonne
À reverdir la bûche où mon grand cœur tisonne.
Est-il de vrais yeux?
Nulle ne songe à m'aimer un peu.

Upset you, have I, a pain?
Come to the fountain's rain
Where moths fly round again,
Elysian Nights the strain.

– Airs-and-graceless shrew, eyes conquered, fop with fine legs,
Give to the flower Regret all your manure, the dregs.

So, then, your breath again
Won't smell of the vervain!
Funny old caper, inane . . .
Next year, eh, once again?

– Yesterday's virgins, this evening's carriers, embryous,
Down on your knees. Time for the moaning Angelus.

We'll go no more to the wood.
The pines are eternal there,
Horns sound on the air! . . .

Snow in pale months stood,
You'll be my book of prayer!
– Till thaw comes everywhere.

COMPLAINT OF MONOTONOUS AUTUMN

Autumn, autumn, goodbye to Goodbye!
The brew boils over, makes my fire die;
The wind huffs till it croaks
To bring to leaf again the log my big heart pokes.
Is there an honest eye?
No girl thinks loving me worth a try.

Milieux aptères,
Ou sans divans;
Regards levants,
Deuils solitaires
Vers des Sectaires!

Le vent, la pluie, oh! le vent, la pluie!
Antigone, écartez mon rideau;
Cet ex-ciel tout suie,
Fond-il *decrescendo, statu quo, crescendo*?
Le vent qui s'ennuie,
Retourne-t-il bien les parapluies?

Amours gibiers!
Aux jours de givre,
Rêver sans livre,
Dans les terriers
Chauds de fumiers!

Plages, chemins de fer, ciels, bois morts,
Bateaux croupis dans les feuilles d'or,
Le quart aux étoiles,
Paris grasseyant par chic aux prises de voiles:
De trop poignants cors
M'ont hallalisé ces chers décors.

Meurtres, alertes,
Rêves ingrats!
En croix, les bras;
Roses ouvertes,
Divines pertes!

Le soleil mort, tout nous abandonne.
Il se crut incompris. Qu'il est loin!
Vent pauvre, aiguillonne
Ces convois de martyrs se prenant à témoins!
La terre, si bonne,
S'en va, pour sûr, passer cet automne.

Apterous zone,
No sofa-bed;
Eye-rise; tread,
Mourning alone,
To Sectarians head.

Wind and rain, and oh, the wind and rain!
Antigone, draw my curtain back;
Does this ex-sky, soot-stain,
Blend *decrescendo*, *status quo*, *crescendo* rack?
The wind that's bored insane:
Does it turn the brollies back again?

Small-game affairs!
On days of frost,
To dream, books lost,
In burrows like theirs,
Dung-warm in pairs!

Shores, railway lines, skies, the woods foundered,
Boats clagged in leaves of gold surrounded,
The watch under the stars,
Paris, gripped in sails, and showily rolling r's:
Too poignant, horns sounded
The mort of these dear scenes they'd hounded.

In bad dreams doss,
Murders, alarms!
Roses' blown charms,
Divine loss!
Your arms cross.

The sun dead, feeling misunderstood.
Everything leaves us. How far it is!
You wretched wind, you should
Spur these trains of martyrs acting as witnesses!
A cert, the earth so good,
Is off to spend the autumn out of the wood.

Nuits sous-marines!
Pourpres forêts,
Torrents de frais,
Bancs en gésines,
Tout s'illumine!

— Allons, fumons une pipette de tabac,
En feuilletant un de ces si vieux almanachs,

En rêvant de la petite qui unirait
Aux charmes de l'œillet ceux du chardonneret.

COMPLAINTE DE L'ANGE INCURABLE

Je t'expire mes Cœurs bien barbouillés de cendres;
Vent esquinté de toux des paysages tendres!

Où vont les gants d'avril, et les rames d'antan?
L'âme des hérons fous sanglote sur l'étang.

Et vous, tendres
D'antan?

Le hoche-queue pépie aux écluses gelées;
L'amante va, fouettée aux plaintes des allées.

Sais-tu bien, folle pure, où sans châle tu vas?
— Passant oublié des yeux gais, j'aime là-bas . . .

— En allées
Là-bas!

Le long des marbriers (Encore un beau commerce!)
Patauge aux défoncés un convoi, sous l'averse.

Submarine nights!
Red forests thresh,
Torrents so fresh,
Shoals' birthing sites,
All interlights!

– Come on now, let's smoke a little pipe, relax,
Leafing through one of these so ancient almanacs,

Dreaming of the pretty little girl who'd clinch
In one the charms of the pink and those of the gold finch.

COMPLAINT OF THE INCURABLE ANGEL

I expire for you, my Loves so smutted with cinders, ashen;
The wind wracked with coughs from regions of tender passion!

Where go the gloves of April, the oars of yesteryear?
The soul of mad herons is sobbing on the mere.

And you, each passion
Of yesteryear?

The wagtail whistles to the locks that the ice packs;
The loved one's going, driven by plaints of the tracks.

And where, pure fool, d'you go without a shawl to wear?
– Stroller forgotten of lively eyes, I love down there . . .

– On the tracks
Down there!

Past monumental masons (A roaring trade as yet!)
A cortège flounders round the potholes in the wet.

Un trou, qu'asperge un prêtre âgé qui se morfond,
Bâille à ce libéré de l'être; et voici qu'on

        Le déverse
          Au fond.

Les moulins décharnés, ailes hier allègres,
Vois, s'en font les grands bras du haut des coteaux maigres!

Ci-gît n'importe qui. Seras-tu différent,
Diaphane d'amour, ô Chevalier-Errant?

        Claque, ô maigre
          Errant!

Hurler avec les loups, aimer nos demoiselles,
Serrer ces mains sauçant dans de vagues vaisselles!

Mon pauvre vieux, il le faut pourtant! et puis, va,
Vivre est encor le meilleur parti ici-bas.

        Non! vaisselles
          D'ici-bas!

Au-delà plus sûr que la Vérité! des ailes
D'Hostie ivre et ravie aux cités sensuelles!

Quoi? Ni Dieu, ni l'art, ni ma Sœur Fidèle; mais
Des ailes! par le blanc suffoquant! à jamais,

        Ah! des ailes
          À jamais!

– Tant il est vrai que que la saison dite d'automne
N'est aux cœurs mal fichus rien moins que folichonne.

An aged priest, frozen bored stiff, asperges the gap
That yawns for someone freed of being; here's the chap

Cast in and let
Down slap.

Their sail-wings spritely yesterday, the bony mills,
Look, spreading wide their arms from tops of barren hills!

Here lies no matter who. Will you, transparent mite
Of love, be any different, you knight-errantite?

Croak with your ills,
Thin errantite.

To love our damsels, howl whenever the wolf-pack wishes,
And clasp those hands that dip in some or other dishes!

My poor old chap, one must, however, and then go;
To live is still the better part for us below.

No, not dishes
Here below!

Beyond and surer than the Truth is! some Host's wings
Drunk and ravished in the sensual city-flings!

What? Not God, Art, nor my loyal Sister; but wings to soar!
Through the white and stifling blankness – ever more,

Ah, but wings
Ever more!

– So very true; the season, autumn, to give its name,
For dodgy hearts is not at all a frolicking game.

COMPLAINTE DES NOSTALGIES PRÉHISTORIQUES

La nuit bruine sur les villes.
Mal repu des gains machinals,
On dîne; et gonflé d'idéal,
Chacun sirote son idylle,
    Ou furtive, ou facile.

Échos des grands soirs primitifs!
Couchants aux flambantes usines,
Rude paix des sols en gésine,
Cri jailli là-bas d'un massif,
    Violuptés à vif!

Dégringolant une vallée,
Heurter, dans des coquelicots,
Une enfant bestiale et brûlée
Qui suce, en blaguant les échos,
    De juteux abricots.

Livrer aux langueurs des soirées
Sa toison où du cristal luit,
Pourlécher ses lèvres sucrées,
Nous barbouiller le corps de fruits
    Et lutter comme essui!

Un moment, béer, sans rien dire,
Inquiets d'une étoile là-haut;
Puis, sans but, bien gentils satyres,
Nous prendre aux premiers sanglots
    Fraternels des crapauds.

Et, nous délèvrant de l'extase,
Oh! devant la lune en son plein,
Là-bas, comme un bloc de topaze,
Fous, nous renverser sur les reins,
    Riant, battant des mains!

COMPLAINT OF PREHISTORIC NOSTALGIAS

Over the towns the drizzling night.
Mechanic gains make no square meal;
You dine; bloated on the ideal,
Each sips his fancy, rose or white,
    Clandestine or light.

Echoes of primitive nights survive!
Sunsets with factories flaming red,
Crude peace of soils in childbed,
Cry from a massif launched in dive,
    Violuptures alive.

And, in a valley tumbling down,
Among the poppies jolt a kid
Sucking, creaturely, tanned brown,
Lush apricots, who parroted
    The echoes as she did.

To liberate in evening languidness
Her locks where glints of crystal ply;
Her sugared lips to lick and press,
And daub ourselves with fruits nearby,
    Tussle each other dry!

One moment gape and no word said,
Disquieted by a star above;
Then gentle satyrs, no aim in head,
To brother toads' first sobs, make love
    Together, hand in glove.

And liperated from joy's thrill,
Oh, under the moon's full round
Up there, a mighty topaze pill,
Madly to turn, backs to the ground,
    Laughing, clap hands and pound!

La nuit bruine sur les villes:
Se raser le masque, s'orner
D'un frac deuil, avec art dîner,
Puis, parmi des vierges débiles,
    Prendre un air imbécile.

AUTRE COMPLAINTE DE L'ORGUE DE BARBARIE

Prolixe et monocorde,
Le vent dolent des nuits
Rabâche ses ennuis,
Veut se pendre à la corde
    Des puits! et puis?
    Miséricorde!

– Voyons, qu'est-ce que je veux?
Rien. Je suis-t-il malhûreux!

Oui, les phares aspergent
Les côtes en sanglots,
Mais les volets sont clos
Aux veilleuses des vierges,
    Orgue au galop,
    Larmes des cierges!

– Après? qu'est-ce qu'on y peut?
– Rien. Je suis-t-il malhûreux!

Vous, fidèle madone,
Laissez! Ai-je assisté,
Moi, votre puberté?
Ô jours où Dieu tâtonne,
    Passants d'été,
    Pistes d'automne!

Over the towns the drizzling night.
To shave the mask, to flaunt a pair
Of mourning tails, to dine, polite,
With art, with sickly virgins wear
    An imbecilic air.

ANOTHER COMPLAINT OF THE BARREL-ORGAN

Prolix and monotone,
The doleful night-wind's mope
Drones tediums of its own,
Wants to swing from the rope –
    Of wells. Well? No hope!
    Mercy! (Not shown!)

– Let's see: what is it I want to do?
Nothing. I'm too un'appy to!

Yes, lighthouses asperge in
Sobs the near shores;
And shutters close their doors
On night-lights of the virgin;
    Organ gallops all fours;
    Candle tears merging.

– And after? What is there one can do?
Nothing. I'm too un'appy to!

You, faithful Virgin? Some hopes!
Skip it. Wasn't it me
Attended your puberty?
Oh, days when God gropes,
    Strollers summery –
    Autumn slopes!

– Eh bien! aimerais-tu mieux . . .
– Rien. Je suis-t-il malhûreux!

    Cultes, Littératures,
    Yeux chauds, lointains ou gais,
    Infinis au rabais,
    Tout train-train, rien qui dure,
        Oh! à jamais
        Des créatures!

– Ah! ça qu'est-ce que je veux?
– Rien. Je suis-t-il malhûreux!

    Bagnes des pauvres bêtes,
    Tarifs d'alléluias,
    Mortes aux camélias,
    Oh! lendemain de fête
        Et paria,
        Vrai, des planètes!

– Enfin! quels sont donc tes vœux?
– Nuls. Je suis-t-il malhûreux!

    La nuit monte, armistice
    Des cités, des labours.
    Mais il n'est pas, bon sourd,
    En ton digne exercice,
        De raison pour
        Que tu finisses?

– Bien sûr. C'est ce que je veux.
– Ah! Je suis-t-il malhûreux!

– Oh well, would you prefer to do . . .
Nothing. I'm too un'appy to.

    Cults and Literatures,
    Warm eyes, distant or bright,
    The cut-price infinite
    All routine, nothing endures,
        Creatures our plight
        Always, no cures!

– Ah, is that then what I want to do?
Nothing. I'm too un'appy to.

    Hard-labour for poor beast,
    Tariffs of alleluias,
    Dead in the camellias,
    Oh, hangover on feast,
        And outcast as
        A planetiste!

In short! Then what are your wishes, you?
None. I'm too un'appy to.

    Night deepens, truce in session
    On cities, farmsteads, here.
    But isn't it, my good cloth-ear,
    Within your worthy profession,
        A reason (hear, hear!)
        To cease from expression?

– Oh, sure. That's what I want to do.
But, ah, I'm too un'appy to.

COMPLAINTE DU PAUVRE CHEVALIER-ERRANT

Jupes des quinze ans, aurores de femmes,
Qui veut, enfin, des palais de mon âme?
Perrons d'œillets blancs, escaliers de flamme,
Labyrinthes alanguis,
Édens qui
Sonneront, sous vos pas reconnus, des airs reconquis.

Instincts-levants souriant par les fentes,
Méditations un doigt à la tempe,
Souvenirs clignotant comme des lampes,
Et, battant les corridors,
Vains essors,
Les Dilettantismes chargés de colliers de remords.

Oui, sans bruit, vous écarterez mes branches,
Et verrez comme, à votre mine franche,
Viendront à vous mes biches les plus blanches,
Mes ibis sacrés, mes chats,
Et, rachats!
Ma Vipère de Lettres aux bien effaçables crachats.

Puis, frêle mise au monde! ô Toute Fine,
Ô ma Tout-universelle orpheline,
Au fond de chapelles de mousseline
Pâle, ou jonquille à pois noirs,
Dans les soirs,
Feu-d'artificeront envers vous mes sens encensoirs!

Nous organiserons de ces parties!
Mes caresses, naïvement serties,
Mourront, de ta gorge aux vierges hosties,
Aux amandes de tes seins!
Ô tocsins,
Des cœurs dans le roulis des empilements de coussins.

COMPLAINT OF THE POOR KNIGHT-ERRANT

Oh, skirts of fifteen, in woman's dawning role,
Who wants, at last, some palaces of my soul?
Steps of white carnations, stairways of flame; stroll
    Languorous labyrinths; tour
        Edens galore
That will resound to your known tread with airs restored once more.

Rising instinct-daybreaks smiling through the chinks;
Finger to the forehead, meditations, thinks,
Souvenirs that twinkle as the lamplight winks.
    And, beating the corridors,
        Vain flight soars,
Dilettantries in penitential collars of remorse.

Yes, without a sound, you will part my branches
And see how at your honest face advances
The whitest of my does towards your glances,
    My sacred ibises, my cats,
        Redemptions! – That's
My Lettered Snake whose spit just wipes off like a prat's.

Then, frail-clad to the world! my All that is Fine,
Altogether-universal orphan, mine,
In chapel depths of pale muslin, or design
    Of black dots on jonquil hue,
        Evenings through
My uncensury senses will firework soft soap for you!

We will organise such parties, oh the most!
My kisses simply set'll give up their ghost
Along your throat and down to your virgin host,
    From breasts to almond eyes!
        Alarm cries,
For hearts that rolling of the cushions may capsize.

Tu t'abandonnes au Bon, moi j'abdique;
Nous nous comblons de nos deux Esthétiques;
Tu condimentes mes piments mystiques,
J'assaisonne tes saisons;
Nous blasons,
À force d'étapes sur nos collines, l'Horizon!

Puis j'ai des tas d'éternelles histoires,
Ô mers, ô volières de ma Mémoire!
Sans compter les passes évocatoires!
Et quand tu t'endormiras,
Dans les draps
D'un somme, je t'éventerai de lointains opéras.

Orage en deux cœurs, ou jets d'eau des siestes,
Tout sera Bien, contre ou selon ton geste,
Afin qu'a peine un prétexte te reste
De froncer tes chers sourcils,
Ce souci:
«Ah! suis-je née, infiniment, pour vivre par ici?»

– Mais j'ai beau parader, toutes s'en fichent!
Et je repars avec ma folle affiche,
Boniment incompris, piteux *sandwiche*:
Au Bon Chevalier-Errant,
Restaurant,
Hôtel meublé, Cabinets de lecture, prix courants.

You throw yourself on the Good, I abdicate;
We fill ourselves with our two Aesthetics straight;
You pep my mystical peppers up a rate,
   I season your season's zest.
    How we crest
Our hills each day we dull the Horizon from east to west!

Then I've everlasting stories, pile on pile,
O seas, O pigeon-runs in Memory's file!
Leave out evocatory passes meanwhile!
   And when you feel sleep win, in
    Bed linen
You'll nap and I'll fan you with distant operas, dimin –

Siestas' fountains or storm in both hearts brewing,
All will be Well, with or without your doing,
So you'll have hardly one excuse for screwing
   Up so much those brows so dear –
    This one fear:
'Ah, but was I infinitely born to live just round here?'

– Vain my parading; women my image pan!
And round I go again, poor sandwich man,
Patter misunderstood, my fool pitch ran:
   At the Good Knight-Errant: Rest-
    Aurant; Guest
And Residential; Reading Rooms; standard rates on request.

COMPLAINTE DES FORMALITÉS NUPTIALES

LUI

Allons, vous prendrez froid.

ELLE

              Non; je suis un peu lasse.
Je voudrais écouter toujours ce cor de chasse!

LUI

Dis, veux-tu te vêtir de mon Être éperdu?

ELLE

Tu le sais; mais il fait si pur à la fenêtre . . .

LUI

Ah! tes yeux m'ont trahi l'Idéal à connaître;
Et je le veux, de tout l'univers de mon être!
       Dis, veux-tu?

ELLE

Devant cet univers, je me veux femme;
C'est pourquoi tu le sais. Mais quoi! ne m'as-tu pas
Prise toute déjà? par tes yeux, sans combats!
À la messe, au moment du grand Alléluia,
       N'as-tu pas eu mon âme?

LUI

Oui; mais l'Unique Loi veut que notre serment
Soit baptisé des roses de ta croix nouvelle;
Tes yeux se font mortels, mais ton destin m'appelle,
Car il sait que, pour naître aux moissons mutuelles,
Je dois te caresser bien singulièrement:

COMPLAINT OF NUPTIAL FORMALITIES

HE

Come on, you'll get cold.

SHE

                      No, I'm tired, just a bit.
I'd always like that hunting horn, the sound of it.

HE

D'you want to wear my roused-up Being? Say if you do,

SHE

You know; yet at the window it's so pure, I feel . . .

HE

Ah, your eyes have betrayed me to know of the Ideal;
With all the universe of my being I wish it real!
       Tell me, do you?

SHE

Before that universe, I want my woman's role;
That's why you know it. But there, haven't you quite
Had all of me already? With your eyes, no fight!
At mass the moment of the Alleluia's height,
       Haven't you had my soul?

HE

Yes, but the Law Unique requires the oath we say
Be baptised with the roses of your new cross here;
Your eyes turn mortal, but your destiny calls me clear.
It knows that to be born of mutual sowings, dear,
I must caress you in a very singular way:

Vous verrez mon palais! vous verrez quelle vie!
J'ai de gros lexicons et des photographies,

> De l'eau, des fruits, maints tabacs,
> Moi, plus naïf qu'hypocondre,
> Vibrant de tact à me fondre,
> Trempé dans les célibats.
> Bon et grand comme les bêtes,
> Pointilleux mais emballé,
> Inconscient mais esthète,
> Oh! veux-tu nous en aller
> Vers les pôles dont vous êtes?

Vous verrez mes voiliers! vous verrez mes jongleurs!
Vous soignerez les fleurs de mon *bateau de fleurs*.

Vous verrez qu'il y en a plus que je n'en étale,
Et quels violets gros deuil sont ma couleur locale,

Et que mes yeux sont ces vases d'Élection
Des Danaïdes où sans fin nous puiserions!

> Des prairies adorables,
> Loin des mufles des gens;
> Et, sous les ciels changeants,
> Maints hamacs incassables!

>> Dans les jardins
>> De nos instincts
>> Allons cueillir
>> De quoi guérir . . .

Cuirassés des calus de mainte expérience,
Ne mettant qu'en mes yeux leurs lettres de créance,
Les orgues de mes sens se feront vos martyrs
Vers des cieux sans échos étoilés à mourir!

You'll see my palace; you'll see the life I lead!
I've photographs and massive dictionaries to read,

Water, fruits, tobacco, Me,
Not hypochondriac – ingenuous,
With tact to melt quite tremulous,
Dampened with this celibacy.
Like beasts, and good and energetic,
Finicking yet headstrong,
Inconscient but aesthetic,
Oh! d'you want us to go along
To whose you are, the poles magnetic?

You'll see my sailers! you'll see my jugglers and their powers;
And you will tend the flowers of my *craft of flowers.*

You'll see there's nothing I've withheld that you'll uncover,
And what deep mourning violets provide my local colour;

And how my eyes are these two great Election urns
For Danaids where endlessly we'd draw by turns.

Adorable prairies there,
Folk's snitches out of range;
And, under skies that change,
Unbreakable hammocks share!

In garden precincts
Of our instincts,
Come, let us pick
A cure that's quick . . .

Armoured with calluses of experience manifold,
And in my eyes the only letters of credit I hold,
The organs of my senses will be your martyrs' breath,
Rising to heavens without echoes starred to death!

ELLE

Tu le sais; mais tout est si décevant! ces choses
Me poignent, après tout, d'un infaillible émoi!
Raconte-moi ta vie, ou bien étourdis-moi.
Car je me sens obscure, et, je ne sais pourquoi,
Je me compare aux fleurs injustement écloses . . .

LUI

Tu verras, c'est un rêve. Et tu t'éveilleras
Guérie enfin du mal de pousser solitaire.
Puis, ma fine convalescente du Mystère,
On vous soignera bien, nuit et jour, seuls sur terre.
    Tu verras?

ELLE

Tu le sais. Ah! – si tu savais! car tu m'a prise!
Bien au-delà! avec tes yeux, qui me suffisent.
Oui, tes yeux francs seront désormais mon église.
   Avec nos regards seulement,
   Alors, scellons notre serment?

LUI

Allons, endormez-vous, mortelle fiancée.
Là, dans mes bras loyaux, sur mon grand cœur bercée,
Suffoquez aux parfums de l'unique pensée
Que la vie est sincère et m'a fait le plus fort.

ELLE

Tiens, on n'entend plus ce cor; vous savez, ce cor . . .

LUI

L'Ange des Loyautés l'a baisée aux deux tempes;
Elle dort maintenant dans l'angle de ma lampe.

SHE

You know; but everything's so disappointing. These things
Shake me, after all, with an infallible emotion!
Tell me your life or else astound me with devotion;
I feel I'm in the dark; and, why I have no notion,
Compare myself with flowers' too early blossomings.

HE

You'll see. It's just a dream, and you'll awaken new,
Cured at last of having to flourish on your own.
And then, my worthy convalescent of the Unknown,
You'll be well cared for, night and day, ourselves alone,
                You'll see, won't you?

SHE

You know. Ah, if you only knew. You've taken me
Quite beyond; your eyes are my sufficiency.
Yes, your honest eyes my church henceforth will be.
            So just with looks then shall we both
            Swear to each other on our oath?

HE

Come, my mortal child betrothed, sleep and take your rest,
Here in my faithful arms, cradled in my heart's deep nest;
Suffocate in the perfume of this one thought pressed:
That life's sincere and has created me the stronger.

SHE

Wait! That horn; you know, that horn . . . it's heard no
    longer . . .

HE

The Angel of Loyalties has kissed her on the brow;
Within the angle of my lamp she's sleeping now.

Ô Nuit,
Fais-toi lointaine
Avec ta traîne
Qui bruit!

Ô défaillance universelle!
Mon unique va naître aux moissons mutuelles!
Pour les fortes roses de l'amour
Elle va perdre, lys pubère,
Ses nuances si solitaires,
Pour être, à son tour,
Dame d'atour
De Maïa!

Alléluia!

COMPLAINTE DES BLACKBOULÉS

«Ni vous, ni votre art, monsieur.» C'était un dimanche,
Vous savez où.
À vos genoux,
Je suffoquai, suintant de longues larmes blanches.

L'orchestre du jardin jouait ce *«si tu m'aimes»*
Que vous savez;
Et je m'en vais
Depuis, et pour toujours, m'exilant sur ce thème.

Et toujours, ce refus si monstrueux m'effraie
Et me confond
Pour vous au fond,
Si Regard-Incarné! si moi-même! si vraie!

Night, night,
You and your brush
That will not hush,
Take flight.

Oh universal decline!
My one and only's to be born of mutual sowings – mine!
For love's strong roses, she,
My nubile lily, will forsake
Her shadows so remote, and take
Her turn to be
Woman in finery
Of Maya.

Alleluia.

COMPLAINT OF THE BLACKBALLED

'Not you, sir, nor your art.' One Sunday. You'd
Remember where.
I gasped for air
Against your knees, and felt long, guileless tears exude.

The garden orchestra played the 'If you love me' air
That you recall;
Once and for all,
Upon that theme, into my exile, then, I fare.

And, ever since, that monstrous denial frightens me,
Confounds me for you
At depth, so true!
So Look-Incarnate! so myself! and so all three!

Bien. – Maintenant, voici ce que je vous souhaite,
　　　　Puisque, après tout,
　　　　En ce soir d'août,
Vous avez craché vers l'Art, par-dessus ma tête.

Vieille et chauve à vingt ans, sois prise pour une autre,
　　　　Et sans raison,
　　　　Mise en prison,
Très loin, et qu'un geôlier, sur toi, des ans, se vautre.

Puis, passe à Charenton, parmi de vagues folles,
　　　　Avec Paris
　　　　Là-bas, fleuri,
Ah! rêve trop beau! Paris où je me console.

Et demande à manger, et qu'alors on confonde!
　　　　Qu'on croie à ton
　　　　Refus! et qu'on
Te nourrisse, horreur! horreur! horreur! à la sonde.

La sonde t'entre par le nez, Dieu vous bénisse!
　　　　À bas, les mains!
　　　　Et le bon vin,
Le lait, les œufs te gavent par cet orifice.

Et qu'après bien des ans de cette facétie,
　　　　Un interne (aux
　　　　Regards loyaux!)
Se trompe de conduit! et verse, et t'asphyxie.

Et voilà ce que moi, guéri, je vous souhaite,
　　　　Cœur rose, pour
　　　　Avoir un jour
Craché sur l'Art! l'Art pur! sans compter le poète.

So. – Now here's what I would wish for you instead,
        Since after all
        On that night-fall
In August you had spat on Art, over my head:

Old and bald at twenty, taken for some other, you,
        No reason given
        Be put in prison,
And far away in there for years a jailer cover you.

Then pass to Charenton, vague maniacs on the shelf,
        With Paris below,
        In flourishing show,
Ah, dream too lovely, Paris, where I console myself.

You ask for something to eat and someone makes a boob!
        Remembers you'd
        Refused, and food
Be forced upon you, horror, horror, with a tube.

The tube by way of the nose, God bless thee this!
        Hands down, hands down!
        And milk and brown
Eggs and the goodly wine bloat through that orifice.

And after years enough of such a practical joke
        A student (with looks
        So loyal) hooks
The tubing up all wrong, and pours, and then you choke.

That's what I wish, now cured, as you should undergo it,
        Rose heart, just that
        Because you spat
One day at Art! pure Art! and never mind the poet.

COMPLAINTE DES CONSOLATIONS

Quia voluit consolari.

Ses yeux ne me voient pas, son corps serait jaloux;
Elle m'a dit: «monsieur . . .» en m'enterrant d'un geste;
Elle est Tout, l'univers moderne et le céleste.
Soit! draguons donc Paris, et ravitaillons-nous,
      Tant bien que mal, du reste.

Les Landes, sans espoir de ses regards brûlés,
Semblaient parfois des paons prêts à mettre à la voile . . .
Sans chercher à me consoler vers les étoiles,
Ah! Je trouverai bien deux yeux aussi sans clés,
      Au Louvre, en quelque toile!

Oh! qu'incultes, ses airs, rêvant dans la prison
D'un *cant* sur le qui-vive au travers de nos hontes! . . .
Mais, en m'appliquant bien, moi dont la foi démonte
Les jours, les ciels, les nuits, dans les quatre saisons
      Je trouverai mon compte.

Sa bouche! à moi, ce pli pudiquement martyr
Où s'aigrissent des nostalgies de nostalgies!
Eh bien, j'irai parfois, très sincère vigie,
Du haut de Notre-Dame aider l'aube, au sortir,
      De passables orgies.

Mais, Tout va la reprendre! – Alors Tout m'en absout.
Mais, Elle est ton bonheur! – Non! je suis trop immense,
Trop chose. Comment donc! mais ma seule présénce
Ici-bas, vraie à s'y mirer, est l'air de Tout:
      De la Femme au Silence!

COMPLAINT OF CONSOLATIONS

Quia voluit consolari.

Her eyes didn't see me; jealous her body would have been;
She merely uttered, 'Sir . . .', with a gesture buried me;
She's the Whole, both modern universe and heavenly.
So be it! Then let's dredge Paris, supply ourselves, I mean,
      Elsewhere, as best as I can see.

Les Landes seemed, lacking any hope in her scorched looks,
From time to time like peacocks ready to take flight . . .
Not seeking my consolation in the stars of night,
Ah! I'll find two eyes all right, also closed books,
      In the Louvre, some canvas-ite!

Oh, how uncouth her airs and graces, dreaming in the prison
Of a *cant* fully alert to see through all our shames! . . .
Yet, with a proper approach, I, whose faith unframes
The days, the skies, and nights, in the all-weather business
      Will get something out of these games.

Her mouth! At me, that fold, so bashfully the martyr
Where nostalgias of nostalgias are turning sour!
Oh well, most sincere look-out, I'll sometimes spend an hour
From high on Notre Dame, to help the dawn's departure
      From orgies of passable power.

– The Whole'll have her again! – So absolves me the role.
But: She's your happiness! – No, I am too immense,
Too thing. Of course! But my being here presents,
True to its reflection there, the appearance of the Whole:
      From Woman to the Silence hence!

COMPLAINTE DES BONS MÉNAGES

L'Art sans poitrine m'a trop longtemps bercé dupe.
Si ses labours sont fiers, que ses blés décevants!
Tiens, laisse-moi bêler tout aux plis de ta jupe
      Qui fleure le couvent.

Le Génie avec moi, serf, a fait des manières;
Toi, jupe, fais frou-frou, sans t'inquiéter pourquoi,
Sous l'œillet bleu de ciel de l'unique théière,
      Sois toi-même, à part moi.

Je veux être pendu, si tu n'es pas discrète
Et *comme il faut*, vraiment! Et d'ailleurs tu m'es tout.
Tiens, j'aimerais les plissés de ta collerette
      Sans en venir à bout.

Mais l'Art, c'est l'Inconnu! qu'on y dorme et s'y vautre,
On peut ne pas l'avoir constamment sur les bras!
Eh bien, ménage au vent! Soyons Lui, Elle et l'Autre.
      Et puis, n'insistons pas.

COMPLAINT OF GOOD COUPLES

Breastless, Art's suckered me too long inert.
If her tillage is fine, how disappointing the wheat!
Here, let me bleat now at the pleats of your skirt
        With its tang of the convent, sweet.

Genius with me, slave, has put on its air.
You, skirt, go rustling, don't worry why, glide,
Under the skeye-blue pink of the teapot there,
        Just be yourself, on my side.

I'll be hanged if you're not totally discreet
And *as one should be*, really. You're otherwise all.
Sure, I'd love the folds of your collar, sweet,
        And they would never pall.

But Art's the Stranger. It's sleep and soak in it,
But can't be on your hands, no second missed!
So, goodbye, bliss. Let's be He, She, the Other bit.
        And then let's not insist.

COMPLAINTE DE LORD PIERROT

Au clair de la lune,
Mon ami Pierrot,
Filons, en costume,
Présider là-haut!
Ma cervelle est morte.
Que le Christ l'emporte!
Béons à la Lune,
La bouche en zéro.

Inconscient, descendez en nous par réflexes;
Brouillez les cartes, les dictionnaires, les sexes.

Tournons d'abord sur nous-même, comme un fakir!
(Agiter le pauvre être, avant de s'en servir.)

J'ai le cœur chaste et vrai comme une bonne lampe;
Oui, je suis en taille-douce, comme une estampe.

Vénus, énorme comme le Régent,
Déjà se pâme à l'horizon des grèves;
Et c'est l'heure, ô gens nés casés, bonnes gens,
De s'étourdir en longs trilles de rêves!
Corybanthe, aux quatre vents tous les draps!
Disloque tes pudeurs, à bas les lignes!
En costume blanc, je ferai le cygne,
Après nous le Déluge, ô ma Léda!
Jusqu'à ce que tournent tes yeux vitreux,
Que tu grelottes en rires affreux,
Hop! enlevons sur les horizons fades
Les menuets de nos pantalonnades!
Tiens! l'Univers
Est à l'envers . . .

– Tout cela vous honore,
Lord Pierrot, mais encore?

COMPLAINT OF LORD PIERROT

In the light of the moon,
My old mate Pierrot,
In costume let's assume
Heights above the flow.
My grey-matter's dead,
Christ receive my head!
Let us gawp the Moon,
The mouth that's in an O.

Inconscient, descend in us by reflexes;
Confuse the cards, the lexicons, the sexes.

And first let's turn upon ourselves like some fakir!
(Shake well before use if the poor being's clear.)

I have a heart that's chaste and true like a good lamp;
Yes, copperplate I am, engraved like a good stamp.

Venus, immense as the Regent, faints away
Already on the sky-line of the sands;
Good folk, born pigeon-holed, it's time of day
To find diversion in dream's long trilling bands.
Corybant, to the four winds, cover, sheet!
Luxate your modesties, lines down! And me,
The swan in whitest costume's what I'll be;
And after us the Deluge, Leda, my sweet!
Until I see the glazing of your eyes,
Until you shake with laughs that terrorise,
Let's up! And on the pallid skyline whiz
Our minuets of pantalooneries!
                    The Universe, no doubt
                    Is turned to inside out.

– Lord P, You're up to scratch,
But now for your next snatch?

– Ah! qu'une, d'elle-même, un beau soir sût venir,
Ne voyant que boire à mes lèvres, ou mourir!

Je serais, savez-vous, la plus noble conquête
Que femme, au plus ravi du Rêve, eût jamais faite!

D'ici là, qu'il me soit permis
De vivre de vieux compromis.

Où commence, où finit l'humaine
Ou la divine dignité?

Jonglons avec les entités,
Pierrot s'agite et Tout le mène!
Laissez faire, laissez passer;
Laisser passer, et laissez faire:
Le semblable, c'est le contraire,
Et l'univers, c'est pas assez!
Et je me sens, ayant pour cible
Adopté la vie impossible,
De moins en moins localisé!

– Tout cela vous honore,
Lord Pierrot, mais encore?

– Il faisait, ah! si chaud si sec.
Voici qu'il pleut, qu'il pleut, bergères!
Les pauvres Vénus bocagères
Ont la roupie à leur nez grec!

– Oh! de moins en moins drôle;
Pierrot sait mal son rôle?

– J'ai le cœur triste comme un lampion forain . . .
Bah! j'irai passer la nuit dans le premier train;

Sûr d'aller, ma vie entière,
Malheureux comme les pierres. *(Bis)*

– If only off her own bat one of them'd dropped by,
Intent on drinking from my lips, or else to die!

You know, I'd be the noblest conquest that could fall
To woman in her most ravishing dream of all!

> So may I be allowed, here on,
> The old compromise to go upon.

> Where does it start, and where closes
> Divine or human dignities?

> Let's juggle with the entities,
> P. proposes, the Whole disposes!
> Give way to it, and let it be;
> Let it be, give way to it:
> Resemblance is the opposite,
> The universe not enough! And me,
> Adopting now as my ideal
> The life not possible, I feel
> Much less of the locality.

> > – Lord P, You're up to scratch,
> > But now for your next snatch?

> It was, ah, dry and very warm.
> Nymphs, here's the rain, here comes the rain!
> Poor bunged-up Venuses complain
> As drops on their Greek noses form!

> > – Oh, less and less amusing soul;
> > Pierrot hardly knows his role?

– I have a heart as sorry as a funfair light . . .
Bah, in the first train come I'll spend the night;

> Certain to go my whole life through
> Unfortunate, as the stones do. *(Repeat)*

AUTRE COMPLAINTE DE LORD PIERROT

Celle qui doit me mettre au courant de la Femme!
Nous lui dirons d'abord, de mon air le moins froid:
«La somme des angles d'un triangle, chère âme,
    Est égale à deux droits.»

Et si ce cri lui part: «Dieu de Dieu! que je t'aime!»
– «Dieu reconnaîtra les siens.» Ou piquée au vif:
– «Mes claviers ont du cœur, tu seras mon seul thème.»
    Moi: «Tout est relatif.»

De tous ses yeux, alors! se sentant trop banale:
«Ah! tu ne m'aimes pas; tant d'autres sont jaloux!»
Et moi, d'un œil qui vers l'Inconscient s'emballe:
    «Merci, pas mal; et vous?»

– «Jouons au plus fidèle!» – «À quoi bon, ô Nature!
Autant à qui perd gagne!» Alors, autre couplet:
– «Ah! tu te lasseras le premier, j'en suis sûre . . .»
    – «Après vous, s'il vous plaît.»

Enfin, si, par un soir, elle meurt dans mes livres,
Douce; feignant de n'en pas croire encor mes yeux,
J'aurai un: «Ah ça, mais, nous avions De Quoi vivre!
    C'était donc sérieux?»

ANOTHER COMPLAINT OF LORD PIERROT

On Woman, that one should bring me up to date!
We'll try out first, my manner the least cool:
'The angles of a triangle, dear soul, equate
               With two right angles as a rule.'

And should this cry escape her: 'God supreme,
How much I love you!' Or, pricked to the quick, she:
'My touch has heart; you'll be my only theme.'
               – 'Relatively speaking,' – me.

With all her eyes, next, feeling very trite:
'Ah! you don't love me; so many others jealous!'
And me, eye flashed to the Inconscient's height:
               'Not bad, thanks. You? Do tell us.'

'Let's play who's truest!' – 'Nature, what's the profit?
The loser wins!' A further couplet, too:
'You'll tire the first; ah, yes, I'm certain of it . . .'
               'Oh, no, please, after you.'

Last, if she dies, one evening, quiet, in my books,
Feigning I don't yet trust my eyes, I'll try:
'Oh, that! but we'd the Wherewithal. It looks
               It was straight, then – as a die?'

COMPLAINTE SUR CERTAINS ENNUIS

Un couchant des Cosmogonies!
Ah! que la Vie est quotidienne . . .
Et, du plus vrai qu'on se souvienne,
Comme on fut piètre et sans génie . . .

On voudrait s'avouer des choses,
Dont on s'étonnerait en route,
Que feraient une fois pour toutes!
Qu'on s'entendrait à travers poses.

On voudrait saigner le Silence,
Secouer l'exil des causeries;
Et non! ces dames sont aigries
Par des questions de préséance.

Elles boudent là, l'air capable.
Et, sous le ciel, plus d'un s'explique,
Par quels gâchis suresthétiques
Ces êtres-là sont adorables.

Justement, une nous appelle,
Pour l'aider à chercher sa bague,
Perdue (où dans ce terrain vague?)
Un souvenir d'AMOUR, dit-elle!

Ces êtres-là sont adorables!

COMPLAINT OVER CERTAIN ENNUIS

A sunset of Cosmogonies!
How mundane life is . . . And of all
The truest things we may recall
How paltry we were, no geniuses . . .

We'd like to confess to some things
Which in their course would stun our ear,
Once and for all would make us hear
Each other through the posturings.

We'd like to bleed the Silence white,
Shake off the exile of small-talk,
And no, not yet! the ladies baulk,
Piqued, to get precedences right;

Air knowing looks and sulking features.
And more than one man's exegesis
States by what superaesthetic greases
These beings are adorable creatures.

Right now one of them gives a call
For us to find her missing ring,
Lost (where in this waste's the thing?)
Keepsake of LOVE, she tells us all.

These beings are adorable creatures!

COMPLAINTE DES NOCES DE PIERROT

Où te flatter pour boire dieu,
Ma provisoire corybante?
Je sauce mon âme en tes yeux,
Je ceins ta beauté pénitente,
Où donc vis-tu? Moi si pieux,
     Que tu m'es lente, lente!

Tes cils m'insinuent: c'en est trop;
Et leurs calices vont se clore,
Sans me jeter leur dernier mot,
Et refouler mes métaphores,
De leur petit air comme il faut?
     Isis, levez le store!

Car cette fois, c'est pour de bon;
Trop d'avrils, quittant la partie
Devant des charmes moribonds,
J'ai bâclé notre eucharistie
Sous les trépieds où ne répond
     Qu'une aveugle Pythie!

Ton tabernacle est dévasté?
Sois sage, distraite égoïste!
D'ailleurs, suppôt d'éternité,
Le spleen de tout ce qui s'existe
Veut qu'en ce blanc matin d'été,
     Je sois ton exorciste!

Ainsi, fustigeons ces airs plats
Et ces dolentes pantomimes
Couvrant d'avance du vieux glas
Mes tocsins à l'hostie ultime!
Ah! tu me comprends n'est-ce pas,
     Toi, ma moins pauvre rime?

COMPLAINT OF PIERROT'S WEDDING

Where touch you up to drink the divine,
My temporary corybantic, you.
I dunk my soul in your eyes so fine,
I wear your hairshirt beauty, too.
Where do you dwell? Such piety, mine,
      Why slow, so slow, come through!

Your lashes hint: over the top;
And won't their chalices now shut,
Their final word to me not drop,
And all my metaphors rebut,
With airs of being right and proper?
      Isis, raise the sun-blind up!

For this time now it is for good.
Too many Aprils, the party missed,
Faced with charms so much dead wood,
I've cobbled together our Eucharist
Before the tripod where there stood
      A mute blind Pythianist.

Your tabernacle's razed, you mean?
Be good, distracted egotist,
Or eternity's henchman, spleen
At all that's existent, will insist,
This summer morning, white and clean,
      That I become your exorcist.

These dull airs, then, let us dispel
And all this doleful pantomime,
Precluding with the same old knell
My tocsins for last host this time!
Ah, you get me, don't you, well,
      You, my least wretched rime?

Introïbo, voici l'Époux!
Hallali! songe au pôle, aspire;
Je t'achèterai des bijoux,
Garde-moi ton *ut* de martyre . . .
Quoi! bébé bercé, c'est donc tout?
      Tu n'as plus rien à dire?

– Mon dieu, mon dieu! je n'ai rien eu,
J'en suis encore aux poncifs thèmes!
Son teint me redevient connu,
Et, sur son front tout au baptême,
Aube déjà l'air ingénu!
L'air vrai! l'air non mortel quand même!

      Ce qui fait que je l'aime,

    Et qu'elle est même vraiment
      La chapelle rose
      Où parfois j'expose
      Le Saint-Sacrement
    De mon humeur du moment.

COMPLAINTE DU VENT QUI S'ENNUIE LA NUIT

Ta fleur se fane, ô fiancée?
Oh! gardes-en encore un peu
La corolle qu'a compulsée
Un soir d'ennui trop studieux!
Le vent des toits qui pleure et rage,
Dans ses assauts et ses remords,
Sied au nostalgique naufrage
Où m'a jeté ta Toison-d'Or.

      Le vent assiège
          Dans sa tour
      Le sortilège

Introibo: the Groom admit!
Halloo! Aspire, the pole muse deep;
I'll buy you jewels, exquisite;
That *do . . . me* martyrdom just keep
For me . . . What, babe? That's all, that's it?
     No word more, not a peep?

– My God, my God, I've had nothing, too.
I'm stuck with this hackneyed to and fro!
Her colour's back to what I knew,
And on her brow, all baptism's glow,
Day-springs the innocent air! The true
Air! that air not mortal even so.

     That makes my love for her grow,

   And makes her truly present
     The chapel of rose
     Where I expose
     The Holy Sacrament,
  Of my present mood and bent.

COMPLAINT OF THE WIND BORED AT NIGHT

Your flower's fading, my elect?
Oh, a bit longer save its buddy
Corolla that's been thoroughly checked
A dull evening with too much study.
Off roofs the wind's assaults, remorse,
Its tears and rage, are of a piece
With that nostalgic shipwrecked course
Where I was cast by your Golden Fleece.

     The siege wind's edge
       Beleaguers Love
    With its sortilege,

De l'Amour;
Et, pris au piège,
Le sacrilège
Geint sans retour.

Ainsi, mon Idéal sans bride
T'ubiquitait de ses sanglots,
Ô calice loyal mais vide
Qui jouais à me rester clos!
Ainsi dans la nuit investie,
Sur tes pétales décevants,
L'Ange fileur d'eucharisties
S'afflige tout le long du vent.

Le vent assiège
Dans sa tour
Le sortilège
De l'Amour,
Et, pris au piège,
Le sacrilège
Geint sans retour.

Ô toi qu'un remords fait si morte,
Qu'il m'est incurable, en tes yeux,
D'écouter se morfondre aux portes
Le vent aux étendards des cieux!
Rideaux verts de notre hypogée,
Marbre banal du lavabo,
Votre hébétude ravagée
Est le miroir de mon tombeau.

Ô vent, allège
Ton discours
Des vains cortèges
De l'humour;
Je rentre au piège,
Peut-être y vais-je,
Tuer l'Amour!

In its tower above;
Snared in the cledge,
There, sacrilege
Whines in rebuff.

Thus, my Ideal without let
With sobs was ubiquating you,
O chalice, loyal but empty yet,
That played at shut to me on cue.
Thus in the beleaguered night,
Over your disappointing bloom,
The Angel that spins communion's rite
Grieves the length of the wind's boom.

The siege wind's edge
Beleaguers Love,
With its sortilege,
In its tower above;
Snared in the cledge,
There, sacrilege
Whines in rebuff.

O you so stone-dead with remorse
It's fatal to me now, in your eyes,
To hear wait freezing at your doors
The wind with the standards of the skies!
Green curtains of our hypogeum,
Plain marble of our lavatory,
Your ravaged hebetude – they seem
The mirror of the tomb for me.

Wind, lighten your sledge-
Hammer stuff,
Your vain cortège
Of humour. Enough!
Re-entering cledge,
Snare, I may edge
There to kill love!

COMPLAINTE DU PAUVRE CORPS HUMAIN

L'Homme et sa compagne sont serfs
De corps, tourbillonnants cloaques
Aux mailles de harpes de nerfs
Serves de tout et que détraque
Un fier répertoire d'attaques.

    Voyez l'homme, voyez!
    Si ça n'fait pas pitié!

Propre et correct en ses ressorts
S'assaisonnant de modes vaines,
Il s'admire, ce brave corps,
Et s'endimanche pour sa peine,
Quand il a bien sué la semaine.

    Et sa compagne! allons,
    Ma bell', nous nous valons.

Faudrait le voir, touchant et nu
Dans un décor d'oiseaux, de roses;
Ses tics réflexes d'ingénu,
Ses plis pris de mondaines poses;
Bref, sur beau fond vert, sa chlorose.

    Voyez l'Homme, voyez!
    Si ça n'fait pas pitié!

Les Vertus et les Voluptés
Détraquant d'un rien sa machine,
Il ne vit que pour disputer
Ce domaine à rentes divines
Aux lois de mort qui le taquinent.

    Et sa compagne! allons,
    Ma bell', nous nous valons.

COMPLAINT OF THE POOR HUMAN BODY

Man and his companion are serfs
Of flesh, are whirling cesspit sacks
In mailcoats linked from harps of nerves,
The slaves of all, and they're on racks
Of a fine repertoire of attacks.

> Look at the man, and look straight!
> If that's not a pitiable state!

Responses proper and unique,
Seasons himself in styles quite vain,
Admires himself, this fine physique,
And Sunday-suits him for his pain,
Though sweating all the week again.

> And his companion! Come, come,
> My beaut, we rate ourselves some.

You ought to see him, touching, bare
In some décor of birds and roses;
His reflex tics are callow there,
Skinfolds derived from routine poses;
In brief, on fine deep green, chlorosis.

> Look at Man, and look straight!
> If that's not a pitiable state!

Virtues and Voluptuous vices wrest
His frame with nothings to and fro;
And all he lives for's to contest
These grounds at holy rents below
With laws of death that plague him so.

> And his companion! Come, come,
> My beaut, we rate ourselves some.

Il se soutient de mets pleins d'art,
Se drogue, se tond, se parfume,
Se truffe tant, qu'il meurt trop tard;
Et la cuisine se résume
En mille infections posthumes.

     Oh! ce couple, voyez!
     Non, ça fait trop pitié.

Mais ce microbe subversif
Ne compte pas pour la Substance,
Dont les déluges corrosifs
Renoient vite pour l'Innocence
Ces fols germes de conscience.

     Nature est sans pitié
     Pour son petit dernier.

COMPLAINTE DU ROI DE THULÉ

Il était un roi de Thulé,
     Immaculé,
Qui, loin des jupes et des choses,
Pleurait sur la métempsychose
     Des lys en roses,
     Et quel palais!

Ses fleurs dormant, il s'en allait,
     Traînant des clés,
Broder aux seuls yeux des étoiles,
Sur une tour, un certain Voile
     De vive toile,
     Aux nuits de lait!

With arty food he feeds his state;
Drugs, barbers himself, perfumes,
Stuffs so much to die too late;
And then the cookery resumes
The thousand illnesses of tombs.

     Look, at the couple, straight, as such!
     Don't! you'd pity them too much.

But this subversive microbe is
As Substance, nothing much indeed,
For which the corrosive deluges
Redrown for Innocence, full speed,
Conscience's foolish germs that breed.

     Nature has no pity, son,
     For her latest little one.

COMPLAINT OF THE KING OF THULE

A king in Thule used to reign –
     Spotless of stain –
Who far from skirts and things like those
Mourned that the lily metempsychose
     Into the rose –
     Some palace-domain!

His flowers sleeping, he would go,
     With keys in tow,
To broider in a tower's height
A certain Sheet by the stars' lone sight,
     In cloth so bright
     On nights milk-white

Quand le Voile fut bien ourlé,
    Loin de Thulé,
Il rama fort sur les mers grises,
Vers le soleil qui s'agonise,
    Féerique Église!
    Il ululait:

«Soleil-crevant, encore un jour,
Vous avez tendu votre phare
Aux holocaustes vivipares,
Du culte qu'ils nomment l'Amour.

«Et comme, devant la nuit fauve,
Vous vous sentez défaillir,
D'un dernier flot d'un sang martyr
Vous lavez le seuil de l'Alcôve!

«Soleil! Soleil! moi je descends
Vers vos navrants palais polaires,
Dorloter dans ce Saint-Suaire
    Votre cœur bien en sang,
      En le berçant!»

Il dit, et, le Voile étendu,
    Tout éperdu,
Vers les coraux et les naufrages,
Le roi raillé des doux corsages,
    Beau comme un Mage
    Est descendu!

Braves amants! aux nuits de lait,
    Tournez vos clés!
Une ombre, d'amour pur transie,
Viendrait vous gémir cette scie:
«Il était un roi de Thulé
    Immaculé . . .»

And when the Sheet was well and sewn
    From Thule alone
He strongly rowed, on grey seas flying,
To where the Sun in pain was dying,
    A fay shrine, crying
    In howl and groan:

'Oh, sun-writhing, one more day again
You've shone your beacon from above
On holocausts that bear in pain
The cult that they have christened Love.

'And as, before wild night's divide,
You feel yourself faint in the head,
With martyr blood in a last tide
You wash the threshold to the Bed.

'Oh Sun! Oh Sun! Me, I descend
To your floating palaces of ice
To coddle in this Shroud of Christ
    Your heart's well bloodied end,
    And cradling, tend!'

And then, with Sheet at full extent,
    Distraught, he went
Towards the coral and the wrecks,
Laughed at by the gentle sex,
    This fine Mage-Rex
    Made his descent.

On nights of milk, bold lovers lain!
    Lock door, fix chain!
Pure love's chill shadow at the latch
Would come to groan for you this catch:
'A king in Thule used to reign,
    Spotless of stain . . .'

COMPLAINTE DU SOIR
DES COMICES AGRICOLES

Deux royaux cors de chasse ont encore un duo
            Aux échos,
Quelques fusées reniflent s'étouffer là-haut!

        Allez, allez, gens de la noce,
        Qu'on s'en donne une fière bosse!

Et comme le jour naît, que bientôt il faudra,
            À deux bras,
Peiner, se recrotter dans les labours ingrats,

        Allez, allez, gens que vous êtes,
        C'est pas tous les jours jour de fête!

Ce violon incompris pleure au pays natal,
            Loin du bal,
Et le piston risque un appel vers l'Idéal . . .

        Mais le flageolet les rappelle,
        Et allez donc, mâl's et femelles!

Un couple erre parmi les rêves des grillons,
            Aux sillons;
La fille écoute en tourmentant son médaillon.

        Laissez, laissez, ô cors de chasse,
        Puisque c'est le sort de la race.

Les beaux cors se sont morts; mais cependant qu'au loin,
            Dans les foins,
Crèvent deux rêves niais, sans maire et sans adjoint.

        Pintez, dansez, gens de la Terre,
        Tout est un triste et vieux Mystère.

COMPLAINT OF THE EVENING
OF THE AGRICULTURAL SHOW

Two royal hunting horns have yet another pair
            In echoes there,
Some rockets sniff up and snuff their sizzling flare.

        You people binging, show your paces,
        Scoff it, scoff it, stuff your faces.

And since the day is breaking when soon enough you must
            Both arms thrust
In thankless furrows, caked again in muck and dust,

        Go it, go it, the men you are,
        Not every day's a feast on par.

Not understood, that violin weeps its home in France
            Far from the dance,
And calling to the Ideal the cornet takes a chance.

        The flageolet brings them back down,
        Now, men and women, go to town!

A couple takes a stroll through dreams of crickets now,
            Fields under plough,
She listens, twisting up her locket anyhow.

        Leave them, leave them, oh hunting horn.
        That's the fate of the whole race born.

The fine horns fade and die; however far away,
            In the hay,
Sans mayor or deputy, two trite dreams turn grey.

        Dance, people of the Earth and swill,
        All is an old, sad Mystery still.

– Ah! le Premier que prit ce besoin insensé
                    De danser
Sur ce monde enfantin dans l'Inconnu lancé!

            Ô Terre, ô terre, ô race humaine,
            Vous me faites bien de la peine.

COMPLAINTE DES CLOCHES

Dimanche, à Liège

            Bin bam, bin bam,
         Les cloches, les cloches,
Chansons en l'air, pauvres reproches!
            Bin bam, bin bam,
         Les cloches en Brabant!

Petits et gros, clochers en fête,
De l'hôpital à l'Évêché,
Dans ce bon ciel endimanché,
Se carillonnent, et s'entêtent,
         À tue-tête! à tue-tête!

Bons vitraux, saignez impuissants
Aux allégresses hosannahlles
Des orgues lâchant leurs pédales,
Les tuyaux bouchés par l'encens!
         Car il descend! il descend!

Voici les lentes oriflammes
Où flottent la Vierge et les Saints!
Les cloches, leur battant des mains,
S'étourdissent en jeunes gammes
         Hymniclames! hymniclames!

– Ah, the First who felt this senseless need advance
                Making him dance
Upon this childish world thrown out to Unknown Chance!

      O Earth, O earth, humanity,
      It's quite a pain you give to me.

COMPLAINT OF BELLS

Sunday, in Liège

        The bells, the bells,
     Ding-dong-ding, dong-ding-dong,
Wretched reproaches, air-borne song!
        The Brabant bells,
     Ding-dong-bong, ding-dong-bong.

In fine and Sunday-suited sky,
Towers, tall and small, in festival,
Cathedral to the hospital,
Carillonnade, persist on high,
      At top voice, top voice cry!

Good windows impotently bleed
To hosannalian sprightliness
As organ pedals press, depress,
And incense blocks up pipe and reed,
      For he descends! Descends, indeed!

Look, gentle banners fluttering
Where Virgin and the Saints drift by!
The bells clap hands for them on high,
Dizzy themselves with callow ring
      Hymn-bellowing, hymn-bellowing!

Va, Globe aux studieux pourchas,
Où Dieu à peine encor s'épèle!
Bondis, Jérusalem nouvelle,
Vers les nuits grosses de rachats,
    Où les lys ne filent pas!

Édens mûrs, Unique Bohême!
Nous, les beaux anges effrénés;
Elles, des Regards incarnés,
Pouvant nous chanter, sans blasphème:
    Que je t'aime! pour moi-même!

Oui, les cloches viennent de loin!
Oui, oui, l'Idéal les fit fondre
Pour rendre les gens hypocondres,
Vêtus de noir, tendant le poing
    Vers un Témoin! Un Témoin!

Ah! cœur-battant, cogne à tue-tête
Vers ce ciel niais endimanché!
Clame, à jaillir de ton clocher,
Et nous retombe à jamais BÊTE.
    Quelle fête! quelle fête!

    Bin bam, bin bam,
    Les cloches! les cloches!
Chansons en l'air, pauvres reproches!
    Bin bam, bin bam,
    Les cloches en Brabant![1]

[1] Et ailleurs.

Get lost, you Globe of studied chases,
Where God hardly spells his name!
Leap, New Jerusalem, and aim
For gross nights of redeeming graces
      Where lilies don't spin out embraces!

Unique Bohemia, Edens ripe!
We, fine, unbridled angels prance;
They, of the incarnate Glance,
Without blaspheming there can pipe,
      How I love you! My own, my type!

From far the bells come harbinger!
Yes, yes, the Ideal had them cast
To turn folk hypochondriac fast,
Dressed in black, fist profferer
      To a Witnesser! A Witnesser!

Ah, clapper-heart, strike till you're creased
Towards this dumb sky Sunday-black!
Bellow, spouting from your stack,
Fall again for us forever BEAST.
      What a feast! What a feast!

      The bells, the bells,
    Ding-dong-ding, dong-ding-dong,
Wretched reproaches, air-borne song!
      The Brabant[1] bells,
    Ding-dong-bong, ding-dong-bong.

---

[1] And elsewhere. (*Author's note.*)

COMPLAINTE DES GRANDS PINS
DANS UNE VILLA ABANDONNÉE
À Bade

Tout hier, le soleil a boudé dans ses brumes,
Le vent jusqu'au matin n'a pas décoléré,
Mais, nous point des coteaux là-bas, un œil sacré
Qui va vous bousculer ces paquets de bitume!

> – Ah! vous m'avez trop, trop vanné,
> Bals de diamants, hanches roses;
> Et, bien sûr, je n'étais pas né
> Pour ces choses.

– Le vent jusqu'au matin n'a pas décoléré.
Oh! ces quintes de toux d'un chaos bien posthume,

> – Prés et bois vendus! Que de gens,
> Qui me tenaient mes gants, serviles,
> À cette heure, de mes argents,
> Font des piles!

– Délayant en ciels bas ces paquets de bitume
Qui grimpaient talonnés de noirs Misérérés!

> – Elles, coudes nus dans les fruits,
> Riant, changeant de doigts leurs bagues;
> Comme nos plages et nos nuits
> Leur sont vagues!

– Oh! ces quintes de toux d'un chaos bien posthume!
Chantons comme Memnon, le soleil a filtré,

> – Et moi, je suis dans ce lit cru
> De chambre d'hôtel, fade chambre,
> Seul, battu dans les vents bourrus
> De novembre.

COMPLAINT OF GREAT PINES
IN A DESERTED VILLA

In Baden

All yesterday, the sun in mists was sulking then,
The wind, till morning, never let its anger die,
But from the hillsides lights on us a blessed eye
Designed to tumble on you these sacks of bitumen!

> – Ah, you've fleeced me much too much,
> Diamond dances, thighs of rose;
> Indeed, I wasn't born for such
> > Things as those.

– The wind, till morning, never let its anger die.
Oh, these coughs of good and posthumous chaos, phlegm,

> – Woods and fields all sold. How many
> Menials who held my gloves out once
> Now make themselves a pretty penny
> > Out of my funds!

– Thinning in louring skies these sacks of bitumen
That, chased by blackest Misereres, climb on high.

> – Girls, bare-armed amid the fruit,
> And swapping rings around with laughter;
> Our beaches, nights that followed suit,
> > How vague to them after!

– Oh these coughs of good and posthumous chaos, phlegm!
Let's sing like Memnon, sun has filtered through the sky,

> – And I, stuck in this hotel room,
> This tawdry room, in this crude bed,
> Alone, thrashed by November's boom
> > Above my head.

– Qui, consolant des vents les noirs Misérérés,
Des nuages en fuite éponge au loin l'écume.

– Berthe aux sages yeux de lilas,
Qui priais Dieu que je revinsse,
Que fais-tu, mariée là-bas,
En province?

– Memnons, ventriloquons! le cher astre a filtré
Et le voilà qui tout authentique s'exhume!

– Oh! quel vent! adieu tout sommeil;
Mon Dieu, que je suis bien malade!
Oh! notre croisée au soleil
Bon, à Bade.

– Il rompt ses digues! vers les grands labours qui fument!
Saint Sacrement! et *Labarum* des *Nox iræ*!

– Et bientôt, seul, je m'en irai,
À Montmartre, en cinquième classe,
Loin de père et mère, enterrés
En Alsace.

COMPLAINTE SUR CERTAINS TEMPS DÉPLACÉS

Le couchant de sang est taché
Comme un tablier de boucher;
Oh! qui veut aussi m'écorcher!

– Maintenant c'est comme une rade!
Ça vous fait le cœur tout nomade,
À cingler vers mille Lusiades!

– Consoling black Misereres for the winds on high,
It mops with clouds in flight the foam in furthest ken.

> – Berthe, of the modest lilac eyes,
> Who prayed that I would reappear
> What are you doing, in marriage ties,
>> In the provinces, dear?

– Let's memnon, ventriloquise! He's filtered through the sky;
The dear star's heats exhuming all authentics again!

> – Oh, what a wind! 'Bye, sleep, you're done;
> My God, I'm feeling awfully ill.
> Oh, our casement in the good sun
>> In Baden still.

– It breaks its banks! for great ploughed lands that steam again!
The Holy Sacrament! And *Labarum* of *Nox Irae*!

> – And soon, alone, I'll slip away,
> To Montmartre, lowest cost – alas,
> Far from mother and father; they
>> Lie in Alsace.

COMPLAINT OF CERTAIN DISPLACED TIMES

The sunset's bed is stained with gore,
It's like a butcher's apron; what's more,
He wants to give me too what for!

– And now it looks like a roadstead!
That gives your heart its rover's head
To sail the thousand Lusiads read!

Passez, ô nuptials appels,
Vers les comptoirs, les Archipels
Où l'on mastique le bétel!

Je n'aurai jamais d'aventures;
Qu'il est petit, dans la Nature,
Le chemin d'fer Paris-Ceinture!

– V'là l'fontainier! il siffle l'air
(Connu) du bon roi Dagobert;
Oh! ces matins d'avril en mer!

– Le vent galope ventre à terre,
En vain voudrait-on le fair' taire!
Ah! nom de Dieu quelle misère!

– Le Soleil est mirobolant
Comme un poitrail de chambellan,
J'en demeure les bras ballants;

Mais jugez si ça m'importune,
Je rêvais en plein de lagunes
De Venise au clair de la lune!

– Vrai! la vie est pour les badauds;
Quand on a du dieu sous la peau,
On cuve ça sans dire mot.

L'obélisque quadrangulaire,
De mon spleen monte; j'y digère,
En stylite, ce gros Mystère.

Head off, oh all you marriage wiles,
Towards the godowns and the isles
Where betel juice stains all the smiles!

Adventures! I'll never get a taste;
How small against all Nature placed
The circle line round Paris' waist!

– There's the turncock whistling the air
(Well known) of good king Dagobert;
Oh, April mornings at sea there.

– The wind gallops, belly to ground;
In vain you'd wish to hush the sound!
Ah, what a god-awful dreary round!

– The Sun's a splendiferous glare
Like breastplates chamberlains would wear;
I live in it, arms dangling spare.

Judge if that bothers me, rise, set, noon;
I was dreaming on the lagoon
Of Venice in the light of the moon!

– True! Life is for loafing in;
When you've some god under the skin,
You sleep it off and make no din.

My spleen's rectangular obelus
Rises; upon its pillar thus
I digest the gross Mysterious.

COMPLAINTE DES CONDOLÉANCES AU SOLEIL

Décidément, bien don Quichotte, et pas peu sale,
Ta Police, ô Soleil! malgré tes grands Levers,
Et tes couchants des beaux Sept-Glaives abreuvés,
Rosaces en sang d'une aveugle Cathédrale!

Sans trêve, aux spleens d'amour sonner des hallalis!
Car, depuis que, majeur, ton fils calcule et pose,
Labarum des glaciers! fais-tu donc autre chose
Que chasser devant toi des dupes de leurs lits?

Certes, dès qu'aux rideaux aubadent tes fanfares,
Ces piteux d'infini, clignant de gluants deuils,
Rhabillent leurs tombeaux, en se cachant de l'œil
Qui cautérise les citernes les plus rares!

Mais tu ne te dis pas que, là-bas, bon Soleil,
L'autre moitié n'attendait que ta défaillance,
Et déjà se remet à ses expériences,
Alléguant quoi? la nuit, l'usage, le sommeil . . .

Or, à notre guichet, tu n'es pas mort encore,
Pour aller fustiger de rayons ces mortels,
Que nos bateaux sans fleurs rerâlent vers leurs ciels
D'où pleurent des remparts brodés contre l'aurore!

Alcôve des Danaïdes, triste astre! – Et puis,
Ces jours où, tes fureurs ayant fait les nuages,
Tu vas sans pouvoir les percer, blême de rage
De savoir seul et tout à ses aises l'Ennui!

Entre nous donc, bien don Quichotte, et pas moins sale,
Ta Police, ô Soleil, malgré tes grands Levers,
Et tes couchants des beaux Sept-Glaives abreuvés,
Rosaces en sang d'une aveugle Cathédrale!

COMPLAINT OF CONDOLENCES FOR THE SUN

Decidedly Quixotic, not unsoiled, unsmutty,
Your Police, O Sun, despite your levees' grand parades;
Your settings with the handsome blood-quenched Seven Blades,
A blind Cathedral's rosace windows, gored and bloody!

Without a let-up, for the love-spleens sound halloo!
For, come of age, your son will calculate and query,
Labarum of glaciers, do you do much else in theory
Than drive the hoodwinked from their beds ahead of you?

Indeed, since on the curtains now aubades your fanfare,
Those, in their clammy mourning, the piteous infinite ones
Put on their tombs again to hide out of your sun's
Eye that can cauterise all cisterns however rare.

But you don't tell yourself, down there, fine Sun, bright Light,
The other half-world merely waits for your decline,
And even now restarts on its experience. The line
It pleads for it is what? Oh, custom, sleep, the night . . .

Well, at our lattice now you're not yet feeling dead
Enough to go and beat those mortals up with beams,
How our flowerless boats fume back at their skies
Where weep embroidered barriers against dawn's red!

Danaidan intimacies, sad star! Then days like these
When though your furies have produced the cloud,
You're there, too weak to pierce them, pale with rage in shroud
To savour, alone and fully, Boredom take its ease.

Between the two of us, Quixotic, and no less smutty,
Your Police, O Sun, despite your levees' grand parades;
Your settings with the handsome blood-quenched Seven Blades,
A blind Cathedral's rosace windows, gored and bloody!

COMPLAINTE DE L'OUBLI DES MORTS

Mesdames et Messieurs,
Vous dont la mère est morte,
C'est le bon fossoyeux
Qui gratte à votre porte.

      Les morts
    C'est sous terre;
        Ça n'en sort
    Guère.

Vous fumez dans vos bocks,
Vous soldez quelque idylle,
Là-bas chante le coq,
Pauvres morts hors des villes!

Grand-papa se penchait,
Là, le doigt sur la tempe,
Sœur faisait du crochet,
Mère montait la lampe.

      Les morts
    C'est discret,
        Ça dort
    Trop au frais.

Vous avez bien dîné,
Comment va cette affaire?
Ah! les petits mort-nés
Ne se dorlotent guère!

Notez, d'un trait égal,
Au livre de la caisse,
Entre deux frais de bal:
Entretien tombe et messe.

COMPLAINT OF FORGETTING THE DEAD

Ladies and Gentlemen,
You whose mother's dead,
It's the good digger then
Scratching your door instead.

> The dead lie
> Underground.
> They'll not try
> Coming round.

You smoke among your bocks.
Settle some idyll, cash down.
Below, that crow's the cock's,
Poor dead outside town.

Grandpa's leaning there,
Finger to temple, right;
Sister crotchets where
Mother turns up the light.

> The dead,
> They're discreet.
> Their bed
> Out of the heat.

You've had an ample fill.
How's that affair go?
Ah, little ones born still
Hardly cuddle, though.

In firm hand in the accounts,
Between two costs of balls,
Note two further amounts:
The mass and funeral's.

      C'est gai,
  Cette vie;
      Hein, ma mie,
  Ô gué?

Mesdames et Messieurs,
Vous dont la sœur est morte,
Ouvrez au fossoyeux
Qui claque à votre porte;

Si vous n'avez pitié,
Il viendra (sans rancune)
Vous tirer par les pieds,
Une nuit de grand'lune!

      Importun
  Vent qui rage!
      Les défunts?
  Ça voyage . . .

COMPLAINTE DU PAUVRE JEUNE HOMME

Sur l'air populaire:
«Quand le bonhomm' revint du bois.»

Quand ce jeune homm' rentra chez lui,
Quand ce jeune homm' rentra chez lui,
Il prit à deux mains son vieux crâne,
Qui de science était un puits!
      Crâne
    Riche crâne,
Entends-tu la Folie qui plane?
Et qui demande le cordon,
Digue dondaine, digue dondaine,
Et qui demande le cordon,
Digue dondaine, digue dondon!

Life's bonny,
Cuts a dash;
Eh, my pash,
Hey-nonny?

Ladies and Gentlemen,
You whose sister's dead,
Let in the digger then
Who knocks your door instead;

If you've no pity to feel,
He'll still come, without spite,
And drag you by the heel,
Some night of full moonlight!

Wind, hot-head,
Battering ram!
And the dead?
They scram . . .

COMPLAINT OF THE POOR YOUNG MAN

Based on the popular song:
'When the young man came back from the wood.'

When the young man came back home,
When the young man came back home,
He took in both hands his old brain
That in knowledge weighed a tome!
Brain,
Rich brain,
D'you hear the Folly soar again?
She wants an entry from now on,
Digue dondaine, digue dondaine,
She wants an entry from now on.
Digue dondaine, digue dondon.

Quand ce jeune homm' rentra chez lui,
Quand ce jeune homm' rentra chez lui,
Il entendit de tristes gammes,
Qu'un piano pleurait dans la nuit!
      Gammes,
      Vieilles gammes,
Ensemble, enfants, nous vous cherchâmes!
Son mari m'a fermé sa maison,
Digue dondaine, digue dondaine,
Son mari m'a fermé sa maison,
Digue dondaine, digue dondon!

Quand ce jeune homm' rentra chez lui,
Quand ce jeune homm' rentra chez lui,
Il mit le nez dans sa belle âme,
Où fermentaient des tas d'ennuis!
      Âme,
      Ma belle âme,
Leur huile est trop sal' pour ta flamme!
Puis, nuit partout! lors, à quoi bon?
Digue dondaine, digue dondaine,
Puis, nuit partout! lors, à quoi bon?
Digue dondaine, digue dondon!

Quand ce jeune homm' rentra chez lui,
Quand ce jeune homm' rentra chez lui,
Il vit que sa charmante femme
Avait déménagé sans lui!
      Dame,
      Notre-Dame,
Je n'aurai pas un mot de blâme!
Mais t'aurais pu m'laisser l'charbon,[1]
Digue dondaine, digue dondaine,
Mais t'aurais pu m'laisser l'charbon,
Digue dondaine, digue dondon.

Lors, ce jeune homme aux tels ennuis,
Lors, ce jeune homme aux tels ennuis;
Alla décrocher une lame,
Qu'on lui avait fait cadeau avec l'étui!

When the young man came back home,
When the young man came back home,
He heard sad scales repeat the same,
A piano wept beneath night's dome!
    Same
     Old scale game,
We sought you, children, one in aim!
Her husband's warned me off now on,
Digue dondaine, digue dondaine,
Her husband's warned me off now on,
Digue dondaine, digue dondon.

When the young man came back home,
When the young man came back home,
He poked his nose in his soul's good name
Where heaps of tediums brewed their foam!
    Shame,
     Fine soul, shame!
Their oil's too dirty for your flame!
Right, night throughout, what good go on?
Digue dondaine, digue dondaine,
Right, night throughout, what good go on?
Digue dondaine, digue dondon.

When the young man came back home,
When the young man came back home,
His charming wife had dumped his name,
Moved out on him with cash and comb!
    Blame,
     No word of blame,
Our Lady, none against her claim.
You might have left me coal and gone,[1]
Digue dondaine, digue dondaine,
You might have left me coal and gone,
Digue dondaine, digue dondon!

Then this man whose tediums foam,
Then this man whose tediums foam,
Went and took a blade to aim,
A present with the sheath its home!

Lame,
Fine lame,
Soyez plus droite que la femme!
Et vous, mon Dieu, pardon! pardon!
Digue dondaine, digue dondaine,
Et vous, mon Dieu, pardon! pardon!
Digue dondaine, digue dondon!

Quand les croq'morts vinrent chez lui,
Quand les croq'morts vinrent chez lui,
Ils virent qu'c'était un'belle âme,
Comme on n'en fait plus aujourd'hui!
Âme,
Dors, belle âme!
Quand on est mort c'est pour de bon,
Digue dondaine, digue dondaine,
Quand on est mort c'est pour de bon,
Digue dondaine, digue dondon!

¹ Pour s'asphyxier.

COMPLAINTE DE L'ÉPOUX OUTRAGÉ

Sur l'air populaire:
«Qu'allais-tu faire à la fontaine?»

– Qu'alliez-vous faire à la Mad'leine,
     Corbleu, ma moitié.
Qu'alliez-vous faire à la Mad'leine?

– J'allais prier pour qu'un fils nous vienne,
     Mon Dieu, mon ami;
J'allais prier pour qu'un fils nous vienne.

Aim,
Fine blade, aim,
Be straighter now than any dame!
And you, my God, forgive what's done,
Digue dondaine, digue dondaine,
And you, my God, forgive what's done
Digue dondaine, digue dondon.

When the bearers reached his home,
When the bearers reached his home,
They saw the fine soul they'd to claim,
The sort not made these days from loam!
Came
Rest, it came,
Fine soul, when dead, all's good and gone,
Digue dondaine, digue dondaine,
Fine soul, when dead, all's good and gone,
Digue dondaine, digue dondon.

---

[1] To suffocate himself. (*Author's note*)

COMPLAINT OF THE OUTRAGED HUSBAND

Based on the popular song:
'What did you do at the fountain?'

'Why at the church of the Magdalen,
Damn odd, my darling dove.
Why at the church of the Magdalen?'

'Went there to pray for a son again,
My God, my only love;
Went there to pray for a son again.'

– Vous vous teniez dans un coin, debout,
    Corbleu, ma moitié!
Vous vous teniez dans un coin, debout.

– Pas d'chaise économis' trois sous,
    Mon Dieu, mon ami;
Pas d'chaise économis' trois sous.

– D'un officier, j'ai vu la tournure,
    Corbleu, ma moitié!
D'un officier, j'ai vu la tournure.

– C'était ce Christ grandeur nature,
    Mon Dieu, mon ami;
C'était ce Christ grandeur nature.

– Les Christs n'ont pas la croix d'honneur,
    Corbleu, ma moitié!
Les Christs n'ont pas la croix d'honneur.

– C'était la plaie du Calvaire, au cœur,
    Mon Dieu, mon ami;
C'était la plaie du Calvaire, au cœur.

– Les Christs n'ont qu'au flanc seul la plaie,
    Corbleu, ma moitié!
Les Christs n'ont qu'au flanc seul la plaie!

– C'était une goutte envolée,
    Mon Dieu, mon ami;
C'était une goutte envolée.

– Aux Crucifix on n'parl' jamais,
    Corbleu, ma moitié!
Aux Crucifix on n'parl' jamais!

– C'était du trop d'amour qu'j'avais,
    Mon Dieu, mon ami,
C'était du trop d'amour qu'j'avais!

'You stood in a corner and never went thence,
    Damn odd, my darling dove!
You stood in a corner and never went thence.'

'No chair's a saving of several pence,
    My God, my only friend;
No chair's a saving of several pence.'

'Officer's figure caught my eyes,
    Damn odd, my darling dove!
Officer's figure caught my eyes.'

'That was some Christ you saw life-size,
    My God, my only love;
That was some Christ you saw life-size.'

'Legion of Honour Christs don't wear,
    Damn odd, my darling dove!
Legion of Honour Christs don't wear.'

'That was Calvary's heart-wound, bare,
    My God, my only love;
That was Calvary's heart-wound, bare.'

'Only the sides of Christs are lanced,
    Damn odd, my darling dove!
Only the sides of Christ are lanced.'

'That was a splash of blood that chanced,
    My God, my only love;
That was a splash of blood that chanced.'

'In Holy Week none speaks of such,
    Damn odd, my darling dove!
In Holy Week none speaks of such!'

'That was a love I felt too much,
    My God, my only love,
That was a love I felt too much.'

– Et moi j'te brûl'rai la cervelle,
       Corbleu, ma moitié,
Et moi j'te brûl'rai la cervelle!

– Lui, il aura mon âme immortelle,
       Mon Dieu, mon ami,
Lui, il aura mon âme immortelle!

COMPLAINTE VARIATIONS SUR LE MOT «FALOT, FALOTTE»

       Falot, falotte!
Sous l'aigre averse qui clapote,
Un chien aboie aux feux-follets,
Et puis se noie, taïaut, taïaut!
La Lune, voyant ces ballets,
       Rit à Pierrot!
       Falot! falot!

       Falot, falotte!
Un train perdu, dans la nuit, stoppe
Par les avalanches bloqué;
Il siffle au loin! et les petiots
Croient ouïr les méchants hoquets
       D'un grand crapaud!
       Falot, falot!

       Falot, falotte!
La danse du bateau-pilote,
Sous l'œil d'or du phare, en péril!
Et sur les *steamers*, les galops
Des vents filtrant leurs longs exils
       Par les hublots!
       Falot, falot!

'And I, in your head'll blast a hole,
 Damn odd, my darling dove,
And I, in your head'll blast a hole!'

'Then he will have my immortal soul,
 My God, my only love,
Then he will have my immortal soul!'

COMPLAINT VARIATIONS ON THE WORDS 'LIGHT BEAM, BEAM LIGHT'

Light beam, beam light!
Under a head wind's gusts tonight,
At will-o'-wisps a mongrel barks
And, tally-ho, drowns in a stream.
The Moon laughs, seeing these larks,
 A clown's laugh-scream.
 Light beam! light beam!

Light beam, beam light!
A lost train stands stock-still tonight.
It's blocked off by a landslide's load;
It shrieks afar, the nippers seem
To hear ill-tempered croaks of a toad
 In size extreme.
 Light beam, light beam!

Light beam, beam light!
The pilot cutter dancing bright
Endangered in the lighthouse gold.
And over *steamers* the winds stream,
Filtering their exiles, long and old,
 Through portholes, hold,
 Light beam, light beam!

Falot, falotte!
La petite vieille qui trotte,
Par les bois aux temps pluvieux,
Cassée en deux sous le fagot
Qui réchauffera de son mieux
    Son vieux fricot!
    Falot, falot!

Falot, falotte!
Sous sa lanterne qui tremblotte,
Le fermier dans son potager
S'en vient cueillir des escargots,
Et c'est une étoile au berger
    Rêvant là-haut!
    Falot, falot!

Falot, falotte!
Le lumignon au vent toussotte,
Dans son cornet de gras papier;
Mais le passant en son pal'tot,
Ô mandarines des janviers,
    File au galop!
    Falot, falot!

Falot, falotte!
Un chiffonnier va sous sa hotte;
Un réverbère près d'un mur
Où se cogne un vague soulaud,
Qui l'embrasse comme un pur,
    Avec des mots!
    Falot, falot!

Falot, falotte!
Et c'est ma belle âme en ribotte,
Qui se sirote et se fait mal,
Et fait avec ses grands sanglots,
Sur les beaux lacs de l'Idéal
    Des ronds dans l'eau!
    Falot, falot!

Light beam, beam light!
The widow woman plodding, slight,
In rainy season through the copse,
Doubled with logs, her load extreme;
They'll do their best to heat the slops
    In her stew of ream.
    Light beam, light beam!

Light beam, beam light!
Using his trembling lantern's sight
The farmer goes to gather snails
That in his kitchen garden gleam,
And it's a star a shepherd hails
    Up there adream.
    Light beam, light beam!

Light beam, beam light!
The candle end in the wind's spite
Coughs in its cardboard tundish placed.
The passer-by, his mack astream,
– Oh, winter mandarins – in haste
    So it would seem!
    Light beam, light beam!

Light beam, beam light!
A dustman goes, his hood drawn tight;
A lamppost close against the wall
A drunk collides with, in his dream,
And hugs it, simpleton, words all
    The usual theme!
    Light beam, light beam!

Light beam, beam light!
And that's my swell soul, good and tight,
Tippling itself, and bad it feels
With its great big sobs that teem
Rounds in the water of the Ideal's
    Fine lakes! Gleam,
    Light beam, light beam!

COMPLAINTE DU TEMPS
ET DE SA COMMÈRE L'ESPACE

Je tends mes poignets universels dont aucun
N'est le droit ou le gauche, et l'Espace, dans un
Va-et-vient giratoire, y détrame les toiles
D'azur pleines de cocons à fœtus d'Étoiles.
Et nous nous blasons tant, je ne sais où, les deux
Indissolubles nuits aux orgues vaniteux
De nos pores à Soleils, où toute cellule
Chante: Moi! Moi! puis s'éparpille, ridicule!

Elle est l'infini sans fin, je deviens le temps
Infaillible. C'est pourquoi nous nous perdons tant.
Où sommes-nous? Pourquoi? Pour que Dieu s'accomplisse?
Mais l'Éternité n'y a pas suffi! Calice
Inconscient, où tout cœur crevé se résout,
Extrais-nous donc alors de ce néant trop tout!
Que tu fisses de nous seulement une flamme,
Un vrai sanglot mortel, la moindre goutte d'âme!

Mais nous bâillons de toute la force de nos
Touts, sûrs de la surdité des humains échos.
Que ne suis-je indivisible! Et toi, douce Espace,
Où sont les steppes de tes seins, que j'y rêvasse?
Quand t'ai-je fécondée à jamais? Oh! ce dut
Être un spasme intéressant! Mais quel fut mon but?
Je t'ai, tu m'as. Mais où? Partout, toujours. Extase
Sur laquelle, quand on est le Temps, on se blase.

Or, voilà des spleens infinis que je suis en
Voyage vers ta bouche, et pas plus à présent
Que toujours, je ne sens la fleur triomphatrice
Qui flotte, m'as-tu dit, au seuil de ta matrice.
Abstraites amours! quel infini mitoyen
Tourne entre nos deux Touts? Sommes-nous deux? ou bien,
(Tais-toi si tu ne peux me prouver à outrance,
Illico, le fondement de la connaissance,

COMPLAINT OF TIME
AND HIS OLD CRONY WOMAN SPACE

I raise my universal fists – neither of which is right
Or left – and Space, in come-and-go, gyrating flight,
Unweaves the azure canvases there that are packed
With the cocoons of foetal Stars. And it's a fact
We bore each other so much – don't ask me where – two bores
Of Indissoluble nights, our vain organs with pores
Of Suns, where each and every single solitary cell
Sings out: 'Me first! Me first!' Then multiplies. Daft spell.

Infallible Time I become; she, boundless infinitude.
That's why we lose each other, hardly rendezvous'd.
Where are we? Why? So God can make himself feel whole?
So eternity wasn't enough! Inconscient Chalice, Bowl
Where every broken heart dissolves away desire,
Extract us next then from this oblivion too entire.
Oh, make us just a flame, or else a tear to roll,
An honest mortal tear, with just a dash of soul.

Yet still with all the force of all our Wholes we bound
Off, sure of deafness in the human echoes that sound.
If only I were not so indivisible of seam.
And, sweetest, where's your bosom's steppes where I may dream?
When've I ever made you pregnant? Oh that must have been
An interesting spasm. What purpose had I seen?
I'm yours, you're mine. But where. Everywhere, ever. Joy, that.
Which, when one's Time becomes a trifle old hat.

For there are infinite spleens that I'm pursuing on
Travels to find your mouth, and, never more foregone
Than now still, never scented the triumphal bloom
Which floats, you told me, on the threshold of your womb.
Such abstract love affairs! What infinite interval
Spins between our two Wholes? And are we two at all?
(Shut up, if you can't test me to the uttermost,
This instant now, consciousness's fundamental post,

Et, par ce chant: Pensée, Objet, Identité!
Souffler le Doute, songe d'un siècle d'été.)
Suis-je à jamais un solitaire Hermaphrodite,
Comme le Ver Solitaire, ô ma Sulamite?
Ma complainte n'a pas eu de commencement,
Que je sache, et n'aura nulle fin; autrement,
Je serais l'anachronisme absolu. Pullule
Donc, azur possédé du mètre et du pendule!

Ô Source du Possible, alimente à jamais
Des pollens des soleils d'exil, et de l'engrais
Des chaotiques hécatombes, l'automate
Universel où pas une loi ne se hâte.
Nuls à tout, sauf aux rares mystiques éclairs
Des Élus, nous restons les deux miroirs d'éther
Réfléchissant, jusqu'à la mort de ces Mystères,
Leurs Nuits que l'Amour distrait de fleurs éphémères.

GRANDE COMPLAINTE DE LA VILLE DE PARIS

PROSE BLANCHE

Bonne gens qui m'écoutes, c'est Paris, Charenton compris.
Maison fondée en . . . à louer. Médailles à toutes les expositions
et des mentions. Bail immortel. Chantiers en gros et en détail de
bonheurs sur mesure. Fournisseurs brevetés d'un tas de majestés.
Maison recommandée. Prévient la chute des cheveux. En loter-
ies! Envoie en province. Pas de morte-saison. Abonnements.
Dépôt, sans garantie de l'humanité, des ennuis les plus comme il
faut et d'occasion. Facilités de paiement, mais de l'argent. De
l'argent, bonne gens.

Et ça se ravitaille, import et export, par vingt gares et douanes.
Que tristes, sous la pluie, les trains de marchandise! À vous,
dieux, chasublerie, ameublements d'église, dragées pour bap-
têmes, le culte est au troisième, clientèle ineffable! Amour, à toi,
des maisons d'or aux hospices dont les langes et loques feront le
papier des billets doux à monogrammes, trousseaux et layettes,

And with this song: 'Thought, Object, Identity!
To diddle Doubt, and dream of a summer century.)
Or am I always now a lone hermaphrodite,
Like the solitary Worm, oh my Shulamite?
And my complaint has hardly got itself quite going,
As far as I can tell, and can't end on this showing;
Or else I'd be the utter anachronism. Pullulate,
Then, azure one, possessed of metre, pendulum, weight.

O Source of Possibility, eternal provender,
Pollens of exile suns, roughage and fattener
For hecatombs of chaos, cosmic automaton
Where not one single law will ever hurry on.
Nothings at all, except to rare and mystic gleams
Of the Elect, we're the two ethereal mirror beams
Reflecting, till the death of these Mysteries of ours,
Their Nights that Love distracts with such ephemeral flowers.

GRAND COMPLAINT OF THE CITY OF PARIS

WHITE PROSE

Good people who are listening, now this is Paris, including
Charenton. Old establishment to let, founded in . . . Medallions
in all the exhibitions and many distinctions. Lease in perpetuity.
Wholesale and retail outlets for limited happinesses. Suppliers by
appointment to a whole heap of majesties. Highly recommended
establishment. Avoid hair loss. Take no risks. Delivery to the
provinces. No off-season. Subscriptions. Wholesalers, without
human guarantee, of tediums, the most respectable and second-
hand. Easy payments but cash only. Above all cash, my good
people.
    And it's supplied, for import and export, with twenty stations
and custom-houses. How sad in the rain the goods trains look!
For you, gods, chasublery, church-furnishings, sweetmeats for
christenings, the cult is situated on the third floor, patronised by
an ineffable clientèle. Love, for dearest you, golden houses with

seules eaux alcalines reconstituantes, ô chlorose! bijoux de sérail, falbalas, tramways, miroirs de poches, romances! Et à l'antipode, qu'y fait-on? Ça travaille, pour que Paris se ravitaille . . .

D'ailleurs, des moindres pavés, monte le Lotus Tact. En bataille rangée, les deux sexes, toilettés à la mode des passants, mangeant dans le ruolz! Aux commis, des Niobides; des faunesses aux Christs. Et sous les futaies seigneuriales des jardins très-publics, martyrs niaisant et vestales minaudières faisant d'un clin d'œil l'article pour l'Idéal et Cie (Maison vague, là-haut), mais d'elles-mêmes absentes, pour sûr. Ah! l'Homme est un singulier monsieur; et elle, sa voix de fausset, quel front désert! D'ailleurs avec du tact . . .

Mais l'inextirpable élite, d'où? pour où? Maisons de blanc: pompes voluptiales; maisons de deuil: spleenuosités, rancœurs à la carte. Et les banlieues adoptives, humus teigneux, haridelles paissant bris de vaisselles, tessons, semelles, de profil sur l'horizon des remparts. Et la pluie! trois torchons à une claire-voie de mansarde. Un chien aboie à un ballon là-haut. Et des coins claustrals, cloches exilescentes des *dies iræmissibles*. Couchants d'aquarelliste distinguée, ou de lapidaire en liquidation. Génie au prix de fabrique, et ces jeunes gens s'entraînent en auto-litanies et formules vaines, par vaines cigarettes. Que les vingt-quatre heures vont vite à la discrète élite! . . .

Mais les cris publics reprennent. Avis important! l'Amortissable a fléchi, ferme le Panama. Enchères, experts. Avances sur titres cotés ou non cotés, achat de nu-propriétés, de viagers, d'usufruit; avances sur successions ouvertes et autres; indicateurs, annuaires, étrennes. Voyages circulaires à prix réduits. Madame Ludovic prédit l'avenir de 2 à 4. Jouets *Au Paradis des enfants* et accessoires pour cotillons aux grandes personnes. Grand choix de principes à l'épreuve. Encore des cris! Seul dépôt! soupers de centième! Machines cylindriques Marinoni! Tout garanti, tout pour rien! Ah! la rapidité de la vie aussi seul dépôt . . .

Des mois, les ans, calendriers d'occasion. Et l'automne s'engrandeuille au bois de Boulogne, l'hiver gèle les fricots des pauvres aux assiettes sans fleurs peintes. Mai purge, la canicule aux brises frivoles des plages fane les toilettes coûteuses. Puis, comme nous existons dans l'existence où l'on paie comptant, s'amènent ces messieurs courtois des Pompes Funèbres, autopsies

their own crèches whose nappies and clouts make paper for mono-grammed love-letters, trousseaux and layettes, exclusive mineral water tonics, oh chlorosis! jewellery suitable for the seraglio, furbe-lows, trams, pocket mirrors, novelettes! And what's going on at the antipodes. It toils away to supply Paris . . .

Elsewhere, from the meanest pavements rises the Lotus Touch. In battle ranged, the two sexes, fashionably styled as visitors, eating off the E.P.N.S. For clerks, the Niobes; fauns for Christs. And, below the manorial timberwoods of widely public parks, trifling martyrs and smirking vestal virgins plugging their goods in the twinkling of an eye for Ideal and Co. (Vacant establishment above) but certainly not all there themselves. Ah, Man is a singu-lar gent; and she with her shrill voice, what a vacant brow! But let's move on with a bit of tact . . .

But the inextirpable élite, where from, where for? Haber-dasheries: voluptual standing on ceremony; mourning houses; spleens and grudges *à la carte*. Adopted suburbs, scurvy soil, old nags grazing broken crocks, bottle ends, old soles, in silhouette upon the sky-line of the ramparts. And the rain! Three ragbags at a mansard lattice. A dog bays at a balloon above. And monas-tic corners, exilent bells of *dies iraemissibles*. Distinguished water-colourist's sunsets or those of a lapidary's clearance sale. Genius at cost price, and young men drawing themselves into auto-litanies and vain formulations by vain cigarette-drags. How quickly fly the twenty-four hours for the discreet élite!

But the public crying starts again. Important warning: The Redeemable has fallen, close the Panama. Bids, auctions, apprais-ers. Advances on securities quoted or not, purchases of bare ownerships, of life-interests; advances on direct inheritances and others; directories, annuals, first deals. Round trips at reduced rates. Madam Ludovic predicts the future from 2 to 4 o'clock. Toys at the *Children's Paradise* and accessories for cotillions of grown-ups. Wide choice of proofed principles. And still the cries! Sole suppliers! Suppers for a shilling! Cylindrical Marinoni machines! All guaranteed; all for nothing! Ah, the speediness of life, sole supplier, too . . .

Months, the years, second-hand almanacs. And autumn full-mourning-dresses herself in the Bois de Boulogne; winter freezes the stew of the poor on plain unflowery plates. May purges, the dog-days with frivolous inshore breezes ruffle expensive dresses.

et convois salués sous la vieille Monotopaze du soleil. Et l'histoire va
toujours dressant, raturant ses Tables criblées de piteux *idem*, –
ô Bilan, va quelconque! ô Bilan, va quelconque . . .

COMPLAINTE DES MOUNIS DU MONT-MARTRE

Dire que, sans filtrer d'un divin Cœur,
Un air divin, et qui veut que tout s'aime,
S'in-Pan-filtre, et sème
Ces vols d'oasis folles de blasphèmes
Vivant pour toucher quelque part un Cœur . . .

Un tic-tac froid rit en nos poches,
Chronomètres, réveils, coucous;
Faut remonter ces beaux joujoux,
Œufs à heures, mouches du coche,
Là-haut s'éparpillant en cloches . . .

Voici le soir,
Grince, musique
Hypertrophique
Des remontoirs!

Dire que Tout est un Très-Sourd Mystère;
Et que le Temps, qu'on ne sait où saisir,
Oui, pour l'avertir!
Sarcle à jamais les bons soleils martyrs,
Ô laps sans digues des nuits du Mystère! . . .

Then, since we exist in this existence where you pay cash down
these old world gents turn up with funeral ceremonies, autopsies,
and respectfully observed cortèges under the old Monotopaze of
the sun. And history continues, listing, deleting its Tables
riddled with pitiful *idems*, Oh, Accounts, push off anywhere! Oh,
Accounts push off anywhere!

COMPLAINT OF HINDU ASCETICS
FROM MONTMARTRE

Just think, not filtered down from any Divine Heart,
But, wanting one to love another, a divine breeze
            Saint-Pan-filtrates, spreading these
Crazily blaspheming flights from oases
Living to touch down somewhere on another Heart . . .

        A chill tick laughs in fobs and climbs,
        Chronometers, alarms, cuckoos;
        Need winding, these fine toys we use,
        Coach-flies that nose, eggs hatching times,
        Sprinkled above in bells and chimes.

                It's evening.
                Grate, music, grate,
                Hypertrophic in state,
                Of winder and spring!

To think the Whole is just a Stone-deaf Mystery;
That Time – of which none knows quite where to seize hold,
            Yes, to warn, get it told! –
Weeds out forever martyr suns as good as gold –
Oh lapse without a bound in nights of Mystery! . . .

Allez, coucous, réveils, pendules;
Escadrons d'insectes d'acier,
En un concert bien familier,
Jouez sans fin des mandibules,
L'Homme a besoin qu'on le stimule!

Sûrs, chaque soir,
De la musique,
Hypertrophique
Des remontoirs!

Moucherons, valseurs d'un soir de soleil,
Vous, tout comme nous, nerfs de la nature,
Vous n'avez point cure
De ce que peut être cette aventure:
Les mondes penseurs s'errant au Soleil!

Triturant bien l'heure en secondes,
En trois mil six-cents coups de dents,
De nos parts au gâteau du Temps
Ne faites qu'un hachis immonde
Devant lequel on se morfonde!

Sûrs, chaque soir,
De la musique
Hypertrophique
Des remontoirs!

Où le trouver, ce Temps, pour lui tout dire,
Lui mettre le nez dans son Œuvre, un peu!
Et cesser ce jeu!
C'est vrai, la Métaphysique de Dieu
Et ses amours sont infinis! – mais, dire . . .

Ah! plus d'heure? fleurir sans âge?
Voir les tableaux lents des Saisons
Régir l'écran des horizons,
Comme autant de belles images
D'un même Aujourd'hui qui voyage?

Come on, alarm, cuckoos, pendulum;
Squadrons of insects made of steel,
In concert with a familiar feel,
Play on your jaws continuo:
Man needs a stimulus, you know!

    Sure, each evening,
    The music will grate,
    Hypertrophic in state,
    Of winder and spring!

Midges, dancers on an evening of sun,
You, just like us the nerves of nature, have no care
    About what this affair
Of random chance may even be, the why or where,
These thinker worlds that lose themselves astray in Sun!

    Grinding to seconds all the hours
    With three thousand six hundred snaps
    Makes nothing but the vilest scraps
    Of the bit of Time's cake that's ours.
    Before that hash one chills and cowers!

    Sure, each evening,
    The music will grate,
    Hypertrophic in state,
    Of winder and spring.

Where will we find this old Timer, to say our piece?
To rub his nose into his Works a little bit!
    And end this game of it!
Granted, the Metaphysics of God are infinite,
And so are his affaires! – and yet, to say our piece . . .

    Ah, time's gone? Ageless flourishing?
    Slow pageants of Seasons to know?
    Make the screen of horizons show
    Like many lovely images that spring
    From one Today that's sojourneying?

Voici le soir!
Grince, musique
Hypertrophique
Des remontoirs!

COMPLAINTE-LITANIES DE MON SACRÉ-CŒUR

Prométhée et Vautour, châtiment et blasphème,
Mon Cœur, cancer sans cœur, se grignotte lui-même.

Mon Cœur est une urne où j'ai mis certains défunts,
Oh! chut, refrains de leurs berceaux! et vous, parfums . . .

Mon Cœur est un lexique où cent littératures
Se lardent sans répit de divines ratures.

Mon Cœur est un désert altéré, bien que soûl
De ce vin revomi, l'universel dégoût.

Mon Cœur est un Néron, enfant gâté d'Asie,
Qui d'empires de rêve en vain se rassasie.

Mon Cœur est un noyé vide d'âme et d'essors,
Qu'étreint la pieuvre Spleen en ses ventouses d'or.

C'est un feu d'artifice hélas! qu'avant la fête,
A noyé sans retour l'averse qui s'embête.

Mon Cœur est le terrestre Histoire-Corbillard,
Que traînent au néant l'instinct et le hasard.

Mon Cœur est une horloge oubliée à demeure,
Qui, me sachant défunt, s'obstine à sonner l'heure!

Mon aimée était là, toute à me consoler;
Je l'ai trop fait souffrir, ça ne peut plus aller.

Here's evening.
Grate, music, grate,
Hypertrophic in state,
Of winder and spring.

LITANY-COMPLAINT OF MY SACRED HEART

Prometheus and Vulture, blasphemy and punishment,
My Heart, a heartless cancer, gnaws itself, intent.

My Heart's an urn where I've put certain of the dead;
Oh, shush, refrains of their lullabies; you scents long fled . . .

A hundred literatures make the canon of my Heart;
Divine deletions without respite lard their art.

My Heart's a dry desert – drunk, though, isn't it just?,
With this regurgitated wine, universal disgust.

My Heart's a Nero as a child, a pampered Asian,
And vainly cloyed with realms of dream to satiation.

My Heart's a drowned man, of soul and lift drained clean,
Grasped in the suckers of the sponging octopus, Spleen.

It's a firework display, alas, before the night,
That headlong rains have drowned beyond all hope to light.

My Heart's the earthbound Hearse of History
Dragged to oblivion by instinct and hazardry.

My Heart's a clock, for good forgotten in its tower,
That, knowing I'm the late, persists to chime the hour.

My love was there just to console me; I know
I've hurt her far too much; no further can that go.

Mon Cœur, plongé au Styx de nos arts danaïdes,
Présente à tout baiser une armure de vide.

Et toujours, mon Cœur, ayant ainsi déclamé,
En revient à sa complainte: Aimer, être aimé!

COMPLAINTE DES DÉBATS
MÉLANCOLIQUES ET LITTÉRAIRES

> *On peut encore aimer, mais confier*
> *toute son âme est un bonheur qu'on*
> *ne retrouvera plus.* —
>
> CORINNE OU L'ITALIE

Le long d'un ciel crépusculâtre,
Une cloche angéluse en paix
L'air exilescent et marâtre
Qui ne pardonnera jamais.

Paissant des débris de vaisselle,
Là-bas, au talus des remparts,
Se profile une haridelle
Convalescente; il se fait tard.

Qui m'aima jamais? Je m'entête
Sur ce refrain bien impuissant,
Sans songer que je suis bien bête
De me faire du mauvais sang.

Je possède un propre physique,
Un cœur d'enfant bien élevé,
Et pour un cerveau magnifique
Le mien n'est pas mal, vous savez!

My Heart, in the Styx of our Danaidan arts, addresses
An empty suit of armour to all and any caresses.

And always, having just declaimed, much as above,
My Heart returns to its complaint: to be loved, to love!

COMPLAINT OF MELANCHOLY
AND LITERARY DEBATES

> *You can still love but to confide*
> *all one's soul is a happiness*
> *you will not find again.*
> MADAME DE STAEL: CORINNE OU L'ITALIE

Along a twilit evening sky
In peace a bell now angeludes
The air, exilient, stepmother sly,
Who'll never have forgiving moods.

Down there upon the rampart's slopes,
Grazing the bits of crock and plate,
An old nag, silhouetted, copes,
Convalescing; it's getting late.

Who ever loved me? I still jam
On this quite impotent refrain,
Not dreaming yet how daft I am
To fret myself so sick again.

I have a pretty good physique,
Heart of a child that's been well bred,
And for a great brain, at the peak,
It's not so bad, you know, my head!

Eh bien, ayant pleuré l'Histoire,
J'ai voulu vivre un brin heureux;
C'était trop demander, faut croire;
J'avais l'air de parler hébreux.

Ah! tiens, mon cœur, de grâce, laisse!
Lorsque j'y songe, en vérité,
J'en ai des sueurs de faiblesse,
À choir dans la malpropreté.

Le cœur me piaffe de génie
Éperdûment pourtant, mon Dieu!
Et si quelqu'une veut ma vie,
Moi je ne demande pas mieux!

Eh va, pauvre âme véhémente!
Plonge, être, en leurs Jourdains blasés,
Deux frictions de vie courante
T'auront bien vite exorcisé.

Hélas, qui peut m'en répondre!
Tenez, peut-être savez-vous
Ce que c'est qu'une âme hypochondre?
J'en suis une dans les prix doux.

Ô Hélène, j'erre en ma chambre;
Et tandis que tu prends le thé,
Là-bas, dans l'or d'un fier septembre,
Je frissonne de tous mes membres,
En m'inquiétant de ta santé.

Tandis que, d'un autre côté . . .

Well, having wept all History's ink,
I wished to live happyish next;
Too much to ask, one needs must think;
I spoke, it seems, some Hebrew text.

Ah, hold on, heart, for mercy sake!
When I imagine it in truth
I'm in a cold sweat and I shake
In fear of acting most uncouth.

My heart paws me with genius,
God! desperate, still – curvetter!
If some woman wants my life, me'n us,
Myself, I wouldn't ask for better.

Come on, poor forceful soul at strife!
And in their blasé Jourdains, plunge!
Two chafings then in running life
You'll quickly exorcise, expunge!

Oh dear, who can respond to me?
Hang on, perhaps you understand
What hypochondriac souls may be?
I'm one in the soft price band.

Oh, Helen, I pace about my room
And while below you sip your tea
In proud September's golden bloom,
I shake in every limb, consume
Myself with how your health may be.

While, on the other hand, you see . . .

COMPLAINTE D'UNE CONVALESCENCE EN MAI

Nous n'avons su toutes
ces choses qu'après sa mort.
MADAME PERIER: VIE DE PASCAL

Convalescent au lit, ancré de courbatures,
Je me plains aux dessins bleus de ma couverture,

Las de reconstituer dans l'art du jour baissant
Cette dame d'en face auscultant les passants:

Si la Mort, de son van, avait chosé mon être,
En serait-elle moins, ce soir, à sa fenêtre? . . .

Oh! mort, tout mort! au plus jamais, au vrai néant
Des nuits où piaule en longs regrets le chat-huant!

Et voilà que mon Âme est tout hallucinée!
Puis s'abat, sans avoir fixé sa destinée.

Ah! que de soirs de mai pareils à celui-ci;
Que la vie est égale; et le cœur endurci!

Je me sens fou d'un tas de petites misères.
Mais maintenant, je sais ce qu'il me reste à faire.

Qui n'a jamais rêvé? Je voudrais le savoir!
Elles vous sourient avec âme, et puis bonsoir,

Ni vu ni connu. Et les voilà qui rebrodent
Le canevas ingrat de leur âme à la mode;

Fraîches à tous, et puis reprenant leur air sec
Pour les christs déclassés et autres gens suspects.

Et pourtant, le béni grand bol de lait de ferme
Que me serait un baiser sur sa bouche ferme!

COMPLAINT OF A CONVALESCENCE IN MAY

All these things were learnt only after
his death.
MADAME PERIER: LIFE OF PASCAL

Now convalescent, still in bed, I just complain,
Anchored by aches, to blue designs of counterpane,

Fagged to reconstitute in the art of declining day
That woman, opposite, sounding all who pass her way.

If Death had thinged my being with its fanning winnow,
Would she be any less, this evening, at her window?

Oh, dead, all dead, in the true void forever gone
Of nights where long regrets of owls go wailing on.

And there it is, my Soul is all hallucinated,
Then, not having fixed its destiny, deflated.

Oh, for evenings of May like this to come again;
For life all of a piece, and heart inured to pain.

I feel I'm going mad from petty ills that pile
But now I know what's left for me to do meanwhile.

Who's never dreamed? I'd like to know exactly who!
They smile with soul at you, and then, good evening, through!,

Not seen nor known. And there they are embroidering
The graceless canvas of their soul in the latest thing:

Blooming with all, then don their desiccated aspects
For has-been Christs and any other human suspects.

And yet, that blessed ample dish of dairy cream,
What it would do for me to kiss her firm mouth's seam!

Je ne veux accuser personne, bien qu'on eût
Pu, ce me semble, mon bon cœur étant connu . . .

N'est-ce pas; nous savons ce qu'il nous reste à faire,
Ô Cœur d'or pétri d'aromates littéraires,

Et toi, cerveau confit dans l'alcool de l'Orgueil!
Et qu'il faut procéder d'abord par demi-deuils . . .

Primo: mes grandes angoisses métaphysiques
Sont passées à l'état de chagrins domestiques;

Deux ou trois spleens locaux. – Ah! pitié, voyager
Du moins, pendant un an ou deux à l'étranger . . .

Plonger mon front dans l'eau des mers, aux matinées
Torrides, m'en aller à petites journées,

Compter les clochers, puis m'asseoir, ayant très chaud,
Aveuglé des maisons peintes au lait de chaux . . .

Dans les Indes du Rêve aux pacifiques Ganges,
Que j'en ai des comptoirs, des hamacs de rechange!

– Voici l'œuf à la coque et la lampe du soir.
Convalescence bien folle, comme on peut voir.

I wouldn't want to blame a soul, and yet, one could
Have, seems to me, my kind heart being understood . . .

Couldn't one? We know what's left for us to do,
O Heart of gold embalmed in bookish spice, and you,

Dear brain, preserved in alcohol of Pride! And how
It must begin at outset in half mourning now . . .

First, my vast metaphysical anxieties
Have reached the level of domestic quandaries;

Two or three local spleens. – Oh for pity's sake, go
Away abroad at least, to spend a year or so . . .

Plunge my head, mornings, in seas of the torrid zone,
And wander off on easy stages on my own,

Count the bell-towers, then sit down, being very warm,
Blinded by houses painted in their white-washed form . . .

In Indias of Dream, the peace of the Ganges,
If only I'd the godowns, a change of hammocks, please!

– Here's the good old hen's egg and the lamp is lit.
This convalescence, as you see, quite a mad fit.

COMPLAINTE DU SAGE DE PARIS

Aimer, uniquement, ces jupes éphémères?
Autant dire aux soleils: fêtez vos centenaires.

Mais tu peux déguster, dans leurs jardins d'un jour,
Comme à cette dînette unique Tout concourt;

Déguster, en menant les rites réciproques,
Les trucs Inconscients dans leur œuf, à la coque.

Soit en pontifiant, avec toute ta foi
D'Exécuteur des hautes-œuvres de la Loi;

Soit en vivisectant ces claviers anonymes,
Pour l'art, sans espérer leur *ut* d'hostie ultime.

Car, crois pas que l'hostie où dort ton paradis
Sera d'une farine aux levains inédits.

Mais quoi, leurs yeux sont tout! et puis la nappe est mise,
Et l'Orgue juvénile à l'aveugle improvise.

Et, sans noce, voyage, curieux, colis,
Cancans, et fadeur d'hôpital du même lit,

Mais pour avoir des vitraux fiers à domicile,
Vivre à deux seuls est encor le moins imbécile.

Vois-la donc, comme d'ailleurs, et loyalement,
Les passants, les mots, les choses, les firmaments.

Vendange chez les arts enfantins; sois en fête
D'une fugue, d'un mot, d'un ton, d'un air de tête.

La science, outre qu'elle ne peut rien savoir,
Trouve, tels les ballons, l'Irrespirable Noir.

COMPLAINT OF THE SAGE OF PARIS

What, these ephemeral skirts, and only these to love?
As good tell suns: mark your centenaries above.

But you could taste, down in their gardens, any day,
The Whole converging on their picnic tray;

Could taste, conforming with reciprocal rites observed,
The tricks of the Inconscient in their egg, soft-served.

Either pontificating, with all your faith and awe
As Executioner of the high deeds of the Law;

Or else, by vivisecting anonymous harpsichords
For art, not hoping for their *do*, last host's awards.

Don't think the host where sleep your paradisal hours
Is baked with unprecedented and unleaven flours.

Then what: their eyes are all! And next the cloth is laid,
The youthful organ, blindly improvising, played.

And, without wedding, travel, sightseers, packages,
Can-cans, and one bed's ward-like sick insipidities,

Yet to install some proud stained glass in your own place,
To live as two loners is still the least mad case.

See her, then, as from elsewhere, and with loyal intent,
Those passing, words and things, the changing firmament.

A vintage of childish arts; celebrate instead
A fugue in flight, a word, a tone, poise of the head.

Science, though its knowledge of anything's a total lack,
Finds, such the balloons show, an unbreathable Black.

Ne force jamais tes pouvoirs de Créature,
Tout est écrit et vrai, rien n'est contre-nature.

Vivre et peser selon le Beau, le Bien, le Vrai?
Ô parfums, ô regards, ô fois! soit, j'essaierai;

Mais, tel Brennus avec son épée, et d'avance,
Suis-je pas dans l'un des plateaux de la balance?

Des casiers de bureau, le Beau, le Vrai, le Bien;
Rime et sois grand, la Loi reconnaîtra les siens.

Ah! démaillotte-toi, mon enfant, de ces langes
D'Occident! va faire une pleine eau dans le Gange.

La logique, la morale, c'est vite dit;
Mais! gisements d'instincts, virtuels paradis,

Nuit des hérédités et limbes des latences!
Actif? passif? ô pelouses des Défaillances,

Tamis de pores! Et les bas-fonds sous-marins,
Infini sans foyer, forêt vierge à tous crins!

Pour voir, jetez la sonde, ou plongez sous la cloche;
Oh! les velléités, les anguilles sous roche,

Les polypes sournois attendant l'hameçon,
Les vœux sans état-civil, ni chair, ni poisson!

Les guanos à Geysers, les astres en syncope,
Et les métaux qui font loucher nos spectroscopes!

Une capsule éclate, un monde de facteurs
En prurit, s'éparpille assiéger les hauteurs;

D'autres titubent sous les butins génitoires,
Ou font un feu d'enfer dans leurs laboratoires!

Never constrain your Creature powers, instinctual;
All is written and true, nothing's counter-natural.

To live and weigh by the Beautiful, the Good, the True?
Oh, perfumes, glances, chances. So be it. I'll try it, too.

But, as with Brennus with his sword, by circumstance
Aren't I in one pan of the scales and in advance?

Office pigeon-holes: the Beautiful, the Good, the True;
Rime and be big; the Law recognises its own, too.

Ah, unwrap yourself, child from this Western woolliness!
Go off and sail the Ganges without storm or stress.

Logic, morality, they're spoken in a trice,
But instinctual bearings, virtual paradise,

Night of heredities, limbo of latences! It's
Active or passive? Oh, lawns of Fainting-Fits,

The sieve of pores! And the shallows under water,
Homeless infinity, forest virgin to the last daughter!

To see it, swing the lead, or plunge in diving-bell;
Oh, the velleities, the something fishy smell,

The torpid polyps awaiting fish-hooks on the prowl;
Wishes without civil status, neither fish nor fowl.

Guanos in Geysers, stars that faint within their stint,
Metals that make our spectroscopes acquire a squint!

A capsule bursts open, a world of carriers itches,
And scatters going to besiege the highest niches.

Others stagger under the engendering loot
Or make hell-fire in their laboratories shoot!

Allez! laissez passer, laissez faire; l'Amour
Reconnaîtra les siens: il est aveugle et sourd.

Car la vie innombrable va, vannant les germes
Aux concurrences des êtres sans droits, sans terme.

Vivottez et passez, à la grâce de Tout;
Et voilà la pitié, l'amour et le bon goût.

L'Inconscient, c'est l'Éden-Levant que tout saigne;
Si la Terre ne veut sécher, qu'elle s'y baigne!

C'est la grande Nounou où nous nous aimerions
À la grâce des divines sélections.

C'est le Tout-Vrai, l'Omniversel Ombelliforme
Mancenilier, sous qui, mes bébés, faut qu'on dorme!

(Nos découvertes scientifiques étant
Ses feuilles mortes, qui tombent de temps en temps.)

Là, sur des oreillers d'étiquettes d'éthiques,
Lévite félin aux égaux ronrons lyriques,

Sans songer: «Suis-je moi? Tout est si compliqué!
Où serais-je à présent, pour tel coche manqué?»

Sans colère, rire, ou pathos, d'une foi pâle,
Aux riches flirtations des pompes argutiales,

Mais sans rite emprunté, car c'est bien malséant,
Sirote chaque jour ta tasse de néant;

Lavé comme une hostie, en quelconques costumes
Blancs ou deuil, bref calice au vent qu'un rien parfume.

– «Mais, tout est un rire à la Justice! et d'où vient
Mon cœur, ah! mon sacré-cœur, s'il ne rime à rien?»

Come on, let it pass, let it happen; Love
Recognises its own; it's blind and deaf enough.

For life innumerably goes on, winnows seeds, germs,
Towards concurrences of beings without rights, or terms.

Scrape by and pass on, by the Whole's favour graced,
And there goes pity, love, and there goes good taste.

Inconscience is the rising Eden everything bleeds;
If Earth would not go dry, there may she bathe her needs!

It's the big Nanny, where all'n' any'd fall in love,
By favour of divine selections, hand in glove.

It's the Whole Truth, the Omniversal Umbelliform
Manchineel beneath which, babes, you must sleep warm!

(The scientific discoveries that we attain
Are just its dead leaves falling now and again.)

There, on pillows of ethical tickets curling,
Feline Levite, with an even lyric purring,

Not thinking: 'Am I me? It's all such a tangled state!
Where should I be at present? For what missed boat late?'

No anger, laughter, pity, of a pale faith there,
In rich flirtations in ceremonies of splitting hair,

But no filched rites – it's quite unseemly, such behaviour –
A sip a day, your cup of full oblivion savour;

Cleansed like a victim in whatever habiliments,
Mourning or white, brief chalice, in wind some nothing scents.

'But all's a jeer at Justice! And where's it from, my heart,
My sacred heart of . . . ? if it rhymes with nothing from the start?'

– Du calme et des fleurs. Peu t'importe de connaître
Ce que tu fus, dans l'à jamais, avant de naître?

Eh bien, que l'autre éternité qui, Très-sans-Toi,
Grouillera, te laisse aussi pieusement froid.

Quant à *ta* mort, l'éclair aveugle en est en route
Qui saura te choser, va, sans que tu t'en doutes.

– «Il rit d'oiseaux, le pin dont *mon* cercueil viendra!»
– Mais *ton* cercueil sera *sa* mort! etc . . .

Allons, tu m'a compris. Va, que ta seule étude
Soit de vivre sans but, fou de mansuétude.

COMPLAINTE DES COMPLAINTES

Maintenant! pourquoi ces complaintes?
Gerbes d'ailleurs d'un défunt Moi
Où l'ivraie art mange la foi?
Sot tabernacle où je m'éreinte
À cultiver des roses peintes?
Pourtant ménage et sainte table!
Ah! ces complaintes incurables,
    Pourquoi? pourquoi?

Puis, Gens à qui les fugues vraies
Que crie, au fond, ma riche voix
– N'est-ce pas, qu'on les sent parfois? –
Attoucheraient sous leurs ivraies
Les violettes d'une Foi,
Vous passerez, imperméables
À mes complaintes incurables?
    Pourquoi? pourquoi?

– From calm and from the flowers. It's precious little worth,
Isn't it, knowing what you'd been forever before your birth?

Well, may the other eternity, Most-Lacking-You,
That soon will swarm, leave you as piously frozen too.

As for *your* death, the blind lightning's on its way,
Knows how, indeed, to thing you, don't you doubt the day.

'The pine my coffin comes from laughs with birds that settle there!'
– But *your* coffin has to be *its* death, et cetera . . .

Come on, you've understood me. May your one study brood
On living with no aim, mad with mansuetude.

COMPLAINT OF COMPLAINTS

Now then, why chunter these complaints?
Sheaves more like of a dead I,
Where arty tares eat faithful rye?
Fool tabernacle where wit taints
In nurturing roses out of paints?
Yet wife and home, Lord's Table, too!
Oh, these deadly complaints you do,
      Why, why?

Well, folks, for whom these fugues' true airs
(That my rich voice from depths cries out
– D'you sometimes feel them round about?)
Would touch upon, beneath their tares,
The violets of a Faith they spout,
Will you folks pass impervious to
My incurable complaints? You do?
      Why, why?

Chut! tout est bien, rien ne s'étonne.
Fleuris, ô Terre d'occasion,
Vers les mirages des Sions!
Et nous, sous l'Art qui nous bâtonne,
Sisyphes par persuasion,
Flûtant des christs les vaines fables,
Au cabestan de l'incurable
      POURQUOI! – Pourquoi?

COMPLAINTE-ÉPITAPHE

La Femme,
Mon âme:
Ah! quels
Appels!

Pastels
Mortels,
Qu'on blâme
Mes gammes!

Un fou
S'avance,
Et danse.

Silence . . .
Lui, où?
Coucou.

Hush! All is well; nothing's astounded.
Flourish, O Earth, the second-hand
To mirages of Sion's land!
And we, beneath Art's cudgel pounded,
Convinced Sisyphians in a band,
Fluting vain fables of christs to you
Around the capstan's incurable cue:
　　　WHY! – Why?

COMPLAINT-EPITAPH

Woman's role,
Oh, my soul,
What a deal
Of appeal!

Pastel-feel,
Mortal-weal –
Such blame they dole
My rigmarole!

A fool who
Advances
And dances.

Silence answers . . .
Him who?
Cuckoo, cuckoo.

L'Imitation de Notre-Dame
la Lune selon Jules Laforgue

The Imitation of Our Lady the Moon
according to Jules Laforgue

Ah! quel juillet nous avons hiverné,
Per amica silentia lunæ!
ÎLE DE LA MAINAU
(Lac de Constance)

À Gustave Kahn
et aussi à la mémoire
de la petite Salammbô, prêtresse de Tanit

What a July we've wintered,
Per amica silentia lunae!
ISLE OF THE MAINAU
(Lake Constance)

To Gustave Kahn
and also to the memory
of little Salambo, priestess of Tanit

UN MOT AU SOLEIL POUR COMMENCER

Soleil! soudard plaqué d'ordres et de crachats,
Planteur mal élevé, sache que les Vestales
À qui la Lune, en son équivoque œil-de-chat,
Est la rosace de l'Unique Cathédrale,

Sache que les Pierrots, phalènes des dolmens
Et les nymphéas blancs des lacs où dort Gomorrhe,
Et tous les bienheureux qui pâturent l'Éden
Toujours printanier des renoncements – t'abhorrent.

Et qu'ils gardent pour toi des mépris spéciaux,
Bellâtre, Maquignon, Ruffian, Rastaquouère
À breloques d'œufs d'or, qui le prends de si haut
Avec la terre et son Orpheline lunaire.

Continue à fournir de couchants avinés
Les lendemains vomis des fêtes nationales,
À styler tes saisons, à nous bien déchaîner
Les drames de l'Apothéose Ombilicale!

Va Phœbus! mais, Dèva, dieu des Réveils cabrés,
Regarde un peu parfois ce Port-Royal d'esthètes
Qui, dans leurs décamérons lunaires au frais,
Ne parlent de rien moins que mettre à prix ta tête.

Certes, tu as encor devant toi de beaux jours;
Mais la tribu s'accroît, de ces vieilles pratiques
De l'À QUOI BON? qui vont rêvant l'art et l'amour
Au seuil lointain de l'Agrégat inorganique.

Pour aujourd'hui, vieux beau, nous nous contenterons
De mettre sous le nez de Ta Badauderie
Le mot dont l'Homme t'a déjà marqué au front;
Tu ne t'en étais jamais douté, je parie?

A WORD TO THE SUN FOR STARTERS

Mercenary Sun, beknighted, gob-gonged, passed up high,
Planter badly raised, know that the Vestals, those
For whom the Moon becomes, with her dubious tiger's eye,
In the Unique Cathedral's rosace the very rose;

Know that the Pierrots, too, the moths of megaliths,
And white chrysalids of lakes in which Gomorrah lies,
And all the lucky types that graze in Eden myths'
Perpetual springtime of renunciations – hate your rise.

Know that they hold for you a special scorn of theirs,
Fop, Pander, Ruffian, Flash Immigré with stuff
Like charms of golden eggs, with high and mighty airs
Towards the earth and her little lunar Orphan-scruff.

You carry on supplying settings – bibulous,
Tomorrows vomited from national festival,
And polish up your seasons to unleash on us
Sensational Apotheosis of the Umbilical.

Go, Phoebal! But, Deva, god of reared arising,
Heed for once this Port-Royal of aesthetes instead;
In lunar open-air decamerons they're devising
Nothing less than the price to fix upon your head.

Yes, true, you've still some splendid days to come, above,
But now the tribe of these old-practised rogues grows still,
The WHAT'S-THE-GOODS?, who go on dreaming art and love
Upon the inorganic Aggregate's far sill.

And so, old Beau, today we'll be content for now
With wagging underneath your Idleness's nose
The word which Man's already branded on your brow;
A thing like that, I bet, you'd never once suppose?

– Sache qu'on va disant d'une belle phrase, os
Sonore mais très-nul comme suc médullaire,
De tout boniment creux enfin: c'est du pathos,
C'est du PHŒBUS! – Ah! pas besoin de commentaires . . .

Ô vision du temps où l'être trop puni,
D'un: «Eh! va donc, Phœbus!» te rentrera ton prêche
De vieux *Crescite et multiplicamini*,
Pour s'inoculer à jamais la Lune fraîche!

LITANIES DES PREMIERS QUARTIERS DE LA LUNE

Lune bénie
Des insomnies,

Blanc médaillon
Des Endymions,

Astre fossile
Que tout exile,

Jaloux tombeau
De Salammbô,

Embarcadère
Des grands Mystères,

Madone et miss
Diane-Artémis,

Sainte Vigie
De nos orgies

Jettatura
Des baccarats,

– So know that there's a fine phrase going round; it's bone
Sonorous but very null like medullar juice,
All humbug hollowed out: Fustian, your own
Phoebal *Sol*ecism! – Further strictures no use . . .

Oh, vision of time when, lashed too often, being flings
A 'Stow it, Sol!' and makes you eat your words and spoon,
Those hoary *Crescite et multiplicaminings*,
And inoculates itself forever with fresh Moon!

LITANIES OF THE MOON'S FIRST QUARTERS

O Moon the blest
Of sleepless rest,

White medallion
Of Endymion,

Fossilised star
Exiled afar,

Envious tomb
Of Salambo's doom,

Port of sail
On Mystery's trail,

Madonna, Miss
Diane-Artemis,

Holy Seer
Of our orgies here,

Evil eye at
Baccarat,

Dame très-lasse
De nos terrasses,

Philtre attisant
Les vers-luisants,

Rosace et dôme
Des derniers psaumes,

Bel œil-de-chat
De nos rachats,

Sois l'Ambulance
De nos croyances!

Sois l'édredon
Du Grand-Pardon!

AU LARGE

Comme la nuit est lointainement pleine
De silencieuse infinité claire!
Pas le moindre écho des gens de la terre,
Sous la Lune méditerranéenne!

Voilà le Néant dans sa pâle gangue,
Voilà notre Hostie et sa Sainte-Table,
Le seul bras d'ami par l'Inconnaissable,
Le seul mot solvable en nos folles langues!

Au-delà des cris choisis des époques,
Au-delà des sens, des larmes, des vierges,
Voilà quel astre indiscutable émerge,
Voilà l'immortel et seul soliloque!

Lady bored, braving
Our café paving,

Philtre igniting
Glow-worm lighting,

Rosace and dome
Where last psalms roam,

Cat's eye gleamings
Of our redeemings,

Be the Ambulance
Of our credulence!

And be the quilt,
Full Pardon for guilt.

OPEN SEA

How far and away full is the night
With the clear silence of infinitude!
Not the slightest sound of men intrude
Under the Moon's Mediterranean light!

There is Oblivion in its pale ore;
There is Our Host and its Communion-Table;
Sole friendly arm in this Unknowable Babel;
The sole word solvent in our fool tongues' store.

Beyond the cries preferred in epochs past,
Beyond the senses, virgins, and the tears,
There what a star beyond dispute appears,
There the immortal, sole, soliloquy cast!

Et toi, là-bas, pot-au-feu, pauvre Terre!
Avec tes essais de mettre en rubriques
Tes reflets perdus du Grand Dynamique,
Tu fais un métier ah! bien sédentaire!

CLAIR DE LUNE

Penser qu'on vivra jamais dans cet astre,
Parfois me flanque un coup dans l'épigastre.

Ah! tout pour toi, Lune, quand tu t'avances
Aux soirs d'août par les féeries du silence!

Et quand tu roules, démâtée, au large
À travers les brisants noirs des nuages!

Oh! monter, perdu, m'étancher à même
Ta vasque de béatifiants baptêmes!

Astre atteint de cécité, fatal phare
Des vols migrateurs des plaintifs Icares!

Œil stérile comme le suicide,
Nous sommes le congrès des las, préside;

Crâne glacé, raille les calvities
De nos incurables bureaucraties;

Ô pilule des léthargies finales,
Infuse-toi dans nos durs encéphales!

Ô Diane à la chlamyde très-dorique,
L'Amour cuve, prend ton carquois et pique

Ah! d'un trait inoculant l'être aptère,
Les cœurs de bonne volonté sur terre!

And, you, below, poor stewpot, wretched Earth!
With your essays to cram in a rubric's slot
Your lost thoughts on the Great Dynamic, what
A trade, ah, what a sedentary berth!

MOONSHINE

To think I'll never live upon that astral
Body can land me one right epigastral.

Ah, I'm all yours, Moon, in your advancement
On August nights in silence of entrancement!

And when you roll on open sea, dismasted,
In the black breakers of the clouds, wind-blasted.

Oh, rapt, to climb, straight to your basin risen,
Drink in beatifications of your baptism.

Star overcome with blindness, fatal beacon
That migrant flights of plaintive Icaruses peak on!

Eye sterile as suicide, we're the forum
Of the bored stiff, preside now on our quorum;

Ice-glazed skull, mock the calvitic pinnacles
Of our deadly bureaucratic finicals.

O pill for terminal lethargies, scatter
Yourself throughout our stubborn cranial matter!

Diana in chlamys of a style most doric,
Ferment the love of you; with barb soporic,

Ah, jab the flightless with inoculations,
Hearts of good will on earth, in all locations!

Astre lavé par d'inouïs déluges,
Qu'un de tes chastes rayons fébrifuges,

Ce soir, pour inonder mes draps, dévie,
Que je m'y lave les mains de la vie !

CLIMAT, FAUNE ET FLORE DE LA LUNE

Des nuits, ô Lune d'Immaculée-Conception,
Moi, vermine des nébuleuses d'occasion,
J'aime, du frais des toits de notre Babylone,
Concevoir ton climat et ta flore et ta faune.

Ne sachant qu'inventer pour t'offrir mes ennuis,
Ô Radeau du Nihil aux quais seuls de nos nuits !

Ton atmosphère est fixe, et tu rêves, figée
En climats de silence, écho de l'hypogée
D'un ciel atone où nul nuage ne s'endort
Par des vents chuchotant tout au plus qu'on est mort ?
Des montagnes de nacre et des golfes d'ivoire
Se renvoient leurs parois de mystiques ciboires,
En anses où, sur maint pilotis, d'un air lent,
Des Sirènes font leurs nattes, lèchent leurs flancs,
Blêmes d'avoir gorgé de lunaires luxures
Là-bas, ces gais dauphins aux geysers de mercure.

Oui, c'est l'automne incantatoire et permanent
Sans thermomètre, embaumant mers et continents,
Étangs aveugles, lacs ophtalmiques, fontaines
De Léthé, cendres d'air, déserts de porcelaine,
Oasis, solfatares, cratères éteints,
Arctiques sierras, cataractes l'air en zinc,
Hauts-plateaux crayeux, carrières abandonnées,
Nécropoles moins vieilles que leurs graminées,

Star, cleansed by deluges unheard of, soon may
You divert a chaste and febrifugal moon-ray,

Tonight, to inundate my sheets and pillows
And wash life off my hands beneath its billows!

CLIMATE, FLORA AND FAUNA OF THE MOON

The nights, Moon of Immaculate Conception above,
That I, vermin of second-hand nebulas, so love
Imagining your climate, flora and fauna, on
The cool roof-tops of our modern Babylon.

Oblivion's Raft, along the lone quays of our nights,
I know my tediums reach you only in fancy's flights.

Your atmosphere is stationary; do you dream
In silent climates, an echo of the hypogeum
Of toneless skies where not a cloud sleeps in its bed
For winds that whisper at the most that one is dead?
Mountains of mother-of-pearl and chasms of ivories
Reflect their rockface back like mystic cibories,
In bays where, with a gentle air, on piling'd banks,
Sirens do their laundry, licking over their flanks,
Blemished with surfeiting on lunar lechery
There, those squiffy dauphins by geysers of mercury.

It's autumn, incantatory and permanent,
Without thermometer, embalming seas and continent,
Blind meres, Lethean fountains, and ophthalmic lakes,
Cindery air, deserts of porcelain that bakes,
Oases, extinct craters, sulphur springs, a rink
Of Arctic sierras, cataracts that look like zinc,
Quarries abandoned long, raised chalk plateaux,
Necropolises not so old as grass they grow,

Et des dolmens par caravanes – et tout très
Ravi d'avoir fait son temps, de rêver au frais.

Salut, lointains crapauds ridés, en sentinelles
Sur les pics, claquant des dents à ces tourterelles
Jeunes qu'intriguent vos airs! Salut, cétacés
Lumineux! et vous, beaux comme des cuirassés,
Cygnes d'antan, nobles témoins des cataclysmes;
Et vous, paons blancs cabrés en aurores de prismes;
Et vous, Fœtus voûtés, glabres contemporains
Des Sphinx brouteurs d'ennuis aux moustaches d'airain,
Qui, dans le clapotis des grottes basaltiques,
Ruminez l'Enfin! comme une immortelle chique!

Oui, rennes aux andouillers de cristal; ours blancs
Graves comme des Mages, vous déambulant,
Les bras en croix vers les miels du divin silence!
Porcs-épics fourbissant sans but vos blêmes lances;
Oui, papillons aux reins pavoisés de joyaux
Ouvrant vos ailes à deux battants d'in-folios;
Oui, gélatines d'hippopotames en pâles
Flottaisons de troupeaux éclaireurs d'encéphales;
Pythons en intestins de cerveaux morts d'abstrait,
Bancs d'éléphas moisis qu'un souffle effriterait!

Et vous, fleurs fixes! mandragores à visages,
Cactus obéliscals aux fruits en sarcophages,
Forêts de cierges massifs, parcs de polypiers,
Palmiers de corail blanc aux résines d'acier!
Lys marmoréens à sourires hystériques,
Qui vous mettez à débiter d'albes musiques
Tous les cent ans, quand vous allez avoir du lait!
Champignons aménagés comme des palais!

Ô Fixe! on ne sait plus à qui donner la palme
Du lunaire; et surtout, quelle leçon de calme!
Tout a l'air émané d'un même acte de foi
Au Néant Quotidien sans comment ni pourquoi!
Et rien ne fait de l'ombre, et ne se désagrège;
Ne naît, ni ne mûrit; tout vit d'un Sortilège

And dolmens by the caravan – all in extreme
Delight of having done their time, in cool to dream.

Hello, wrinkled distant toads on sentry-go
Upon the peaks, grinding your teeth at young doves so
Intrigued by all your songs. Hello, luminous
Cetaceans! And you, like breast-plates splendiferous,
Swans of yester-year, fine witness of cataclysms;
And you, white peacocks, reared auroras made of prisms;
And you, stooping Foetus contemporaries, glabrous as glass,
Of Sphinxes, browsers of boredoms, moustached with brass,
That, by the lapping of basaltic grottoes, nod
And ruminate the Infinal! like an immortal wad.

Yes, reindeers with crystal antlers; polar bears
Grave as the Magi, you, strolling from your lairs,
Arms crossed, to honeys of divine silence; porcupines
That furnish endlessly your ghastly spikes and spines.
Yes, butterflies with backs inlaid with jewelled shows
Opening your wings in two beats of folios.
Yes, gelatines of hippopotamus in wan
Flotsam of lightning troops of encephalon;
Pythons – extracted intestine shapes of dead brains,
Banks of elephants a sigh would crumble into grains.

You, fixed flowers! mandrakes with the faces, I salute:
Obeliskoid cactus with your sarcophagal fruit,
Forests of massive candles, and you parks of polyps,
Palms of white coral with steely sap in dollops,
Marmoreal lilies with hysteric smiles that make
You lilt your musical albas out until you take
A hundred years a time whenever you have milk,
And mushrooms appointed like palaces and their ilk.

Oh, Eyes front! What else deserves the lunar palm
I've no idea – but over all, what lessons there in calm!
It seems to issue from the same act of faith there, for
The Daily Oblivion, without a why or wherefore!
And nothing casts a shadow, won't disintegrate;
Nothing is born, nor ripens; all lives by turn of Fate

Sans foyer qui n'induit guèrc à se mettre en frais
Que pour des amours blancs, lunaires et distraits . . .

Non, l'on finirait par en avoir mal de tête,
Avec le rire idiot des marbres Égynètes
Pour jamais tant tout ça stagne en un miroir mort!
Et l'on oublierait vite comment on en sort.

Et pourtant, ah! c'est là qu'on en revient encore
Et toujours, quand on a compris le Madrépore.

GUITARE

Astre sans cœur et sans reproche,
Ô Maintenon de vieille roche!

Très-Révérende Supérieure
Du cloître où l'on ne sait plus l'heure,

D'un Port-Royal port de Circée
Où Pascal n'a d'autres *Pensées*

Que celles du roseau qui jase
Ne sait plus quoi, ivre de vase . . .

Oh! qu'un Philippe de Champaigne,
Mais né pierrot, vienne et te peigne!

Un rien, une miniature
De la largeur d'une tonsure;

Ça nous ferait un scapulaire
Dont le contact anti-solaire,

Par exemple aux pieds de la femme,
Ah! nous serait tout un programme!

Without a home that scarcely induces you to action
Except for odd affaires of lunar blank distraction . . .

No, you would surely end up with a splitting head
With the idiot smirk of Aeginite marbles spread
Forever as if all were stuck in a dead mirror's plain!
And you would soon forget how to get out again.

And yet, ah, it's just where you end up once more
And always, when you've understood the Madrepore.

ONE-STRING GUITAR

Star without heart and without blame,
O Maintenon of tough old stock and frame!

Prioress, Right Reverend and sublime,
Of the convent where none knows the time,

Of some Circean Port-Royal port
Where Pascal has no other *Thought*

Than has a reed dead drunk with slime,
Chattering of nothing all the time . . .

If only Philip of Champaigne,
But born a clown, could paint again

A miniature, a nothingness,
Size of a tonsure, more or less;

That would become our scapular charm
Whose touch, against all solar harm,

For example from a woman's feet,
Would be, ah, quite a scheme to beat!

PIERROTS

I

C'est, sur un cou qui, raide, émerge
D'une fraise empesée *idem*,
Une face imberbe au cold-cream,
Un air d'hydrocéphale asperge.

Les yeux sont noyés de l'opium
De l'indulgence universelle,
La bouche clownesque ensorcèle
Comme un singulier géranium.

Bouche qui va du trou sans bonde
Glacialement désopilé,
Au transcendental en-allé
Du souris vain de la Joconde.

Campant leur cône enfariné
Sur le noir serre-tête en soie,
Ils font rire leur patte d'oie
Et froncent en trèfle leur nez.

Ils ont comme chaton de bague
Le scarabée égyptien,
À leur boutonnière fait bien
Le pissenlit des terrains vagues.

Ils vont, se sustentant d'azur!
Et parfois aussi de légumes,
De riz plus blanc que leur costume,
De mandarines et d'œufs durs.

Ils sont de la secte du Blême,
Ils n'ont rien à voir avec Dieu,
Et sifflent: «Tout est pour le mieux,
Dans la meilleur' des mi-carême!»

PIERROTS

I

There, on a neck that, stiff, pokes spare
From ruff that's *idem* starched and creased,
A beardless face with cold cream greased –
A hydrocephalic beanpole's air.

The eyes are drowned in opium
That universal licence grants;
The clown mouth spell-binds and enchants
Like a singular geranium.

Mouth runs from bore, without known spile,
Frozenly worked round its laughing-rink,
To transcendental gone-for-a-drink
Of Mona Lisa's feint, vain smile.

Sticking their cone, all floured white,
On a black silk pirate's scarf,
They're going to make their crow's feet laugh
And pucker up their noses tight.

For stones set in their rings they've found
The scarabs that Egyptians loved;
Shown off in button-holes, they've shoved
The dandelions of waste ground.

Living on air, they taste their legs
And vegetables once or twice,
And whiter than their costumes, rice,
And mandarins and hard-boiled eggs.

Their Sect is the Cadaveral,
They have no truck with God or missal;
'Everything's for the best,' they whistle,
'In the best mid-Lenten festival.'

II

Le cœur blanc tatoué
De sentences lunaires,
Ils ont: «Faut mourir, frères!»
Pour mot-d'ordre-Évohé.

Quand trépasse une vierge,
Ils suivent son convoi,
Tenant leur cou tout droit
Comme on porte un beau cierge.

Rôle très-fatigant,
D'autant qu'ils n'ont personne
Chez eux, qui les frictionne
D'un conjugal onguent.

Ces dandys de la Lune
S'imposent, en effet,
De chanter «s'il vous plaît?»
De la blonde à la brune.

Car c'est des gens blasés;
Et s'ils vous semblent dupes,
Çà et là, de la Jupe
Lange à cicatriser,

Croyez qu'ils font la bête
Afin d'avoir des seins,
Pis-aller de coussins
À leurs savantes têtes.

Écarquillant le cou
Et feignant de comprendre
De travers, la voix tendre,
Mais les yeux si filous!

II

White hearts, tattoo-darned
With maxims of the moon,
They have: 'Must die, soon,
Brothers!' as Bacchantic command.

And should a virgin die
They join the funeral gait,
Holding their necks up straight,
As a good candle's held high.

Most tiring, the appointment,
More so since no one's living
With them who'll be giving
Massage with conjugal ointment.

These lunar dandies set
Themselves to sing this measure
In fact: 'What is your pleasure?'
From blond through to brunette.

For blasé types they are,
And if they seem the dupes
For swaddling Skirt's hoops –
Here and there – to scar,

They play the fool, suppose,
Merely to have some breasts
As makeshift cushions, rests,
Where their wise heads may doze.

Stretching the neck to look,
Feigning to comprehend her
Amiss, the voice so tender,
The eyes so much the crook.

– D'ailleurs, de mœurs très-fines,
Et toujours fort corrects,
(École des cromlechs
Et des tuyaux d'usines).

III

Comme ils vont molester, la nuit,
Au profound des parcs, les statues,
Mais n'offrant qu'aux moins dévêtues
Leurs bras et tout ce qui s'ensuit,

En tête-à-tête avec la femme
Ils ont toujours l'air d'être un tiers,
Confondent demain avec hier,
Et demandent *Rien* avec âme!

Jurent «je t'aime!» l'air là-bas,
D'une voix sans timbre, en extase,
Et concluent aux plus folles phrases
Par des: «Mon Dieu, n'insistons pas?»

Jusqu'à ce qu'ivre, Elle s'oublie,
Prise d'on ne sait quel besoin
De lune! dans leurs bras, fort loin
Des convenances établies.

IV

Maquillés d'abandon, les manches
En saule, ils leur font des serments,
Pour être vrais trop véhéments!
Puis, tumultuent en gigues blanches,

Beuglant: «Ange! tu m'as compris,
À la vie, à la mort!» – et songent:
Ah! passer là-dessus l'éponge! . . .
Et c'est pas chez eux parti-pris,

– Else, manners most becoming
And always most correct,
(Style of the cromlech sect
And factory plumbing.)

III

Since they're going to molest,
Tonight, the statues deep in the park,
Yet offering only the least stark
Naked their arms and all the rest,

In twosomes with women, the role
Of third party's what they play,
Blur tomorrow with yesterday,
And ask for *Nothing* with some soul.

They swear: 'I love you!', look distant,
Their voice ecstatic, lacking in tone,
And end the daftest phrases known
With 'God, aren't we to be insistent?'

Till, drunk, She forgets herself quite,
Taken, by some or other need
Of the Moon, in their arms indeed,
Far from the conventional polite.

IV

Make-up thrown on, their sleeves drooping
Like willows, they give them their promise,
Too vehement to be honest!
Then tumult in white shanks, whooping:

'Angel, you've understood me, kiss,
For life, till death!' – Yet pondering:
Ah, of all that scotch everything! . . .
And this with them's no prejudice,

Hélas! mais l'idée de la femme
Se prenant au sérieux encor
Dans ce siècle, voilà, les tord
D'un rire aux déchirantes gammes!

Ne leur jetez pas la pierre, ô
Vous qu'affecte une jarretière!
Allez, ne jetez pas la pierre
Aux blancs parias, aux purs pierrots!

V

Blancs enfants de chœur de la Lune,
Et lunologues éminents,
Leur Église ouvre à tout venant,
Claire d'ailleurs comme pas une.

Ils disent, d'un œil faisandé,
Les manches très-sacerdotales,
Que ce bas-monde de scandale
N'est qu'un des mille coups de dé

Du jeu que l'Idée et l'Amour,
Afin sans doute de connaître
Aussi leur propre raison d'être,
Ont jugé bon de mettre au jour.

Que nul d'ailleurs ne vaut le nôtre,
Qu'il faut pas le traiter d'hôtel
Garni vers un plus immortel,
Car nous sommes faits l'un pour l'autre;

Qu'enfin, et rien du moins subtil,
Ces gratuites antinomies
Au fond ne nous regardant mie,
L'art de tout est l'*Ainsi soit-il*;

Alas, but the thought of the female
Taking herself on the level yet
This century, look, shakes this set
With laughter of ear-splitting scale.

Don't cast the first stone here, oh
You that a garter stirs a bit!
Come on, don't cast a stone to hit
The white parias, the pure pierrot.

                V

White children of the Moon's choir,
And eminent lunologists,
For all comers, their Church exists,
Clear, too, like none else, now or prior.

They say, with looks so full of spice
And really sacerdotal sleeves:
This lower world where scandal heaves
Is one of a thousand throws at dice

In Love and Idea's game that they
Judged good – to find without doubt
Their own reason for being out –
To bring into the light of day.

And nothing elsewhere has its worth;
It's not for use as furnished pad
Till something more immortal's had.
We're made for each other on earth.

And lastly, not a subtle bit,
These antinomies, gratuitous,
At bottom disregarding us,
The whole art is the *So-be-it*;

Et que, chers frères, le beau rôle
Est de vivre de but en blanc
Et, dût-on se battre les flancs,
De hausser à tout les épaules.

PIERROTS

(On a des principes)

Elle disait, de son air vain fondamental:
«Je t'aime pour toi seul!» – Oh! là, là, grêle histoire;
Oui, comme l'art! Du calme, ô salaire illusoire
       Du capitaliste l'Idéal!

Elle faisait: «J'attends, me voici, je sais pas» . . .
Le regard pris de ces larges candeurs des lunes;
– Oh! là, là, ce n'est pas peut-être pour des prunes,
       Qu'on a fait ses classes ici-bas?

Mais voici qu'un beau soir, infortunée à point,
Elle meurt! – Oh! là, là; bon, changement de thème!
On sait que tu dois ressusciter le troisième
       Jour, sinon en personne, du moins

Dans l'odeur, les verdures, les eaux des beaux mois!
Et tu iras, levant encor bien plus de dupes
Vers le Zaïmph de la Joconde, vers la Jupe!
       Il se pourra même que j'en sois.

That, dear brothers, the finest role
Is living with no aim, no rut,
And, even though you bust a gut,
To shrug your shoulders at the whole.

PIERROTS

(One has principles)

Her manner essentially fake, this was her gist:
'I love you for yourself!' – Oh, dear, a likely pass!
Yes, like art, too! Calm down, illusory brass
        Of Ideal the Capitalist!

Next ploy: 'I'm here and waiting, I'm not clear . . .'
Her look filching the wide blankness of moons;
– Oh dear, oh dear, it's not perhaps for prunes
        One's gone to classes here?

Then comes a fine night, luckless, in a nick,
She dies! – Oh dear, oh dear, good, change of tune!
We know you must revive, the third forenoon,
        If not in person quick,

At least in odour, verdure, fine-weather watering places!
And go round raising still more suckers to divert
Towards Gioconda's Zaïmph, towards the Skirt!
        Me, maybe, one of those cases.

PIERROTS

(Scène courte mais typique)

Il me faut vos yeux! Dès que je perds leur étoile,
Le mal des calmes plats s'engouffre dans ma voile,
Le frisson du *Væ soli!* gargouille en mes moelles . . .

Vous auriez dû me voir après cette querelle!
J'errais dans l'agitation la plus cruelle,
Criant aux murs: Mon Dieu! mon Dieu! Que dira-t-elle?

Mais aussi, vrai, vous me blessâtes aux antennes
De l'âme, avec les mensonges de votre traîne,
Et votre tas de complications mondaines.

Je voyais que vos yeux me lançaient sur des pistes,
Je songeais: oui, divins, ces yeux! mais rien n'existe
Derrière! Son âme est affaire d'oculiste.

Moi, je suis laminé d'esthétiques loyales!
Je hais les trémolos, les phrases nationales;
Bref, le violet gros deuil est ma couleur locale.

Je ne suis point «ce gaillard-là!» ni Le Superbe!
Mais mon âme, qu'un cri un peu cru exacerbe,
Est au fond distinguée et franche comme une herbe.

J'ai des nerfs encor sensibles au son des cloches,
Et je vais en plein air sans peur et sans reproche,
Sans jamais me sourire en un miroir de poche.

C'est vrai, j'ai bien roulé! j'ai râlé dans des gîtes
Peu vous; mais, n'en ai-je pas plus de mérite
À en avoir sauvé la foi en vos yeux? dites . . .

– Allons, faisons la paix, Venez, que je vous berce,
Enfant. Eh bien?
                          – C'est que, votre pardon me verse
Un mélange (confus) d'impressions . . . diverses . . .

                                                    (Exit)

PIERROTS

(Scene short but typecast)

I needs must have your eyes! For since I lost their star
The doldrums of dead calm engulf me, sail and spar,
And in my bones the gargles of *Vae soli* jar.

After that last row, you should have seen me perplexed!
I wandered in the cruellest agitation vexed,
Crying at walls: My God, what'll she say next?

But also, really, you'd hurt the antennae of my soul
With all the lies that followed on your train, the whole
Heap of your worldly complications' rigmarole.

I saw your eyes were launching me on turns and twists.
I thought, yes, eyes divine but nothing else exists
Behind. Her soul is matter for the oculist's.

But me and the aesthetics of loyalty are laminate!
Vox humana, national slogans are my hate;
My local colour's purple in full mourning state.

I'm not at all 'that strapping fellow' nor The Superb!
And yet my soul – that somewhat coarse cries can perturb –
Is, underneath it all, distinguished, frank as a herb.

My nerves can still react to bells once in a while;
Without reproach or fear I walk abroad in style;
Nor ever give myself a pocket mirror smile.

It's true, I've knocked about! knackered myself a lot
In joints not you; but out of that, haven't I got
Some merit, keeping faith in your eyes? Say what? . . .

– Come on. Let's make it up. Come, child, and let me nurse
You. What now?
                    – It's just that your pardon seems to immerse
Me in a mess (confused) of impressions . . . most diverse. . .

                                                  (Exit)

LOCUTIONS DES PIERROTS

I

Les mares de vos yeux aux joncs de cils,
   Ô vaillante oisive femme,
   Quand donc me renverront-ils
La Lune-levante de ma belle âme?

Voilà tantôt une heure qu'en langueur
   Mon cœur si simple s'abreuve
   De vos vilaines rigueurs,
Avec le regard bon d'un terre-neuve.

Ah! madame, ce n'est vraiment pas bien,
   Quand on n'est pas la Joconde,
   D'en adopter le maintien
Pour induire en spleens tout bleus le pauv' monde!

II

Ah! le divin attachement
Que je nourris pour Cydalise,
Maintenant qu'elle échappe aux prises
De mon lunaire entendement!

Vrai, je me ronge en des détresses,
Parmi les fleurs de son terroir
À seule fin de bien savoir
Quelle est sa faculté-maîtresse!

– C'est d'être la mienne, dis-tu?
Hélas! tu sais bien que j'oppose
Un démenti formel aux poses
Qui sentent par trop l'impromptu.

ASIDES OF PIERROTS

I

Lashes for reeds, your stagnant ponds of eyes,
    Hard, idle woman, make it plain:
    When'll they give the Moon-rise
Of my fine soul back to me again?

An hour gone nearly while in listlessness
    My all too simple heart here sogs
    Itself in all your vile duress
With faithful looks like some newfoundland dog's.

Ah, madam, no, this really will not do,
    When no Gioconda by any means,
    Trying that poise of hers on you
To bring the poor ol' world abysmal spleens!

II

Ah, the attachment so divine
I nurture here for Cydalise,
Now she escapes the clutch of these
Lunar intentions that are mine!

Indeed I'm gnawed by agonies
Among the flowers of her land
In order just to understand
What her mistress-faculty is!

– It is to be my own, you say?
Too bad! You know that I riposte
A lie direct at poses tossed
Off too impromptu in their way.

III

Ah! sans Lune, quelles nuits blanches,
Quels cauchemars pleins de talent!
Vois-je pas là nos cygnes blancs?
Vient-on pas de tourner la clanche?

Et c'est vers toi que j'en suis là,
Que ma conscience voit double,
Et que mon cœur pêche en eau trouble,
Ève, Joconde et Dalila!

Ah! par l'infini circonflexe
De l'ogive où j'ahanne en croix,
Vends-moi donc une bonne fois
La raison d'être de Ton Sexe!

IV

Tu dis que mon cœur est à jeun
De quoi jouer tout seul son rôle,
Et que mon regard ne t'enjôle
Qu'avec des infinis d'emprunt!

Et tu rêvais avoir affaire
À quelque pauvre in-octavo . . .
Hélas! c'est vrai que mon cerveau
S'est vu, des soirs, trois hémisphères.

Mais va, l'œillet de tes vingt ans,
Je l'arrose aux plus belles âmes
Qui soient! – Surtout, je n'en réclame
Pas, sais-tu, de ta part autant!

III

Moonless, what white-out nights, bad patch!
What nightmares full of talent stream!
There, don't I see our white swans gleam?
Hasn't someone just raised the latch?

And it's by you I've come to this,
That my conscience is seeing double,
And heart is angling pools of trouble,
Eve, Gioconda, Delilah, miss!

Ah, by the infinite circumflex,
The arch in which cross-wise I groan,
Sell me, once for all, the known
Object in life of all Your Sex.

IV

You say my heart is on a fast
From what would, solo, play its role,
And how my look can but cajole
With filched infinities recast.

And you had dreamed of an affair
With some octavo wretch . . . Oh dear!
It's true my mind's passed evenings here
With three hemispheres somewhere.

Come now, the pink of your twenty years
With finest souls there are I'm sprinkling!
– What's more, you know, don't ask an inkling
As much from you as your arrears!

V

T'occupe pas, sois Ton Regard,
Et sois l'âme qui s'exécute;
Tu fournis la matière brute,
Je me charge de l'œuvre d'art.

Chef-d'œuvre d'art sans idée-mère
Par exemple! Oh! dis, n'est-ce pas,
Faut pas nous mettre sur les bras
Un cri des Limbes prolifères?

Allons, je sais que vous avez
L'égoïsme solide au poste,
Et même prêt aux holocaustes
De l'ordre le plus élevé.

VI

Je te vas dire: moi, quand j'aime,
C'est d'un cœur, au fond sans apprêts,
Mais dignement élaboré
Dans nos plus singuliers problèmes.

Ainsi, pour mes mœurs et mon art,
C'est la période védique
Qui seule à bon droit revendique
Ce que j'en «attelle à ton char».

C'est comme notre Bible hindoue
Qui, tiens, m'amène à caresser,
Avec ces yeux de cétacé,
Ainsi, bien sans but, ta joue.

V

Don't fash yourself. Be your own Look,
And be the soul that's executive;
The raw material you give;
I'll do the art bit for the book.

Masterpiece without mother-thought
For instance! Say that's how it stands:
We needn't, need we, place on our hands
A cry from teeming Limbo brought?

Come on. I know you have, and own
The egoism staunch at its post,
And even ready for the most
Exalted order of holocausts known.

VI

Me, when I love, I'm telling you,
It's with a heart at base without frills
But with worthily developed skills
In our most singular problems, too.

So, in my manners and my art,
It is the Vedic period which,
Alone, has rights to what I 'hitch
In harness to your apple-cart'.

It's like our Hindu Bible, now,
Which, here, gives me the inclination,
With those eyes like some cetacean,
Thus, pointlessly to kiss your brow.

VII

Cœur de profil, petite âme douillette,
Tu veux te tremper un matin en moi,
Comme on trempe, en levant le petit doigt,
Dans son café au lait une mouillette!

Et mon amour, si blanc, si vert, si grand,
Si tournoyant! ainsi ne te suggère
Que pas-de-deux, silhouettes légères
À enlever sur ce solide écran!

Adieu. – Qu'est-ce encor? Allons bon, tu pleures!
Aussi pourquoi ces grands airs de vouloir,
Quand mon Étoile t'ouvre son peignoir,
D'Hélas, chercher midi flambant à d'autres heures!

VIII

Ah! tout le long du cœur
Un vieil ennui m'effleure . . .
M'est avis qu'il est l'heure
De renaître moqueur.

Eh bien? je t'ai blessée?
Ai-je eu le sanglot faux,
Que tu prends cet air sot
De *La Cruche cassée*?

Tout divague d'amour;
Tout, du cèdre à l'hysope,
Sirote sa syncope;
J'ai fait un joli four.

VII

Heart in profile, dainty soul in plush,
You want to dunk yourself a morning in me
As one would dunk, raising the pinky free,
A sippet in one's coffee till it's mush.

And so my love – so great, so white, so green,
So dizzying! – only means to you, then, sets
Of pas-de-deux, the lightest silhouettes
To lightning-sketch across this solid screen!

Goodbye. – Now what? Oh, I say, tear-showers!
What's more: why giving out desire's grand airs,
When my Star gapes for you the wrap it wears,
And then Alas, requiring noon to keep your hours?

VIII

Ah, the length of the heart
An old boredom touches me . . .
Tells me it's time to be
Reborn in my mocker's part.

Well, hurt you, have I? Sure?
And had the crocodile flow
To match this stupid show,
Just like *The Broken Ewer*?

With love all turns gibberish
All, cedar to hyssop, we
Sip our own syncope;
I've made a kettle of fish.

IX

Ton geste,
Houri,
M'a l'air d'un *memento mori*
Qui signifie au fond: va, reste . . .

Mais je te dirai ce que c'est,
Et pourquoi je pars, foi d'honnête
            Poète
            Français.

Ton cœur a la conscience nette,
Le mien n'est qu'un individu
            Perdu
            De dettes.

X

Que loin l'âme type
Qui m'a dit adieu
Parce que mes yeux
Manquaient de principes!

Elle, en ce moment,
Elle, si pain tendre,
Oh! peut-être engendre
Quelque garnement.

Car on l'a unie
Avec un monsieur,
Ce qu'il y a de mieux,
Mais pauvre en génie.

IX

        Your gesture,
        Houri,
Seems to me some *memento mori*
Which means at bottom: stay, rest your . . .

But how it is I'll have you know it,
And why I'm leaving, my honest word
        Averred
        As French poet.

Your heart has a conscience finely set;
But mine is only the sort of bloke
        Who's broke
        With debt.

        X

Way out the soulicle
Who said her goodbyes
Just because my eyes
Lacked all principle!

She, at this second –
Tender morsel, that –
With somebody's brat,
Oh, maybe fecund.

For she has been joined
To an eligible
With all that is coined;
Genius negligible.

XI

Et je me console avec la
       Bonne fortune
       De l'alme Lune.
Ô Lune, *Ave Paris stella!*

Tu sais si la femme est cramponne;
       Eh bien, déteins,
       Glace sans tain,
Sur mon œil! qu'il soit tout atone,

Qu'il déclare: ô folles d'essais,
       Je vous invite
       À prendre vite,
Car c'est à prendre et à laisser.

XII

Encore un livre; ô nostalgies
Loin de ces très-goujates gens,
Loin des saluts et des argents,
Loin de nos phraséologies!

Encore un de mes pierrots mort;
Mort d'un chronique orphelinisme;
C'était un cœur plein de dandysme
Lunaire, en un drôle de corps.

Les dieux s'en vont; plus que des hures;
Ah! ça devient tous les jours pis;
J'ai fait mon temps, je déguerpis
Vers l'Inclusive Sinécure!

XI

And I console myself, poor fellah,
    With the lucky boon
    Of the bountiful Moon.
Oh Moon, *Ave Paris stella!*

You know if she's a hanger on;
    Well, then, you drain,
    Unsilvered pane,
Into my eyes till, expression gone,

They declare: fool woman tryer,
    I invite you, quick,
    To make your pick.
It's take it or leave it, good-buyer.

XII

Another book; oh, nostalgiaries
Far from the loutish and the brash,
Far from the accolades and cash,
Far from our phraseologies!

Another of my pierrots dead,
Dead of a chronic orphancy;
His heart was full of lunary
Dandiness in an odd fish bred.

The gods have gone; just mugs secure;
Ah, every day gets worse with it;
I've done my time; I'll do a flit
To the All-Inclusive Sinecure!

XIII

Eh bien oui, je l'ai chagrinée,
Tout le long, le long de l'année;
Mais quoi! s'en est-elle étonnée?

Absolus, drapés de layettes,
Aux lunes de miel de l'Hymette,
Nous avions par trop l'air vignette!

Ma vitre pleure, adieu! l'on bâille
Vers les ciels couleur de limaille
Où la Lune a ses funérailles.

Je ne veux accuser nul être,
Bien qu'au fond tout m'ait pris en traître.
Ah! paître, sans but là-bas! paître . . .

XIV

Les mains dans les poches,
Le long de la route,
J'écoute
Mille cloches
Chantant: «les temps sont proches,
Sans que tu t'en doutes!»

Ah! Dieu m'est égal!
Et je suis chez moi!
Mon toit
Très-natal
C'est Tout. Je marche droit,
Je fais pas de mal.

Je connais l'Histoire,
Et puis la Nature,
Ces foires

XIII

Oh well, yes, I've upset her, true,
The whole way, the whole year through;
So what? Does that amaze her, too?

All fixed, festooned in the layette,
On Hymettan honeymoons all set,
We seemed too meadowsweet a vignette!

My window weeps, goodbye! Yawns fly
To iron-filing-coloured sky
Where the Moon has obsequies on high.

There's none I want to give the blame,
Though all betrayed me just the same.
Ah, graze, to graze, there, without aim . . .

XIV

Hands in pockets, along
The street's full length I hear,
Singing clear,
A thousand strong,
Bells: 'The end is nigh, not long,
Never doubt it here!'

God – I don't give a jot!
And I'm home, my space!
My place,
Of birth, hearth, spot,
It's All. I act with good grace;
I'm not a bad lot.

History I can spout,
And Nature Study, too –
Those crossed-out

   Aux ratures;
Aussi je vous assure
   Que l'on peut me croire!

  XV

J'entends battre mon Sacré-Cœur
Dans le crépuscule de l'heure,
Comme il est méconnu, sans sœur,
Et sans destin, et sans demeure!

J'entends battre ma jeune chair
Équivoquant par mes artères,
Entre les Édens de mes vers
Et la province de mes pères.

Et j'entends la flûte de Pan
Qui chante: «bats, bats la campagne!
Meurs, quand tout vit à tes dépens;
Mais entre nous, va, qui perd gagne!»

  XVI

Je ne suis qu'un viveur lunaire
Qui fait des ronds dans les bassins,
Et cela, sans autre dessein
Que devenir un légendaire.

Retroussant d'un air de défi
Mes manches de mandarin pâle,
J'arrondis ma bouche et – j'exhale
Des conseils doux de Crucifix.

Ah! oui, devenir légendaire,
Au seuil des siècles charlatans!
Mais où sont les Lunes d'antan?
Et que Dieu n'est il à refaire?

Markets scratched through;
Also, I swear there's no doubt
That what I say is true!

XV

My Sacred Heart I hear it pound
Now, in the hour of dusk, the grouse
That it's misunderstood all round,
No sister, destiny or house.

I hear my youthful pulses pound
Dithering in veins from toe to crown,
Between my verse's Eden ground
And my ancestors' country town.

And also hear the pipes of Pan
Sing: 'Ramble, head, and ramble land!
Die when all lives off you, man;
On the q.t.: loser wins the hand!'

XVI

I'm only a man about the moon
Who makes circles in pool and pond
And does so with no design beyond
Being a legendary soon.

Tucking up, air defiant as poss.,
My sleeves of mandarin, pale,
I round my lips and – then exhale
The sweet counsels of the Cross.

Ah, be a legendary one,
Just as the phoney times appear!
But where are the Moons of yesteryear?
And why's God not to be redone?

DIALOGUE AVANT LE LEVER DE LA LUNE

– Je veux bien vivre; mais vraiment,
L'Idéal est trop élastique!

– C'est l'Idéal, son nom l'implique,
Hors son non-sens, le verbe ment.

– Mais, tout est conteste; les livres
S'accouchent, s'entretuent sans lois!

– Certes! l'Absolu perd ses droits,
Là où le Vrai consiste à vivre.

– Et, si j'amène pavillon
Et repasse au Néant ma charge?

– L'Infini, qui souffle du large,
Dit: «pas de bêtises, voyons!»

– Ces chantiers du Possible ululent
À l'Inconcevable, pourtant!

– Un degré, comme il en est tant
Entre l'aube et le crépuscule.

– Être actuel, est-ce, du moins,
Être adéquat à Quelque Chose?

– Conséquemment, comme la rose
Est nécessaire à ses besoins.

– Façon de dire peu commune
Que Tout est cercles vicieux?

– Vicieux, mais Tout!
                    – J'aime mieux
Donc m'en aller selon la Lune.

DIALOGUE BEFORE MOONRISE

– I really want to live, and yet indeed
The Ideal's too elastic, all the same!

– It's the Ideal, that's implied in its name;
Outside its nonsense the word must mislead.

– But all is conflict; and the books are giving
Birth to themselves, lawlessly kill and fight!

– Of course; the Absolute must lose its right
Precisely where the truth consists of living.

– And if I strike my colours, reinstate
My charge upon the Void's non-entity?

– The Infinite that blows from open sea
Says: 'No, don't be silly, come now, let's wait.'

– The stockyards of the Possible ululate,
However, for what is Inconceivable.

– Partly because it is so plentiful.
Between the dawn and dusk whatever date.

– But living for the present's equivalent,
Isn't it, of being adequate as Some Thing?

– That follows, as the rose in flowering
Is necessary to its needful bent.

– A variation on a common tune:
That vicious circles only make the Whole!

– Vicious, but the Whole!
                              – The role
That I prefer is going by the Moon.

LUNES EN DÉTRESSE

Vous voyez, la Lune chevauche
Les nuages noirs à tous crins,
Cependant que le vent embouche
Ses trente-six mille buccins!

Adieu, petits cœurs benjamins
Choyés comme Jésus en crèche,
Qui vous vantiez d'être orphelins
Pour avoir toute la brioche!

Partez dans le vent qui se fâche,
Sous la Lune sans lendemains,
Cherchez la pâtée et la niche
Et les douceurs d'un traversin.

Et vous, nuages à tous crins,
Rentrez ces profils de reproche,
C'est les trente-six mille buccins
Du vent qui m'ont rendu tout lâche.

D'autant que je ne suis pas riche,
Et que Ses yeux dans leurs écrins
Ont déjà fait de fortes brèches
Dans mon patrimoine enfantin.

Partez, partez, jusqu'au matin!
Ou, si ma misère vous touche,
Et bien, cachez aux traversins
Vos têtes, naïves autruches,

Éternelles, chères embûches
Où la Chimère encor trébuche!

MOONS IN DISTRESS

The Moon is riding, just you watch,
The black clouds, all with flowing mane,
While still the wind blasts out full pitch
Its umpteen thousand bugle strain.

'Bye, junior little hearts again,
Fallen like Jesus in the crèche;
You boast of being waifs, it's plain,
To corner all the bread in reach!

Leave, in the wind's furious screech,
Under the morrowless Moon again;
Search out the scraps, the kennel, hutch,
A bolster's softness entertain.

And you, black clouds with flying mane,
Suppress your looks of such reproach.
The umpteen thousand bugle strain
Of wind made me this coward wretch.

And inasmuch as I'm not rich,
And since the caskets that contain
Her Eyes have made a hefty breach
In infant legacies that remain.

Leave, leave, as soon as day is plain!
Or, if my misery moves you much,
Well, in the bolsters hide your brain,
Simple ostriches with the stitch,

Eternal, dear ambushes in which
Illusion is still drawn to pitch.

PETITS MYSTÈRES

Chut! Oh! ce soir, comme elle est près!
Vrai, je ne sais ce qu'elle pense,
Me ferait-elle des avances?
Est-ce là le rayon qui fiance
Nos cœurs humains à son cœur frais?

Par quels ennuis kilométriques
Mener ma silhouette encor,
Avant de prendre mon essor
Pour arrimer, veuf de tout corps,
À ses dortoirs madréporiques.

Mets de la Lune dans ton vin,
M'a dit sa moue cadenassée;
Je ne bois que de l'eau glacée,
Et de sa seule panacée
Mes tissus qui stagnent ont faim.

Lune, consomme mon baptême,
Lave mes yeux de ton linceul;
Qu'aux hommes, je sois ton filleul;
Et pour nos compagnes, le seul
Qui les délivre d'elles-mêmes.

Lune, mise au ban du Progrès
Des populaces des Étoiles,
Volatilise-moi les moelles,
Que je t'arrive à pleines voiles,
Dolmen, Cyprès, Amen, au frais!

LITTLE MYSTERIES

Hush! She's so near tonight, in the flesh!
True, she's thinking god knows what;
Would she make me passes or not?
And is it there, the ray to knot
Our human hearts to hers so fresh?

Through what kilometric boredoms
To lead my silhouette to and fro,
Before taking my flight to stow –
Bereft of body top to toe,
In cabins of the madreporedoms.

Put some Moon into your wine,
Her tight-lipped pouting said to me;
My drink's iced water. Stagnantly,
For her exclusive panacea,
I hunger in these tissues of mine.

Consummate my baptism, Moon;
Cleanse my eyes in your shroud; let me
Become to men your godson; be
For our fair friends the one to free
Them from themselves and make it soon.

Moon, outcast from the Progression
In populations of the Stars,
Volatilise my medullars,
Bring me to you, sail on all spars,
Dolmen, Cypress, Amen; freshen!

NUITAMMENT

Ô Lune, coule dans mes veines
Et que je me soutienne à peine,

Et croie t'aplatir sur mon cœur!
Mais, elle est pâle à faire peur!

Et montre par son teint, sa mise,
Combien elle en a vu de grises!

Et ramène, se sentant mal,
Son cachemire sidéral,

Errante Delos, nécropole,
Je veux que tu fasses école;

Je te promets en ex-voto
Les Putiphars de mes manteaux!

Et tiens, adieu; je rentre en ville
Mettre en train deux ou trois idylles,

En m'annonçant par un Péan
D'épithalame à ton Néant.

NIGHTLY

O Moon, into my veins now flow
And I may just about bear up so,

And think I press you to my heart!
But she's so dreadfully pale, apart!

She shows me by her dress, look, pace,
She's had some rough to-dos to face!

And now pulls on, not well at all,
Her sidereal cashmere shawl;

Wandering Delos, necropolis,
I wish you'd start a trend of this.

As votive gifts I pledge to you
Potiphars of my coats as due.

And now goodbye; to town again
To put a romance or two in train,

By marriage-paean announcing me
At the feast of your Non-Entity.

ÉTATS

Ah! ce soir, j'ai le cœur mal, le cœur à la Lune!
Ô Nappes du silence, étalez vos lagunes;
Ô toits, terrasses, bassins, colliers denoués
De perles, tombes, lys, chats en peine, louez
La Lune, notre Maîtresse à tous, dans sa gloire:
Elle est l'Hostie! et le silence est son ciboire!
Ah! qu'il fait bon, oh! bel et bon, dans le halo
De deuil de ce diamant de la plus belle eau!
Ô Lune, vous allez me trouver romanesque,
Mais voyons, oh! seulement de temps en temps est-c'que
Ce serait fol à moi de me dire, entre nous,
Ton Christophe Colombe, ô Colombe, à genoux?
Allons, n'en parlons plus; et déroulons l'office
Des minuits, confits dans l'alcool de tes délices.
Ralentendo vers nous, ô dolente Cité,
Cellule en fibroïne aux organes ratés!
Rappelle-toi les centaures, les villes mortes,
Palmyre, et les sphinx camards des Thèbes aux cent portes;
Et quelle Gomorrhe a sous ton lac de Léthé
Ses catacombes vers la stérile Astarté!
Et combien l'homme, avec ses relatifs «Je t'aime»,
Est trop anthropomorphe au-delà de lui-même,
Et ne sait que vivotter comm' ça des bonjours
Aux bonsoirs tout en s'arrangeant avec l'Amour.
– Ah! Je vous disais donc, et cent fois plutôt qu'une,
Que j'avais le cœur mal, le cœur bien à la Lune.

STATES

Ah, tonight, I'm sick at heart, heart like the Moon's!
Oh, Sheets of silence, spread out your lagoons;
Oh, roofs, pearl necklaces unstrung, heights, bays,
And tombs and lilies, cats in pain, oh praise
The Moon, our Mistress of all, in majesty:
She is the Host, silence her cibory!
Halo'd in mourning of this diamond of the first water,
How good it is, lovely and good this quarter!
Oh Moon, ah, you will find me some romantic,
But come now, would it be in me a rum antic,
Just between us now and then, a crazy feeling,
To say I'm your Columbus, Columbe, kneeling?
Well, let's say no more; let's unroll the midnights
Prepared in alcohols of your delights.
Rallentando to us, city of wail and whine,
Cell in fibroids of organs in decline!
Recall the centaurs, the ghost-town city-states,
Palmyra, Death's head sphinx of Thebes' Hundred Gates;
And what Gomorrah has, on your Lethe bed,
Its catacombs for barren Astarte spread!
How man with all his relative 'I-love-yous'
Is much too anthropomorphic in his views,
And only knows how to scrape by from good day
To good evening by arrangement with Love some way.
– Ah, told you, a hundred times if once, this tune:
I've a sick heart, a heart just like the Moon.

LA LUNE EST STÉRILE

Lune, Pape abortif à l'amiable, Pape
Des Mormons pour l'art, dans la jalouse Paphos
Où l'État tient gratis les fils de la soupape
D'échappement des apoplectiques Cosmos!

C'est toi, léger manuel d'instincts, toi qui circules,
Glaçant, après les grandes averses, les œufs
Obtus de ces myriades d'animalcules
Dont les simouns mettraient nos muqueuses en feu!

Tu ne sais que la fleur des sanglantes chimies;
Et perces nos rideaux, nous offrant le lotus
Qui constipe les plus larges polygamies,
Tout net, de l'excrément logique des fœtus.

Carguez-lui vos rideaux, citoyens de mœurs lâches;
C'est l'Extase qui paie comptant, donne son Ut
Des deux sexes et veut pas même que l'on sache
S'il se peut qu'elle ait, hors de l'art pour l'art, un but.

On allèche de vie humaine, à pleines voiles,
Les Tantales virtuels, peu intéressants
D'ailleurs, sauf leurs cordiaux, qui rêvent dans nos moelles;
Et c'est un produit net qu'encaissent nos bons sens.

Et puis, l'atteindrons-nous, l'Oasis aux citernes,
Où nos cœurs toucheraient les payes qu'On leur doit?
Non, c'est la rosse aveugle aux cercles sempiternes
Qui tourne pour autrui les bons chevaux de bois.

Ne vous distrayez pas, avec vos grosses douanes;
Clefs de fa, clefs de sol, huit stades de claviers,
Laissez faire, laissez passer la caravane
Qui porte à l'Idéal ses plus riches dossiers!

THE MOON IS STERILE

Moon, Pope abortive for all of friendly intent,
Pope of Mormons for art, in the jealous Paphos where
The State keeps sons of the subpope safety valve, vent
Of apoplectic Cosmoses, free of board and care!

It's you, light manual of instincts, circling round,
Freezing the obtuse eggs, after the great rains,
Of all these myriad animalcules that abound,
Simooms of which inflame our mucous membranes!

And all you know's the flower of bloody alchemies;
You pierce our curtains, offering a lotus-worth
That constipates the largest of polygamies
At one fell swoop of the logical excrement of birth.

You easy-going citizens, brail up your curtain.
It's Ecstasy; she pays cash-down, utters her *Do*,
For both the sexes; doesn't want it known for certain
If be she have, past art for art's sake, an aim in view.

One lures from human life, under full sail and steam,
Real Tantaluses – little interest they offer
Except as pick-me-ups – that in our marrows dream;
And it's a net yield that our good senses coffer.

So, shall we reach it, the Oasis with those cisterns
Wherein our hearts would touch the profit owed them still
By One? No, it's the blind screw's sempiternal twistings
Turning for others the fine carved horses with its mill.

So don't distract yourselves with customs' clumsy checks;
Bass clef and treble clef, eight steps on the keyboard,
Let it be, let the caravan pass on, its trek's
Bearing to the Ideal the richest dossier-hoard!

L'Art est tout, du droit divin de l'Inconscience;
Après lui, le déluge! et son moindre regard
Est le cercle infini dont la circonférence
Est partout, et le centre immoral nulle part.

Pour moi, déboulonné du pôle de stylite
Qui me sied, dès qu'un corps a trop de son secret,
J'affiche: celles qui voient tout, je les invite
À venir, à mon bras, des soirs, prendre le frais.

Or voici: nos deux Cris, abaissant leurs visières,
Passent mutuellement, après quiproquos,
Aux chers peignes du cru leurs moelles épinières
D'où lèvent débusqués tous les archets locaux.

Et les ciels familiers liserés de folie
Neigeant en charpie éblouissante, faut voir
Comme le moindre appel: c'est pour nous seuls! rallie
Les louables efforts menés à l'abattoir!

Et la santé en deuil ronronne ses vertiges,
Et chante, pour la forme: «Hélas! ce n'est pas bien,
Par ces pays, pays si tournoyants, vous dis-je,
Où la faim d'Infini justifie les moyens.»

Lors, qu'ils sont beaux les flancs tirant leur révérence
Au sanglant capitaliste berné des nuits,
En s'affalant cuver ces jeux sans conséquence!
Oh! n'avoir à songer qu'à ses propres ennuis!

– Bons aïeux qui geigniez semaine par semaine,
Vers mon Cœur, baobab des védiques terroirs,
Je m'agite aussi! mais l'Inconscient me mène;
Or, il sait ce qu'il fait, je n'ai rien à y voir.

Art's everything by divine right of Inconscience;
And after that the deluge! And its slightest stare
Is the infinite circle whose circumference
Is everywhere with its immoral centre nowhere.

For me, knocked off my most becoming Stylite pole,
And since a body has too much of its secrecy,
I here announce: All girls who see into the whole
Lean on my arm and take the evening air with me.

Well, here we go: our visors lowered, our two Cries
Mutually put – after various quidproquos –
Their spinal marrow through dear vintage combs whence rise,
Driven out of ambush all the local bows.

And then the usual skies with folly hemmed and sewn,
Snowing with dazzling lint, and then must it be thought –
As being the least appeal: It's up to us alone!
Rally the laudable efforts brought to face the slaughter!

And health in mourning purrs out its vertigo:
'Alas, it is not well,' it sings for the form's sake,
'In these countries, such turbulent countries, no,
Where thirst for Infinity justifies the means to take.'

So, beautiful the thighs are, offering their respects
To the gory capitalist blanket-tossed by night,
In slumping to sleep off games that leave no after-effects!
Oh, if you could mind just your own boredoms outright!

– Good forebears who groaned, week come, week gone,
Over my Heart, the Vedic soil's own baobab tree,
I'm fretting, too! But it's Inconscience leads me on;
Well, it knows what it's doing;'s nothing to do with me.

STÉRILITÉS

Cautérise et coagule
     En virgules
Ses lagunes des cerises
Des félines Ophélies
Orphelines en folie.

Tarentule de feintises
     La remise
Sans rancune des ovules
Aux félines Ophélies
Orphelines en folie.

Sourd aux brises des scrupules,
     Vers la bulle
De la lune, adieu, nolise
Ces félines Ophélies
Orphelines en folie! . . .

STERILITIES

Congeal the springs and cauterise
    To comma size
Each bright lagoon of cherryings
In Ophelias of feline grace
Orphans in folly's beeline race.

Tarantulise with sham strings
    The deliverings
No spite impugning ovule-wise
In Ophelias of feline grace
Orphans in folly's beeline race.

Deaf to wind-swings of doubt that rise
    Say your goodbyes,
To bubble moon now ship the things
These Ophelias of feline grace
Orphans in folly's beeline race! . . .

LES LINGES, LE CYGNE

     Ce sont les linges, les linges,
Hôpitaux consacrés aux cruors et aux fanges;
     Ce sont les langes, les langes,
Où l'on voudrait, ah! redorloter ses méninges!

Vos linges pollués, Noëls de Bethléem!
De la lessive des linceuls des requiems
De nos touchantes personnalités, aux langes
Des berceaux, vite à bas, sans doubles de rechange,
Qui nous suivent, transfigurés (fatals vauriens
Que nous sommes) ainsi que des Langes gardiens.
C'est la guimpe qui dit, même aux trois quarts meurtrie:
«Ah! pas de ces familiarités, je vous prie . . .»
C'est la peine avalée aux édredons d'eider;
C'est le mouchoir laissé, parlant d'âme et de chair
Et de scènes! (Je vous pris la main sous la table,
J'eus même des accents vraiment inimitables),
Mais ces malentendus! l'adieu noir! – Je m'en vais!
– Il fait nuit! – Que m'importe! à moi, chemins mauvais!
Puis, comme Phèdre en ses illicites malaises:
«Ah! que ces draps d'un lit d'occasion me pèsent!»
Linges adolescents, nuptiaux, maternels;
Nappe qui drape la Sainte-Table ou l'autel,
Purificatoire au calice, manuterges,
Refuges des baisers convolant vers les cierges.
Ô langes invalides, linges aveuglants!
Oreillers du bon cœur toujours convalescent
Qui dit, même à la sœur, dont le toucher l'écœure:
«Rien qu'une cuillerée, ah! toutes les deux heures . . .»
Voie Lactée à charpie en surplis; lourds jupons
À plis d'ordre dorique à lesquels nous rampons
Rien que pour y râler, doux comme la tortue
Qui grignotte au soleil une vieille laitue.
Linges des grandes maladies; champ-clos des draps
Fleurant: soulagez-vous, va, tant que ça ira!
Et les cols rabattus des jeunes filles fières,
Les bas blancs bien tirés, les chants des lavandières,

LINEN, SWAN

This is the linen, this is the linen,
Hospitals consecrated to filth and to gore;
    These are the swaddlings, swaddlings for –
Ah, one would want one's meninges recoddled in 'em!

Your filthy linen, Christmas Bethlehems!
From laundering shrouds of requiems
For our touching personalities, to gear
From cradles quickly down, no clothes-change here,
Which follow us, transfigured (worthless louts
Such as we are) to Guardian Anus-Clouts.
It's the wimple saying, though three-parts murdered off:
'No liberties, I beg you; do not scoff.'
It's pain in eiderdowns swallowed up whole;
It's the dropped glove speaking body and soul,
And rows! (I took your hand beneath the table;
Even had truly inimitable accents, most able)
But still cross-purposes! Black farewells! – I quit!
– It's night! – So what! For me the rough roads bit.
And next, like Phèdre in illicit anxiety:
'Ah, how the sheets of a used bed weigh on me.'
Adolescent linen, nuptial, maternal sheets;
Cloth of communion table, altar pleats,
The chalice napkins, manuterges, lair
Of kisses marrying in the candle flare.
Invalid clouts, sheets blinding, incandescent!
Pillows of the kind heart, always convalescent,
Who, even to the sister of sickening touch,
Says, 'Just a spoonful every two hours, not much.'
Lint Milky Way like surplices; Doric pleats
Of heavy skirts we crawl to in our retreats
Just for our death-rattles, quiet as tortoise nibbles,
In sunshine a limp lettuce into fribbles.
Linen of grave illness; tiltyard tang of bed,
Relieve yourselves, all that you can; go right ahead!
And turned-down collars proud young girls parade,
White stockings sleek, songs of the laundry maid,

Le peignoir sur la chair de poule après le bain,
Les cornettes des sœurs, les voiles, les béguins,
La province et ses armoires, les lingeries
Du lycée et du cloître; et les bonnes prairies
Blanches des traversins rafraîchissant leurs creux
De parfums de famille aux tempes sans aveux.
Et la Mort! pavoisez les balcons de draps pâles,
Les cloches! car voici que des rideaux s'exhale
La procession du beau Cygne ambassadeur
Qui mène Lohengrin au pays des candeurs!

       Ce sont les linges, les linges,
Hôpitaux consacrés aux cruors et aux fanges:
       Ce sont les langes, les langes,
Où l'on voudrait, ah! redorloter ses méninges.

NOBLES ET TOUCHANTES DIVAGATIONS SOUS LA LUNE

Un chien perdu grelotte en abois à la Lune . . .
Oh! pourquoi ce sanglot quand nul ne l'a battu?
Et, nuits! que partout la même Âme! En est-il une
Qui n'aboie à l'Exil ainsi qu'un chien perdu?

Non, non; pas un caillou qui ne rêve un ménage,
Pas un soir qui ne pleure: encore un aujourd'hui!
Pas un Moi qui n'écume aux barreaux de sa cage
Et n'épluche ses jours en filaments d'ennui.

Et les bons végétaux! des fossiles qui gisent
En pliocènes tufs de squelettes parias,
Aux printemps aspergés par les steppes kirghyses,
Aux roses des contreforts de l'Hymalaya!

The dressing gown a bird wears after her soak,
Sister's mobcaps, veil, bonnet, and poke,
The province with its cupboards, underwear
Of school and cloisters, the good prairies' glare,
White with bolsters refreshing hollows stowed
With family smells for brows without abode.
And Death! Deck with pale drapes the balcony railing;
Bells now! For here from curtains it's exhaling:
The noble Swan's procession – ambassador
Who pilots Lohengrin to the innocents' white shore!

      This is the linen, this is the linen,
Hospitals consecrated to filth and to gore;
      These are the swaddlings, swaddlings for –
Ah, one would want one's meninges recoddled in 'em.

NOBLE AND TOUCHING DIGRESSIONS
UNDER THE MOON

A lost dog shivers baying at the Moon . . .
Oh, why such whining when it has no punisher?
And, nights, how everywhere's one Spirit and one tune?
Who doesn't bay at Exile just like this lost cur?

No, not a stone that isn't dreaming of a pair,
Not a night that doesn't weep: another day.
Not an I that doesn't foam at the bars that snare
And into tedious peelings pare its days away.

And the fine vegetatives! From fossils in the depths
Of Pliocene strata of pariah skeletons, bones,
To springs that are asperged from the Kirghese steppes,
To roses of the Himalayan foothill zones.

Et le vent qui beugle, apocalyptique Bête
S'abattant sur des toits aux habitants pourris,
Qui secoue en vain leurs huis-clos, et puis s'arrête,
Pleurant sur son cœur à Sept-Glaives d'incompris.

Tout vient d'un seul impératif catégorique,
Mais qu'il a le bras long, et la matrice loin!
L'Amour, l'amour qui rêve, ascétise et fornique;
Que n'aimons-nous pour nous dans notre petit coin?

Infini, d'où sors-tu? Pourquoi nos sens superbes
Sont-ils fous d'au-delà des claviers octroyés,
Croient-ils à des miroirs plus heureux que le Verbe,
Et se tuent? Infini, montre un peu tes papiers!

Motifs décoratifs, et non but de l'Histoire,
Non le bonheur pour tous, mais de coquets moyens
S'objectivant en nous substratums sans pourboires,
Trinité de Molochs, le Vrai, le Beau, le Bien.

Nuages à profils de kaïns! vents d'automne
Qui, dans l'antiquité des Pans soi-disant gais,
Vous lamentiez aux toits des temples heptagones,
Voyez, nous rebrodons les mêmes Anankès.

Jadis les gants violets des Révérendissimes
De la Théologie en conciles cités,
Et l'évêque d'Hippone attelant ses victimes
Au char du Jaggernaut Œcuménicité;

Aujourd'hui, microscope de télescope! Encore,
Nous voilà relançant l'Ogive au toujours Lui,
Qu'il y tourne casaque, à neuf qu'il s'y redore
Pour venir nous bercer un printemps notre ennui.

Une place plus fraîche à l'oreille des fièvres,
Un mirage inédit au détour du chemin,
Des rampements plus fous vers le bonheur des lèvres,
Et des opiums plus longs à rêver. Mais demain?

And the wind, Beast of Apocalypse, forever bawling,
Menaces the roofs of mouldered tenants unbudged,
And shakes their locked-up doors in vain, then stalling,
Weeps over its heart as if the Seven Blades misjudged.

From one categorical imperative all is bound,
But what a long arm it has, what a distant womb!
Love, love that dreams, asceticises, sleeps around;
Are we just to love each other in our bit of room?

Where're you from, Infinity? Why so madly spurred,
Our swell senses, to reach past range of organ-keys?
Why'd they believe in mirrors happier than the Word
And kill themselves? Infinity, your papers, please!

Decorative motifs, and not the aim of History,
Not happiness for all, but coquetry and cuty
To objectify in us substrata without gratuity,
The trinity of Molochs: Truth, and Good and Beauty.

Clouds with kainite profiles! autumn winds that storm,
You, who in Pan the so-called merry's olden day,
Wailed on the roofs of temples heptagonal in form,
Look, it's the same Anangkes we embroider away.

Once, it was purple gloves of Reverendissimusses
Of Theology, in councils cited, taught,
The Bishop of Hippo strapping his victims into trusses
To drag along the Oecumenical Juggernaut.

Now, microscope to telescope, here we are
Still throwing up the Ogive to the always He,
So he'll turn tail, so that again he'll gild his car
To come one spring and lull for us our ennui.

Some place that's cooler on the fevered ear,
Unheard-of mirage in a turning of the way,
Crazier scrabblings towards the joy of lips here
And opiums of longer lasting dreams. But next day?

Recommencer encore? Ah! lâchons les écluses,
À la fin! Oublions tout! nous faut convoyer
Vers ces ciels où, s'aimer et paître étant les Muses,
Cuver sera le dieu pénate des foyers!

Ô! l'Éden immédiat des braves empirismes!
Peigner ses fiers cheveux avec l'arête des
Poissons qu'on lui offrit crus dans un paroxysme
De dévouement! s'aimer sans serments, ni rabais.

Oui, vivre pur d'habitudes et de programmes,
Paccageant mes milieux, à travers et à tort,
Choyant comme un beau chat ma chère petite âme,
N'arriver qu'ivre-mort de Moi-même à la mort!

Oui, par delà nos arts, par delà nos époques
Et nos hérédités, tes îles de candeur,
Inconscience! et elle, au seuil, là, qui se moque
De mes regards en arrière, et fait: n'aie pas peur.

Que non, je n'ai plus peur; je rechois en enfance;
Mon bateau de fleurs est prêt, j'y veux rêver à
L'ombre de tes maternelles protubérances,
En t'offrant le miroir de mes *et cætera* . . .

Another go? Ah, let us open up the sluices,
The end! Let's forget it. We must convoy all parties
Towards those skies where, Love and Grub being the Muses,
Sleep-it-off will be our household Penates.

Oh, instant Eden of brave and straight empiricisms!
To comb her proud hair with a fishbone rake,
Fish that's been offered raw in devotion's paroxysms!
To love each other and no vows, no bargains, make.

Yes, live quite free of habits, programmes, goal,
And browse my patch at random, no shibboleth.
Pet, like a beautiful cat, my darling little soul,
And only dead drunk with the Self arrive at death.

Yes, from beyond our arts, and from beyond our epochs
And our heredities, your isles of guilelessness,
Inconscience! and, at the entrance there, she mocks
My looking-back again: don't be afraid, she says.

No, not afraid; the relapse into childhood it is;
My boat of flowers is ready, I'll dream in the plethora
Of shade beneath your maternal protuberances
Offering you the mirror of my *etcetera* . . .

JEUX

Ah! la Lune, la Lune m'obsède . . .
Croyez-vous qu'il y ait un remède?

Morte? Se peut-il pas qu'elle dorme
Grise de cosmiques chloroformes?

Rosace en tombale efflorescence
De la Basilique du Silence,

Tu persistes dans ton attitude,
Quand je suffoque de solitude!

Oui, oui, tu as la gorge bien faite;
Mais, si jamais je ne m'y allaite? . . .

Encore un soir, et mes berquinades
S'en iront rire à la débandade,

Traitant mon platonisme si digne
D'extase de pêcheur à la ligne!

Salve Regina des Lys! reine,
Je te veux percer de mes phalènes!

Je veux baiser ta patène triste,
Plat veuf du chef de Saint Jean Baptiste!

Je veux trouver un *lied!* qui te touche
À te faire émigrer vers ma bouche!

– Mais, même plus de rimes à Lune . . .
Ah! quelle regrettable lacune!

GAMES

The Moon! The Moon is my obsession . . .
Is there a cure for this confession?

Dead? Or could it be pissed sedation
With cosmic chloroform inhalation?

Rosace in tombly efflorescence
Of Silence's Basilica, essence,

You keep this pose with such persistence
While I am choked in lonely distance.

Yes, yes, you have a lovely breast bare
But if I'm never suckled, pressed there?

Another evening, my Berquinading
Will go off laughing, routed, evading,

Treat my worthy platonic wishing
With the ecstatics of line-fishing!

Salve Regina of Lilies, Empress,
I want my moths to pierce you, Temptress!

I want to kiss your tristful paten,
Widowed-of-St John's-head platter.

I want a *lied*, *bed*rousing, bringing
You migrant to my lips still singing.

– What, still at all this rhyming Moon? Ah,
What a most regrettable lacuna!

LITANIES DES DERNIERS QUARTIERS DE LA LUNE

Eucharistie
De l'Arcadie,

Qui fais de l'œil
Aux cœurs en deuil,

Ciel des idylles
Qu'on veut stériles,

Fonts baptismaux
Des blancs pierrots,

Dernier ciboire
De notre Histoire,

Vortex-nombril
Du Tout-Nihil,

Miroir et Bible
Des Impassibles,

Hôtel garni
De l'infini,

Sphinx et Joconde
Des défunts mondes,

Ô Chanaan
Du bon Néant,

Néant, la Mecque
Des bibliothèques,

Léthé, Lotos,
Exaudi nos!

LITANIES OF THE MOON'S LAST QUARTERS

Arcadist
Eucharist,

Which winks at hearts
That mourning parts,

Sky of idylls
Wished barren vigils,

Baptismal font
White clowns want,

Last ciborium,
History's moratorium,

Vortex-Fix
Of the Whole-Nix,

Impassives' tribal
Mirror and Bible,

Infinity's well–
Furnished hotel,

Gioconda, Sphinx
Of worlds extinct,

O Promised Land,
Oblivion at hand,

Oblivion, Mecca,
Where libraries trek,

Lethe and Lotus,
Exaudi, note us!

AVIS, JE VOUS PRIE

Hélas! des Lunes, des Lunes,
Sur un petit air en bonne fortune . . .
Hélas! de choses en choses
Sur la criarde corde des virtuoses! . . .

Hélas! agacer d'un lys
La voilette d'Isis! . . .
Hélas! m'esquinter, sans trêve, encore,
Mon encéphale anomaliflore
En floraisons de chair par guirlandes d'ennuis! . . .
Ô Mort, et puis?

Mais! j'ai peur de la vie
Comme d'un mariage!
Oh! vrai, je n'ai pas l'âge
Pour ce beau mariage! . . .

Oh! j'ai été frappé de CETTE VIE À MOI,
L'autre dimanche, m'en allant par une plaine!
Oh! laissez-moi seulement reprendre haleine,
Et vous aurez un livre enfin de bonne foi.

En attendant, ayez pitié de ma misère!
Que je vous sois à tous un être bienvenu!
Et que je sois absous pour mon âme sincère,
Comme le fut Phryné pour son sincère nu.

ADVISE, I BEG YOU

Oh dear, Moon after Moon
In good fortune's little tune,
Oh dear, from thing to thing
On a virtuoso's shrilling string! . . .

Oh dear me, with a pale
Lily to stir up Isis' veil! . . .
Oh dear, no let-up, flogging on and on
My anomalifloral encephalon
In florescences of flesh with garlands of tedia! . . .
O Death, then the . . . a . . . ?

But! life scares me like the idea
Of a marriage. Oh, it's true
I'm not of age yet to
Go for this marriage-do! . . .

Oh, I've been very struck by *This Life of Mine*,
The other Sunday, it was, leaving across a plain!
Oh, just let me be to get my breath again,
At last you'll have a book sincere in every line.

And while you wait, take pity on my misery!
May I be welcome to you all no less
And may I be absolved for my soul's sincerity,
As Phryne was for sincere nakedness!

Des Fleurs de bonne volonté

Flowers of Good Will

(*Hamlet exit*)
OPHELIA: O, what a noble mind is here o'erthrown!

HAMLET: Had I but time!
            O, I could tell you, –
    But let it be.

I AVERTISSEMENT

Mon père (un dur par timidité)
Est mort avec un profil sévère;
J'avais presque pas connu ma mère,
Et donc vers vingt ans je suis resté.

Alors, j'ai fait d' la littérature;
Mais le Démon de la Vérité
Sifflotait tout l' temps à mes côtés:
«Pauvre! as-tu fini tes écritures . . .»

Or, pas le cœur de me marier,
Étant, moi, au fond, trop méprisable!
Et elles, pas assez intraitables!!
Mais tout l' temps là à s'extasier! . . .

C'est pourquoi je vivotte, vivotte,
Bonne girouette aux trent' six saisons,
Trop nombreux pour dire oui ou non . . .
– Jeunes gens! que je vous serv' d'Ilote!

Copenhague, Elseneur
1ᵉʳ janvier 1886

II FIGUREZ-VOUS UN PEU

Oh! qu'une, d'Elle-même, un beau soir, sût venir,
Ne voyant que boire à Mes Lèvres! ou mourir . . .

Je m'enlève rien que d'y penser! Quel baptême
De gloire intrinsèque, attirer un «Je vous aime»!

(L'attirer à travers la société, de loin,
Comme l'aimant la foudre; un', deux! ni plus, ni moins.)

I ADVERTISEMENT

My father (hard through timidity)
Is dead of a profile most severe;
I hardly knew my mother here,
And nearing twenty was stuck with me.

And so I tried to write a bit;
But the Demon of the Truth
Kept whispering beside my youth:
'Given up scribbling yet, poor twit?'

Well, had no heart for marriage, me:
Being of too despicable stuff!
Girls not intractable enough!!
All the time game for ecstasy! . . .

That's why I scrape along, scrape by,
Fine weathercock of seasons galore,
Too many for yes or no . . . – As your
Helot may I serve, young fry!

Copenhagen, Elsinore
1st January 1886

II IMAGINE A BIT

If only one of her Own Accord, one night, dropped by,
Saw nothing for it but to drink at my Lips or die . . .

It lifts me even thinking of it. Some baptism, that,
Of intrinsic glory: to draw an 'I-love-you' pat.

(Despite society, to draw it out of the blue,
As lover, lightning, no more no less: one, two!)

Je t'aime! comprend-on? Pour moi tu n'es pas comme
Les autres; jusqu'ici c'était des messieurs, l'Homme . . .

Ta bouche me fait baisser les yeux! et ton port
Me transporte! (et je m'en découvre des trésors . . .)

Et c'est ma destinée incurable et dernière
D'épier un battement *à moi* de tes paupières!

Oh! je ne songe pas au reste! J'attendrai,
Dans la simplicité de ma vie faite exprès . . .

Te dirai-je au moins que depuis des nuits je pleure,
Et que mes parents ont bien peur que je n'en meure? . . .

Je pleure dans des coins; je n'ai plus goût à rien;
Oh! j'ai tant pleuré, dimanche, en mon paroissien!

Tu me demandes pourquoi Toi? et non un autre . . .
Je ne sais; mais c'est bien Toi, et point un autre!

J'en suis sûre comme du vide de mon cœur,
Et . . . comme de votre air mortellement moqueur . . .

– Ainsi, elle viendrait, évadée, demi-morte,
Se rouler sur le paillasson qu'est à ma porte!

Ainsi, elle viendrait à Moi! les yeux bien fous!
Et elle me suivrait avec cet air partout!

I love you, understand? For me you're other than
The rest; now on, of gentlemen, you are The Man . . .

Your mouth induces me to lower my eyes; your bearing
Gets me raring! (And I reveal it treasures unsparing . . .)

It's my incurable and final destiny
To catch a batting of your eyelid over *me*.

And oh, I never think about the rest. I wait
In the simplicity of life made clear and straight . . .

Yet shall I tell you, though, the nights I weep and cry,
And how my parents have real fear that I may die? . . .

I have no taste for anything; in any nook
And corner weep; on Sunday in my prayer-book!

You ask me why it's You I love and not some other?
I don't know, but it's You indeed and not another.

I feel as sure of this as of the void that's there
Within my heart – and of your mortal mocking air.

– That's how she'd come, escaped, and more than half-way dead,
To roll upon my doormat as though it were a bed!

That's how she'd come to Me – with really crazy stare
And she would tag me with that look just everywhere.

III   METTONS LE DOIGT SUR LA PLAIE

Que le pur du bonheur m'est bien si je l'escompte!
Ou ne le cueille qu'en refrains de souvenance!...
Ô rêve, ou jamais plus! Et fol je me balance
Au-dessus du Présent en Ariel qui a honte.

Mais, le cru, quotidien, et trop voyant Présent!
Et qui vous met au pied du mur, et qui vous dit:
«À l'instant, ou bonsoir!» et ne fait pas crédit,
Et m'étourdit le cœur de ses airs suffisants!

Tout vibrant de passé, tout pâle d'espérance,
Je fais signe au Présent: «Oh! sois plus diaphane?»
Mais il me bat la charge et mine mes organes!
Puis, le bateau parti, j'ulule: «Oh! recommence...»

Et lui seul est bien vrai! – mais je me mords la main
Plutôt (je suis trop jeune... ou, trop agonisant...)
Ah! rien qu'un pont entre Mon Cœur et le Présent!
Ô lourd Passé, combien ai-je encor de demains?...

> Ô cœur aride
> Mais sempiterne,
> Ô ma citerne
> Des Danaïdes!...

IV   MANIAQUE

> POLONIUS (aside): *Though this be madness,*
> *yet there is method in't.*

Eh oui que l'on en sait de simples,
Aux matins des villégiatures,
Foulant les prés! et dont la guimpe
A bien quelque âme pour doublure...

III LET'S PUT THE FINGER ON THE WOUND

The pure in happiness, how very me if I discount it! . . .
Or gather it only in the memory's repeats! . . .
Oh, dream, or never more! And, mad, in dangling feats
Above the Present, shameful Ariel, I surmount it.

But ah, too-seeing Present, quotidian and raw!
It puts you up against the wall and then it says it:
'It's now or never!' and will not give you any credit;
Its bumptious airs then slug my heart right on the jaw.

All pale with hope, all trembling with the past,
I signal the Present: 'More transparency perhaps?'
But it mounts the charge at me and all my organs saps!
Then, the boat missed, I yowl: 'Oh, start again! . . . Oh, blast!' . . .

And only it is real! – but still, I bite my thumb
Rather (I'm much too young . . . or too near final pangs)
Ah, just a day-break bridge mid Heart and Present hangs
Oh heavy Past, how many tomorrows have I to come? . . .

> Oh, heart arid
> But sempiternal,
> My urn infernal
> Danaids married! . . .

IV MANIAC

> POLONIUS (aside): *Though this be madness,*
> *yet there is method in't.*

Ah, yes, you know what simples you get
Those mornings on a country stroll,
Trampling the fields! whose chemisette
Has for the lining quite some soul . . .

Mais, chair de pêche, âme en rougeurs!
Chair de victime aux Pubertés,
Âmes prêtes, d'un voyageur
Qui passe, prêtes à dater!

Et Protées valseurs sans vergogne!
Changeant de nom, de rôle (d'âme!)
Sœurs, mères, veuves, Antigones,
Amantes! mais jamais ma Femme.

Des pudeurs devant l'Homme?... – et si
J'appelle, moi, ces falbalas,
La peur d'examens sans merci?
Et si je ne sors pas de là!

V   LE VRAI DE LA CHOSE

Ah! c'est pas sa chair qui m'est tout,
Et suis pas qu'un grand cœur pour elle;
Non, c'est d'aller faire les fous
Dans des histoires fraternelles!

Oh! vous m'entendez bien!
Oh! vous savez comme on y vient;
Oh! vous savez parfaitement qu'il y a moyen,
Et comme on s'y attelle.

Lui défeuiller quel Tout je suis,
Et que ses yeux, perdus, m'en suivent!
Et puis un soir: «Tu m'as séduit
Pourtant!» – et l'aimer toute vive.

Et s'aimer tour à tour,
Au gras soleil des basses-cours,
Et vers la Lune, et puis partout! avec toujours
En nobles perspectives ...

But soul in blushes, flesh of peach!
Body the victim to Puberties,
Souls ready, a stroller may reach,
Ready for date-stamping offices.

Protean waltzers, shameless shes!
Changers of name, of part, (of soul!)
Sisters, mothers, widows, Antigones,
Lovers! – My Woman never the role. .

Modesties before Man? . . . And me,
If I should call these furbelows
The fear of merciless scrutiny?
And if I won't shift ground, suppose!

V   THE TRUTH OF THE MATTER

To me her body isn't all there is,
And I'm not just a good heart for her;
No, it's to go and in the histories
Of brotherhood play fools as never were.

You understand what I say!
You know just how one comes to it some day;
Oh, you know perfectly well how there's a way,
How pull your weight, concur.

To strip whatever All-I-am for him,
And have his lost eyes follow limb by limb!
Then say: 'Yet you seduced me, though!' one dim
Evening – and next to love him all keen.

And love each other, one to one,
In the lusty sun of farmyards just begun
And till the Moon, then everywhere! with always done
In noble perspectives seen . . .

Oh! c'est pas seulement la chair,
Et c'est pas plus seulement l'âme;
C'est l'Esprit édénique et fier
D'être un peu l'Homme avec la Femme.

VI RIGUEURS À NULLE AUTRE PAREILLES

Dans un album,
Mourait fossile
Un géranium
Cueilli aux Îles.

Un fin Jongleur
En vieil ivoire
Raillait la fleur
Et ses histoires . . .

– «Un requiem!»
Demandait-elle.
– «Vous n'aurez rien,
Mademoiselle!» . . .

Oh, it's not merely body, flesh,
Nor any longer just the soul in it;
It's the Spirit, proud and Eden-fresh,
To be Man with Woman just a bit.

VI   RIGOURS LIKE NO OTHER

In an album's files,
A geranium lying,
Picked in the Isles,
Was pressed and dying.

A fine troubadour,
Ivory, old,
Mocked the flower for
The tales she told . . . .

'A requiem!'
She asked just this.
'Oh, none of them
Will you have, miss!'

VII   AQUARELLE EN CINQ MINUTES

> OPHELIA: *'Tis brief, my Lord.*
> HAMLET: *As woman's love.*

Oh! oh! le temps se gâte,
L'orage n'est pas loin,
Voilà que l'on se hâte
    De rentrer les foins! . . .

        L'abcès perce!
        Vl'à l'averse!
        Ô grabuges
        Des déluges! . . .

Oh! ces ribambelles
        D'ombrelles! . . .

        Oh! cett' Nature
En déconfiture! . . .

Sur ma fenêtre,
Un fuchsia
À l'air paria
Se sent renaître . . .

VII WATER-COLOUR IN FIVE MINUTES

OPHELIA: *'Tis brief, my Lord.*
HAMLET: *As woman's love.*

Ho, ho, the weather'll worsen,
The storm's not far away.
That's what drives a person
    To gather the hay!

        The abscess breaks!
        The shower rakes!
        Oh, rumpus roars
        Of these downpours!

Oh these tarantellas
    Of umbrellas! . . .

    Oh, this Nature, you're
In such discomfiture! . . .

Beyond my pane
A fuchsia there
With outcast air
Feels born again . . .

VIII   ROMANCE

HAMLET: *To a nunnery, go.*

J'ai mille oiseaux de mer d'un gris pâle,
Qui nichent au haut de ma belle âme,
Ils en emplissent les tristes salles
De rythmes pris aux plus fines lames . . .

Or, ils salissent tout de charognes,
Et aussi de coraux, de coquilles;
Puis volent en ronds fous, et se cognent
À mes probes lambris de famille . . .

Oiseaux pâles, oiseaux des sillages!
Quand la fiancée ouvrira la porte,
Faites un collier des coquillages
Et que l'odeur de charogn's soit forte! . . .

Qu'Elle dise: «Cette âme est bien forte
Pour mon petit nez . . . – je me r'habille.
Mais ce beau collier? hein, je l'emporte?
Il ne lui sert de rien, pauvre fille . . .»

IX   PETITES MISÈRES DE JUILLET

(Le Serpent de l'Amour
Monte, vers Dieu, des linges.
Allons, rouges méninges,
Faire un tour.)

Écoutez, mes enfants! – «Ah! mourir, mais me tordre
Dans l'orbe d'un exécutant de premier ordre!»
Rêve la Terre, sous la vessie de saindoux
De la Lune laissant fuir un air par trop doux,

VIII ROMANCE

HAMLET: *To a nunnery, go.*

I have a thousand seabirds of pale grey
That nest toward the top of my fine soul.
They fill its saddest rooms up with the play
Of rhythms from the finest waves that roll.

And then they soil the whole with carrion meat
And with the coral and the shells they bring.
They fly around in insane circles, beat
Themselves on my upright family panelling.

Pale birds, birds of the wash and wake!
When the intended opens the door, you thong
Your shells into a necklace for her sake,
And may the stench of carrion be strong! . . .

And may She say: This soul is pretty strong
For my dainty nose . . . I'll get back in my gear.
But this fine necklace? What, take it along?
It's precious little use to her, poor dear . . .'

IX PETTY MISERIES OF JULY

(The Serpent of Love would soar
Godwards from linen. Come on,
Blushing meninges, let's swan
Off on a tour.)

Listen, kiddies! – 'Ah, die but writhing in the sphere
Of an executant of the very top notch here!'
Earth dreams, beneath the Moon's bladder of lard,
Letting escape an air that is too sweet by far,

Vers les Zéniths de brasiers de la Voie Lactée
(Autrement beaux ce soir que les Lois constatées) . . .
Juillet a dégainé! Touristes des beaux yeux,
Quels jubés de bonheur échafaudent ces cieux,
Semis de pollens d'étoiles, manne divine
Qu'éparpille le Bon Pasteur à ses gallines! . . .
Et puis, le vent s'est tant surmené l'autre nuit!
Et demain est si loin! et ça souffre aujourd'hui!
Ah! pourrir! . . . – Vois, la Lune-même (cette amie)
Salive et larmoie en purulente ophtalmie . . .

Et voici que des bleus sous-bois ont miaulé
Les mille nymphes! et (qu'est-ce que vous voulez)
Aussitôt mille touristes des yeux las rôdent,
Tremblants, mais le cœur harnaché d'âpres méthodes!
Et l'on va. Et les uns connaissent des sentiers
Qu'embaument de trois mois les fleurs d'abricotiers;
Et les autres, des parcs où la petite flûte
De l'oiseau bleu promet de si frêles rechutes
(Oh! ces lunaires oiseaux bleus dont la chanson
Lunaire, après dégel, vous donne le frisson!)
Et d'autres, les terrasses pâles où le triste
Cor des paons réveillés fait que Plus Rien n'existe!
Et d'autres, les joncs des mares où le sanglot
Des rainettes vous tire maint sens mal éclos;
Et d'autres, les prés brûlés où l'on rampe; et d'autres,
La Boue où, semble-t-il, Tout! avec nous se vautre! . . .

Les capitales échauffantes, même au frais
Des Grands Hôtels tendus de pâles cuirs gaufrés,
Faussent. – Ah! mais ailleurs, aux grandes routes,
Au coin d'un bois mal famé, rien n'est aux écoutes . . .
Et celles dont le cœur gante six et demi,
Et celles dont l'âme est gris-perle, en bons amis,
Et d'un port panaché d'édénique opulence,
Vous brûlent leurs vaisseaux mondains vers des Enfances! . . .

«Oh! t'enchanter un peu la muqueuse du cœur!»
«Ah! Vas-y, je n'ai plus rien à perdre à cett' heur',
La Terre est en plein air et ma vie est gâchée,

To zeniths of the cressets of the Milky Way
(Otherwise lovely tonight than laws established say) . . .
July has now unsheathed! Tourists of lovely eyes,
What rood-screens of submissive happiness frame these skies,
Broadcast with seeds of stars, the divine manna, He,
The Good Shepherd throws his gallinaceae! . . .
And then the wind, so overworked the other night!
And tomorrow's far! And today it hurts all right!
Ah, rot! . . . The very Moon, that friendly she, look, drivels
And with a purulent ophthalmia she snivels . . .

'Here, from the blue brushwood has emerged the miaow
Of nymphs in thousands and (that is what you want now)
At once a thousand tourists of idling eyes again
Prowl trembling, but with hearts pulled back with savage rein.
But one moves on. And others know of ways and bowers
Fragrant for three months with scent of apricot flowers;
Others know parks in which the bluebird's tiny tune
Is promising the frailest of backslidings soon;
(Oh, these lunar bluebirds with that lunar trill
That, when the thaw has come, can give you such a thrill!)
And others know pale terraces where, sad melodist,
The horn of woken peacocks makes Naught Else exist!
Some know the reeds of ponds where croaking frogs draw tight
For you so many senses poorly brought to light
Some know of parching meadows where one crawls the levels;
Some know the Mud in which the Whole makes us its revels! . . .

The capitals now warming even with the fresh air
Of Grand Hotels, tense with embossed leatherware,
Play false. – Ah, but down major routes elsewhere, some nook
Of some notorious wood, nothing's alert to look . . .
And those whose heart takes six and a half in gloves,
And those whose soul's pearl grey in good friends, loves,
Who, from a port in paradisal riches crowned,
Burn for you their worldly boats on Childhoods bound! . . .

'Oh, to enchant the membrane of your heart!'
'Come off it. Now I've nothing more with which to part.
The Earth is in the open, and my life's a mess,

Ne songe qu'à la Nuit, je ne suis point fâchée.»
Et la vie et la Nuit font patte de velours ...
Se dépècent d'abord de grands quartiers d'amour ...
Et lors, les chars de foin, pleins de bluets, dévalent
Par les vallons des moissons équinoxiales ...
Ô lointains balafrés de bleuâtres éclairs
De chaleur! puis ils regrimperont, tous leurs nerfs
Tressés, vers l'hostie de la Lune syrupeuse ...
– Hélas! tout ça, c'est des histoires de muqueuses ...

– Détraqué, dites-vous? Ah! par rapport à Quoi?
– D'accord; mais le Spleen vient, qui dit que l'on déchoit
Hors des fidélités noblement circonscrites.
– Mais le Divin chez nous confond si bien les rites!
– Soit; mais le Spleen dit vrai: ô surplis des Pudeurs,
C'est bien dans vos plis blancs tels quels qu'est le Bonheur!
– Mais, au nom de Tout! on ne peut pas! La Nature
Nous rue à dénouer dès janvier leur ceinture!
– Bon! si le Spleen t'en dit, saccage universel!
Nos êtres vont par sexe, et sont trop usuels,
Saccagez! – Ah! saignons, tandis qu'elles déballent
Leurs serres de Beauté pétale par pétale!
Les vignes de nos nerfs bourdonnent d'alcools noirs,
Ô Sœurs, ensanglantons la Terre, ce pressoir
Sans Planteur de Justice! – Ah? tu m'aimes, je t'aime!
Que la Mort ne nous ait qu'IVRES-MORTS DE NOUS-MÊMES!

> (Le Serpent de l'Amour
> Cuve Dieu dans les linges;
> Ah! du moins nos méninges
> Sont à court.)

No, I'm not angry; just think of the Night, no less.'
And life and Night draw in their claws of vicious points . . .
First thing, great quarters of love cut up their joints . . .
And next, the wains of hay full of cornflowers wend,
Along the valleys of the harvest-seasons tend . . .
Oh, distant sabre cuts, of bluish summer lightning!
And then they'll climb again, all their nerve-strings heightening,
Entwined, towards the host of the syrupy Moon . . .
– Alas, all that's affairs of mucous membranes' rheum . . .

– Unhinged, you say, all this? But ah, compared with What?
– Okay, but Spleen comes on, says status forfeits a lot
Outside fidelities we nobly circumscribe.
– But the Divine confounds the rites of all our tribe!
– Just so; but Spleen speaks right: O surplice of Modesties,
In your white pleats such as they are's where happiness is!
– But in the name of All, we can't. Nature hurtles
Us from January on to loosen all their girdles!
– Good! If Spleen tells you so, then universal pillage!
We beings work by sex, too normal in that tillage,
So pillage! – Ah, let's bleed as long as they disclose
Petal by petal their Beauty's long pressed rose!
Dark alcohols are humming in our vines of nerves,
Oh, sisters, let us bloody Earth, this press that serves
No Planter who is Just! – Ah? You love me; I, you!
So only DEAD DRUNK WITH OURSELVES may Death take two.

> (Love's Serpent sleeps off God
> Under the bed-sheets' pall;
> At least our meninges fall
>   Short of that cod . . .)

X   ESTHÉTIQUE

Je fais la cour à ma Destinée;
Et demande: «Est-ce pour cette année?»

Je la prends par la douceur, en Sage,
Tout aux arts, au bon cœur, aux voyages . . .

Et vais m'arlequinant des défroques
Des plus grands penseurs de chaque époque . . .

Et saigne! en jurant que je me blinde
Des ritcs végétatifs de l'Inde . . .

Et suis digne, allez, d'un mausolée
En pleine future Galilée!

De la meilleure grâce du monde,
Donc, j'attends que l'Amour me réponde . . .

Ah! tu sais que Nul ne se dérange,
Et que, ma foi, vouloir faire l'ange . . .

Je ferai l'ange! Oh! va, Destinée,
Ta nuit ne m'irait pas chiffonnée!

Passe! et grâce pour ma jobardise . . .
Mais, du moins, laisse que je te dise,

Nos livres bons, entends-tu, nos livres
Seuls, te font ces yeux fous de Survivre

Qui vers ta Matrice après déchaînent
Les héros du viol et du sans-gêne.

Adieu. Noble et lent, vais me remettre
À la culture des Belles-Lettres.

X   AESTHETIC

Again, I'm paying court to my Destiny
And ask her: 'This year, then, is it to be?'

As Sage, I take her by the gentle graces
All to the arts, to kind heart, and places . . .

I scamper harlequinning in cast-off knee-socks
Of all the greatest thinkers of the epochs . . .

And bleed, vowing I'll case myself – in tin, dear,
Made of the vegetative rites from India . . .

And I'm worthy, come now, of a sepulchre
In some thorough future Galilean stir!

With the best will in the world, you see,
I'm waiting, then, till Love may answer me . . .

Ah, you know None from the straight and narrow quit,
And that, my word, wishing to act the angel bit . . .

I'll act the angel! Come off it, Destiny;
Your night'd never get ruffled with me!

Skip it. And do excuse my blathering . . .
But, at the least, just let me say one thing:

Our good books, do you understand? our books
Alone, give you these mad-on-Survival looks

That to your Womb attract and then let loose
Heroes of rape and more thick-skinned abuse.

'Bye. Noble and calm, I'll realign
Myself to hone the art of Writing (Fine!).

XI DIMANCHES

Ô Dimanches bannis
De l'Infini
Au-delà du microscope et du télescope,
Seuil nuptial où la chair s'affale en syncope . . .

Dimanches citoyens
Bien quotidiens
De cette école à vieux cancans, la vieille Europe,
Où l'on tourne, s'en tricotant des amours myopes . . .

Oh! tout Lois sans appel,
Je sais, ce Ciel,
Et non un brave toit de famille, un bon dôme
Où s'en viennent mourir, très-appréciés, nos psaumes!

C'est fort beau comme fond
À certain fronts,
Des Lois! et pas de plus bleue matière à diplômes . . .
– Mais, c'est pas les Lois qui fait le bonheur, hein, l'Homme?

XII DIMANCHES

Oh! ce piano, ce cher piano,
Qui jamais, jamais ne s'arrête,
Oh! ce piano qui geint là-haut
Et qui s'entête sur ma tête!

Ce sont de sinistres polkas,
Et des romances pour concierge,
Des exercices délicats,
Et *La Prière d'une vierge*!

XI SUNDAYS

Oh, Sundays, banished from sight
      Of the Infinite
Beyond the microscope and telescopic stare,
The nuptial threshold where the body faints for air . . .

      Oh, citizen Sundays,
           Humdrum done days
Of this school of old cancans, old Europe where
One sours, in knitting myopic loves by the pair . . .

      All Law with no appeal,
           I know, for real,
This Sky, no trusty family home, nice dome where, quick,
Our psalms arrive, so well esteemed, to die out sick!

      It's as fine as it's deep
           To certain people,
Laws, Laws! And not the subtlest matter for matric . . .
– But, Man, it's never Laws, eh, makes your happiness tick?

XII SUNDAYS

Oh that piano, dear piano-ing,
That's never going to stop dead;
Oh that piano up there snivelling
And going headstrong at my head.

Now polkas very sinister,
For concierge a romantic air,
Delicate practices now recur,
And now we get *A Virgin's Prayer*!

Fuir? où aller, par ce printemps?
Dehors, dimanche, rien à faire . . .
Et rien à fair' non plus dedans . . .
Oh! rien à faire sur la Terre! . . .

Ohé, jeune fille au piano!
Je sais que vous n'avez point d'âme!
Puis pas donner dans le panneau
De la nostalgie de vos gammes . . .

Fatals bouquets du Souvenir,
Folles légendes décaties,
Assez! assez! vous vois venir,
Et mon âme est bientôt partie . . .

Vrai, un Dimanche sous ciel gris,
Et je ne fais plus rien qui vaille,
Et le moindre orgu' de Barbari
(Le pauvre!) m'empoigne aux entrailles!

Et alors, je me sens trop fou!
Marié, je tuerais la bouche
De ma mie! et, à deux genoux,
Je lui dirais ces mots bien louches:

«Mon cœur est trop, ah trop central!
Et toi, tu n'es que chair humaine;
Tu ne vas donc pas trouver mal
Que je te fasse de la peine!»

Escape? In spring-time? Where to?
Nothing, Sundays, to do outside,
And nothing much indoors to do . . .
Nothing on Earth to do, world-wide! . . .

Piano-girl, hey, hold it there!
I know you have no soul, no inkling! . . .
Else you'd not spring nostalgia's snare
With all those scales you keep on tinkling . . .

Deadly bouquets of Remembrance,
Mad, back-number legends flit.
Enough! enough! I see your entrance
And soon enough my soul has quit . . .

True, one Sunday under grey sky,
I'm doing nothing much at all,
And a barrel-organ, poor guy,
Can clench my guts up in a ball.

And, there and then, quite mad I feel!
Married, I'd tire the mouth so dear
Of my beloved! With both legs kneel,
And these right shifty words she'd hear:

'My heart is too, ah, much too central!
And you, just flesh and blood, that's plain;
So you'll not think it's detrimental
If I should give you a bit of pain!'

XIII   AVANT-DERNIER MOT

L'Espace?
– Mon cœur
Y meurt
Sans traces . . .

En vérité, du haut des terrasses,
Tout est bien sans cœur.

La Femme?
– J'en sors,
La mort
Dans l'âme . . .

En vérité, mieux ensemble on pâme
Moins on est d'accord.

Le Rêve?
– C'est bon
Quand on
L'achève . . .

En vérité, la Vie est bien brève,
Le Rêve bien long.

Que faire
Alors
Du corps
Qu'on gère?

En vérité, ô mes ans, que faire
De ce riche corps?

Ceci,
Cela,
Par-ci
Par-là . . .

XIII   WORD BEFORE LAST

What of Space?
– Some part
My heart
Dies sans trace? . . .

In actual fact, right from the highest place,
All is without heart.

Woman's role?
– I quit,
Death fit
In the soul . . .

In actual fact, the closer that you loll
Less the accord in it.

As for Dream?
– Good fun
If one
Ever see'em . . .

In actual fact, Life is just a brief gleam,
The Dream's never done.

Do what here
In mesh
Of flesh
That you steer?

In actual fact, oh my years, do what here
With this precious flesh?

Now here,
Now there,
Now near,
Now where? . . .

En vérité, en vérité, voilà,
Et pour le reste, que Tout m'ait en sa merci.

XIV   L'ÉTERNEL QUIPROQUO

Droite en selle
A passé
Mad'moiselle
Aïssé!

Petit cœur si joli!
Corps banal mais alacre!
Un colis
Dans un fiacre.

Ah! les flancs
Tout brûlants
De fringales
Séminales,

Elle écoute
Par les routes
Si le cor
D'un Mondor

Ne s'exhale
Pas encor!
– Oh! raffale-
Moi le corps

Des salives
Corrosives
Dont mes flancs
Vont bêlant!

In fact, in actual fact, that's the affair;
As for the rest, the Whole have mercy on me here.

XIV   THE ETERNAL QUIDPROQUO

Straight in the seat
She went her way
Along the street,
Miss Aïssé!

Little heart so pretty,
Body banal but dab,
Parcel in a city
Hackney cab.

Ah, thighs burning,
All yearning
With cravings all
Seminal,

Her ears acute
Along the route
If some Mondor
Might not once more

Give the horn vent.
– Oh, drain me out
Till body's spent,
And put to rout

The salivas, those
Corrosive flows
For which my thighs
Bleat out their sighs!

– Ô vous Bon qui passez
Donnez-moi des nouvelles
    De ma Belle
    Mad'moiselle
    Aïssé.

    Car ses épaules
    Sont ma console,
    Mon Acropole!

XV   PETITE PRIÈRE SANS PRÉTENTIONS

Notre Père qui étiez aux cieux . . .
PAUL BOURGET

Notre Père qui êtes aux cieux (Oh! là-haut,
Infini qui êtes donc si inconcevable!)
Donnez-nous notre pain quotidien . . . – Oh! plutôt,
Laissez-nous nous asseoir un peu à Votre Table! . . .

Dites! nous tenez-vous pour de pauvres enfants
À qui l'on doit encor cacher les Choses Graves?
Et *Votre Volonté* n'admet-elle qu'esclaves
Sur cette terre comme au ciel? . . . – C'est étouffant!

Au moins, *Ne nous induisez pas*, par vos sourires
En la tentation de baiser votre cœur!
Et laissez-nous en paix, morts aux mondes meilleurs,
Paître, dans notre coin, et forniquer, et rire! . . .

Paître, dans notre coin, et forniquer, et rire! . . .

– Good men who pass this way,
Give me all news to tell
  Of my swell
  Mademoiselle
  Aïssé.

  For my console is
  Her shoulders – this
  My Acropolis!

XV   SMALL PRAYER WITHOUT PRETENSIONS

Notre Père qui étiez aux cieux . . .
PAUL BOURGET

Our Father who art in heaven (oh, up there, father,
Infinite conception of which we are not able!)
Give us this day our daily bread . . . Oh, we'd rather
You let us for a bit sit ourselves round Your Table! . . .

Say, d'you take us for such wretched kids and trifling
From whom the Serious Things are to be hidden still?
And only slaves may be admitted by *Your Will*
On earth as it is in Heaven? . . . It's so stifling.

At least, though, by your smiling *lead us not* hereafter
Into temptation where we might embrace your heart!
Leave us in peace, to better worlds dead from the start,
To graze our patch and fornicate and roar with laughter! . . .

To graze our patch and fornicate and roar with laughter! . . .

XVI DIMANCHES

HAMLET: *Have you a daughter?*
POLONIUS: *I have, my lord.*
HAMLET: *Let her not walk i' the sun;*
conception is a blessing; but not as your
daughter may conceive.

Le ciel pleut sans but, sans que rien l'émeuve,
Il pleut, il pleut, bergère! sur le fleuve . . .

Le fleuve a son repos dominical;
Pas un chaland, en amont, en aval.

Les Vêpres carillonnent sur la ville,
Les berges sont désertes, sans idylles.

Passe un pensionnat (ô pauvres chairs!)
Plusieurs ont déjà leurs manchons d'hiver.

Une qui n'a ni manchon, ni fourrures
Fait, tout en gris, une pauvre figure.

Et la voilà qui s'échappe des rangs,
Et court! ô mon Dieu, qu'est-ce qu'il lui prend?

Et elle va se jeter dans le fleuve.
Pas un batelier, pas un chien Terr' Neuve.

Le crépuscule vient; le petit port
Allume ses feux. (Ah! connu, l' décor!)

La pluie continue à mouiller le fleuve,
Le ciel pleut sans but, sans que rien l'émeuve.

XVI SUNDAYS

> HAMLET: *Have you a daughter?*
> POLONIUS: *I have, my lord.*
> HAMLET: *Let her not walk i' the sun;*
> *conception is a blessing; but not as your*
> *daughter may conceive.*

Sky rains unmoved, unending, without remorse,
Rains, rains, shepherdess, on the river's course.

The river takes its Sunday of repose;
No lighter up the stream or downstream goes.

Over the town the Vespers carillonnade;
The banks deserted, no romances made.

A file of boarders passes (poor little scruffs)
Several already wear their winter muffs.

One, who has no muff nor furs to wear,
Makes, all in grey, a sorry figure there.

And, her, look, suddenly she's breaking rank
And running! God, what takes her to the bank?

She's going to throw herself straight in and drown.
No boatman, no newfoundland dog dives down.

The dusk comes on; lamps in the little port
Begin to light. (Ah, the scene's a common sort.)

The rain continues to damp the river's course;
Sky rains unmoved, unending, without remorse.

XVII CYTHÈRE

Quel lys sut ombrager ma sieste?
C'était (ah! ne sais plus comme!) au bois trop sacré
Où fleurir n'est pas un secret.
Et j'étais fui comme la peste.
«Je ne suis pas une âme leste!»
Ai-je dit alors et leurs chœurs m'ont chanté: «Reste.»

Et la plus grande, oh! si mienne! m'a expliqué
La floraison sans commentaires
De cette hermétique Cythère
Au sein des mers comme un bosquet,
Et comment quelques couples vraiment distingués
Un soir ici ont débarqué . . .

Non la nuit sait pas de pelouses
D'un velours bleu plus brave que ces lents vallons!
Plus invitant au: dévalons!
Et déjoueur des airs d'épouse!
Et qui telle une chair jalouse,
En ses accrocs plus éperdûment se recouse! . . .

Et la faune et la flore étant comme ça vient,
On va comme ça vient; des roses
Les sens; des floraisons les poses;
Nul souci du tien et du mien;
Quant à des classements en chrétiens et païens,
Ni le climat ni les moyens.

Oui, fleurs de vie en confidences,
Mains oisives dans les toisons aux gros midis,
Tatouages des concettis;
L'un mimant d'inédites danses,
L'autre sur la piste d'essences . . .
— Eh quoi? Nouveau-venu, vous larmes recommencent!

XVII CYTHERA

What lily bed could shade my siesta?
It was in that too holy wood (how, I don't know)
    Where flowering was no secret, though;
    They fled me like the plague or pest.
    'I'm not a nimble soul at best,'
I said, then, and their choir heart-chorused: 'Rest!'

The tallest – oh, so mine! – explained to me
    The floral, without a single note,
    Of this hermetic Cythera afloat
    In deep sea like a shrubbery,
And how couples of some celebrity
    Landed one night from off the sea . . .

    The night knows no lawns elsewhere
Of sprucer blue velvet than these valleys slow!
    Nor more inviting: 'Down we go!'
    More thwarter of the wifely air!
    None more in transports to repair
In such a jealous body the wear and tear! . . .

The flora and the fauna being as it is,
    You do as it does there; from roses
    The senses; from the florals poses;
    Of yours and mine, no niceties,
As for Christian and pagan categories
    Neither climate nor ways for this.

    Yes, living flowers with confidences,
Hands idling in hair in broad noon light;
    Conceits in tattoos strike the sight;
    One in unheard-of dancing tenses;
    On track of essence one commences . . .
– What's up? Newcomer, you're weeping more drenches!

– Réveil meurtri, je m'en irai je sais bien où;
    Un terrain vague, des clôtures,
    Un âne plein de foi pâture
    Des talons perdus sans dégoût,
Et brait vers moi (me sachant aussi rosse et doux)
    Que je desserre son licou.

XVIII   DIMANCHES

    Je m'ennuie, natal! je m'ennuie,
    Sans cause bien appréciable,
Que bloqué par les boues, les dimanches, les pluies,
En d'humides tabacs ne valant pas le diable.

    Hé là-bas, le prêtre sans messes!...
    Ohé, mes petits sens hybrides!...
Et je bats mon rappel! et j'ulule en détresse,
Devant ce Moi, tonneau d'Ixion des Danaïdes.

    Oh! m'en aller, me croyant libre,
    Désattelé des bibliothèques,
Avec tous ces passants cuvant en équilibre
Leurs cognacs d'Absolu, leurs pâtés d'Intrinsèque!...

    Messieurs, que roulerais tranquille,
    Si j'avais au moins ma formule,
Ma formule en pilules dorées, par ces villes
Que vont pavant mes jobardises d'incrédule!...

    (Comment lui dire: «Je vous aime»?
    Je me connais si peu moi-même.)
Ah! quel sort! Ah! pour sûr, la tâche qui m'incombe
M'aura sensiblement rapproché de la tombe.

– Awaking, bruised, I'm going I know where;
   A waste full of enclosures – a mass,
   Where crammed with good faith, an ass
   Without disgust crops scrag-end fare,
And (knowing me a docile nag confrère)
   Brays that I let him loose from there.

XVIII   SUNDAYS

   I weary myself, birthday, weary myself again
   With no appreciable reason quite
Except I'm blocked in by the mud, Sundays, and rain,
Stuck with these tobacco fugs not worth a light.

   Hi, massless priest, down there! . . .
   Halloo, my mongrel senses. Gee! . . .
And then I beat retreat! and yowl out in despair
Before this Ixion's cask for Danaids, this Me.

   Oh, to go, thinking I'm free,
   Libraries unhitched from my back,
With all these passing by who walk off equably
Their patés of Essences, their Absolute cognac!

   Gentlemen, how calm my ups and downs
   Had I my formula; in brief,
My formula of gilded pills about these towns
Which my bamboozling goes paving with disbelief.

   (How say to her: 'I do love you.'?
   I know myself so little.) Rum do,
Ah, what a fate! Ah, sure, the duty I must assume
Will sensibly have made advances to the tomb.

XIX   ALBUMS

On m'a dit la vie au Far-West et les Prairies,
Et mon sang a gémi: «Que voilà ma patrie!...»
Déclassé du vieux monde, être sans foi ni loi,
Desperado! là-bas, là-bas, je serais roi!...
Oh là-bas, m'y scalper de mon cerveau d'Europe!
Piaffer, redevenir une vierge antilope,
Sans littérature, un gars de proie, citoyen
Du hasard et sifflant l'argot californien!
Un colon vague et pur, éleveur, architecte,
Chasseur, pêcheur, joueur, au-dessus des Pandectes!
Entre la mer, et les États Mormons! Des venaisons
Et du whisky! vêtu de cuir, et le gazon
Des Prairies pour lit, et des ciels des premiers âges
Riches comme des corbeilles de mariage!...
Et puis quoi? De bivouac en bivouac, et la Loi
De Lynch; et aujourd'hui des diamants bruts aux doigts,
Et ce soir nuit de jeu, et demain la refuite
Par la Prairie et vers la folie des pépites!...
Et, devenu vieux, la ferme au soleil-levant,
Une vache laitière et des petits-enfants...
Et, comme je dessine au besoin, à l'entrée
Je mettrais: «Tatoueur des bras de la contrée»!
Et voilà. Et puis, si mon grand cœur de Paris
Me revenait, chantant: «Oh! pas encor guéri!
Et ta postérité, pas pour longtemps coureuse!...»
Et si ton vol, Condor des Montagnes-Rocheuses,
Me montrait l'Infini ennemi du comfort,
Eh bien, j'inventerais un culte d'Âge d'or,
Un code social, empirique et mystique
Pour des Peuples Pasteurs, modernes et védiques!...

Oh! qu'ils sont beaux les feux de paille! qu'ils sont fous,
Les albums! et non incassables, mes joujoux!...

XIX   ALBUMS

Someone spoke of the Prairies, the Far West,
And my heart groaned: 'My country, that, the best!'
Declassed from the old world, lawless, faithless, me
A *desperado!* King out there I'd be! . . .
Out there, I'd scalp all Europe off my head,
Paw earth, a virgin antelope instead,
Bookless, a fellow of prey, and in the gang
Of chance, wheezing Californian slang!
The colonist's life, stock-breeder's, architect's,
Hunter, fisher, gamester, above the Pandects!
Between the deep sea and Mormon states. Venison
And whisky! Prairie grass for bed, a denizen
Of leathers; primordial climates like baskets
Filled with the wedding gifts, rich caskets! . . .
And what then? Bivouac on bivouac, Lynch Law,
Today rough diamonds upon the paw,
This evening a gambling night, next day skedaddle
On the Prairie, nugget-crazy in the saddle! . . .
And then when old, a farm in the rising sun,
A good milch cow and toddlers one by one . . .
And, since I sketch as needed, on the gate
I'd put: 'Tattooist to best arms in the State'!
And there we are. If my Parisian heart (tenor)
Then came and sang: 'Ah, not yet cured, partner!
Your offspring not such wanderers quite!'
And, Condor of the Rockies, if your flight
Showed me the Infinite foe to comfort, well,
I'd found a cult of the Golden Age's Spell,
A social code pragmatical and mystic
For Pastor Peoples, vedantic and modernistic . . .

Oh, how beautiful the straw fires burn, no Troys,
How mad the albums, nor unbreakable my toys! . . .

XX   CÉLIBAT, CÉLIBAT, TOUT N'EST QUE CÉLIBAT

Sucer la chair d'un cœur élu,
Adorer de souffrants organes,
Être deux avant qu'on se fane!
Ne serai-je qu'un monomane
    Dissolu
Par ses travaux de décadent et de reclus?

Partout, à toute heure, le thème
De leurs toilettes, de leurs airs,
Des soirs de plage aux bals d'hiver,
Est: «Prenez! ceci est ma chair!»
    Et nous-mêmes,
Nous leur crions de tous nos airs: «À moi! je t'aime!»

Et l'on se salue, et l'on feint . . .
Et l'on s'instruit dans des écoles,
Et l'on s'évade, et l'on racole
De vénales et tristes folles;
    Et l'on geint
En vers, en prose. Au lieu de se tendre la main!

Se serrer la main sans affaires!
Selon les cœurs, selon les corps!
Trop tard. Des faibles et des forts
Dans la curée des durs louis d'or . . .
    Pauvre Terre!
Histoire Humaine: – histoire d'*un* célibataire . . .

XX   CELIBATE, CELIBATE, ALL'S
JUST CELIBATE

To drain a chosen heart's juice,
And suffering organs adore,
Be back to two before you bore!
Won't I be monomanic and more,
    Dissolute, loose,
From all these actions decadent and most recluse?

Everywhere, any hour, one call
From their toilette, their manner, glances,
From evening sands to winter dances:
'This is my body, take it,' advances.
    And we, we bawl
To them in all our ways: 'I love you! Be mine, my all!'

You greet each other and you feign . . .
And teach each other all the arts;
Evade each other, and one starts
Picking up dumb, sad venal tarts;
    Then you complain
In verse and prose, instead of clasping hands again.

To clasp the hands, and no more spats!
Straight from the body, straight from the heart!
Too late! Both weak and strong apart
The scramble for hard sovereigns start . . .
    Poor Earth! But that's
Human History: story that's *one* celibate's . . .

XXI DIMANCHES

Je ne tiens que des mois, des journées et des heures . . .
Dès que je dis oui! tout feint l'en-exil . . .
    Je cause de fidèles demeures,
        On me trouve bien subtil;
        Oui ou non, est-il
D'autres buts que les mois, les journées et les heures?

L'âme du Vent gargouille au fond des cheminées . . .
    L'âme du Vent se plaint à sa façon;
    Vienne Avril de la prochaine année
        Il aura d'autres chansons! . . .
        Est-ce une leçon,
Ô Vent qui gargouillez au fond des cheminées?

Il dit que la Terre est une simple légende
    Contée au Possible par l'Idéal . . .
    – Eh bien, est-ce un sort, je vous l' demande?
        – Oui, un sort! car c'est fatal.
        – Ah! ah! pas trop mal,
Le jeu de mots! – mais folle, oh! folle, la Légende . . .

XXI SUNDAYS

I'm only keeping now the months, the days, the hours . . .
　　All fakes the in-exile since I said yes . . .
　　　　I chat about faithful bowers;
　　　　　　They see I have finesse;
　　　　　　　　Yes or no express,
But are there other ends than months, the days, the hours?

The soul of the Wind gargles in the chimney flues . . .
　　After its fashion, moans like anything;
　　　　Come April next he'll choose
　　　　　　Another song to sing! . . .
　　　　　　　　A lessoning,
Is that? O Wind, that gargles in the chimney flues?

The Earth is a simple legend, so he stated,
　　The Ideal to the Possible has spun . . .
　　　　– I ask you: Is this fated?
　　　　　　– Yes, fate! Since fatal. – Pun,
　　　　　　　　Not a bad one,
The word-play! – But mad, ah mad, the Legend stated . . .

XXII   LE BON APÔTRE

Nous avons beau baver nos plus fières salives,
Leurs yeux sont tout! Ils rêvent d'aumônes furtives!

Ô chairs de sœurs, ciboires de bonheur! On peut
Blaguer, la paire est là; comme un et un font deux.

– Mais ces yeux, plus on va, se fardent de mystère!
– Eh bien, travaillons à les ramener sur Terre!

– Ah! la chasteté n'est en fleur qu'en souvenir!
– Mais ceux qui l'ont cueillie en renaissent martyrs!

Martyres mutuels! de frère à sœur, sans Père!
Comment ne voit-on pas que c'est là notre terre?

Et qu'il n'y a que ça! que le reste est impôts
Dont nous n'avons pas même à chercher l'à-propos!

Il faut répéter ces choses! Il faut qu'on tette
Ces choses! jusqu'à ce que la Terre se mette,

Voyant enfin que Tout vivotte sans Témoin,
À vivre aussi pour Elle, et dans son petit coin!

Et c'est bien dans ce sens, moi, qu'au lieu de me taire,
Je persiste à narrer mes petites affaires.

XXII   THE GOOD APOSTLE

We have to drool our haughtiest saliva in vain;
Their eyes are everything. They dream of furtive gain.

O sister bodies, cibories of joy! And you
Could cod: it's down to pairs; as one and one make two.

– Those eyes, though, the more one lives, doll up their mystique.
– Well, then, let's work to bring them down to Earth some week!

– Ah! chastity is not in flower but memory's head!
– But those who've picked it are born again in martyrs' red!

Mutual martyrdoms! brother to sister without Father!
Why don't we see our Earth lies there, without palaver?

And that it's all there is! The rest just tax to pay
And tax for which we never meet the final day!

One must repeat these things and drain the issue dry
Until the Earth eventually may go and try,

Seeing the Whole is scraping by without a Witness,
To live for just Herself on her own patch and fitness.

So, it's on this understanding I won't stay mute
But of my own affairs keep telling the whole shoot!

XXIII   PETITES MISÈRES D'OCTOBRE

Octobre m'a toujours fiché dans la détresse;
Les Usines, cent goulots fumant vers les ciels ...
    Les poulardes s'engraissent
      Pour Noël.

Oh! qu'alors, tout bramant vers d'albes atavismes,
Je fonds mille Icebergs vers les septentrions
    D'effarants mysticismes
      Des Sions! ...

Car les seins distingués se font toujours plus rares;
Le légitime est tout, mais à qui bon ma cour?
    De qui bénir mes Lares
      Pour toujours?

Je ferai mes oraisons aux Premières Neiges;
Et je crierai au Vent: «Et toi aussi, forçat!»
    Et rien ne vous allège
      Comme ça.

(Avec la Neige, tombe une miséricorde
D'agonie; on a vu des gens aux cœurs de cuir
    Et méritant la corde
      S'en languir.)

Mais vrai, s'écarteler les lobes, jeu de dupe ...
Rien, partout, des saisons et des arts et des dieux,
    Ne vaut deux sous de jupe,
      Deux sous d'yeux.

Donc, petite, deux sous de jupe en œillet tiède
Et deux sous de regards, et tout ce qui s'ensuit ...
    Car il n'est qu'un remède
      À l'ennui.

XXIII   PETTY MISERIES OF OCTOBER

October's always landed me up in despair:
Factories, hundred gullets fuming skies grey . . .
      Pullets fattening fare
          For Christmas Day.

Oh, how, then, troating out to albescent atavisims
I melt a thousand Icebergs towards the northmost stars
      With frightening mysticisms
          From Sion spas!

For then outstanding breasts less often cross our path.
Legitimacy's all but whose good is my court for?
      Take whom to bless my Hearth
          For ever more?

So I will make my prayers unto the First of Snows;
And cry unto the Wind: 'And you, drudge, you too!'
      Nothing else lightens woes
          Like that for you.

(And with the Snow falls a mercy of death anguish;
You've seen the sort of people with their hearts of leather,
      Deserving more rope, languish
          At the end of their tether.)

True, quartering lobes is fool's play for a cert . . .
Nothing anywhere, arts, gods, seasons, skies,
      Is worth two penn'orth of skirt,
          Two penn'orth of eyes.

So now, two penn'orth of skirt, warm eyelets, sweet,
Two penn'orth of looks and all that follows it . . .
      As it's just physic to treat
          Ennui's fit.

XXIV   GARE AU BORD DE LA MER

Korsör. Côtes du Danemark
Aube du 1ᵉʳ janvier 1886

On ne voyait pas la mer, par ce temps d'embruns,
Mais on l'entendait maudire son existence,
«Oh! beuglait-elle, qu'il fût seulement Quelqu'Un!» . . .
Et elle vous brisait maint bateau pas-de-chance.

Et, ne pouvant mordre le steamer, les autans
Mettaient nos beaux panaches de fumée en loques!
Et l'Homme renvoyait ses comptes à des temps
Plus clairs, sifflotant: «Cet univers se moque,

«Il raille! Et qu'il me dise où l'on voit Mon Pareil!
Allez, boudez, chez vos parades sidérales,
Infini! Un temps viendra que l'Homme, fou d'éveil,
Fera pour les Pays Terre-à-Terre ses malles!

«Il crut à l'Idéal! Ah! milieux détraquants
Et bazars d'oripeaux! Si c'était à refaire,
Chers madrépores, comme on ficherait le camp
Chez vous! Oh! même vers la Période Glaciaire! . . .

«Mais l'Infini est là, gare de trains ratés,
Où les gens, aveuglés de signaux, s'apitoient
Sur le sanglot des convois, et vont se hâter
Tout à l'heure! et crever en travers de la voie . . .

«— Un fin sourire (tel ce triangle d'oiseaux
D'exil sur ce ciel gris!) peut traverser mes heures;
Je dirai: passe, oh! va, ne fais pas de vieux os
Par ici, mais vide au plus tôt cette demeure . . .»

Car la vie est partout la même. On ne sait rien!
Mais c'est la Gare! et faut chauffer qui pour les fêtes
Futures, qui pour les soi-disant temps anciens.
Oh! file ton rouet, et prie et reste honnête.

XXIV   STATION BESIDE THE SEA

Korsör. Coast of Denmark
Dawn, 1st January 1886

You couldn't clock the sea during this spell of spray
But heard it cursing its existence in the ruck:
'If only Someone had been there!' it groused away . . .
And smashed you up many a boat, the bad luck.

Failing to spike the steamer, the gales took its feathers,
Its splendid plumes of smoke and tore them into rags!
And Man shelving his reckonings till clearer weathers,
Was wheezing out: 'The universe just sneers and brags;

'It's mocking! means to tell me where to see my Peer!
Go on, Infinity, sulk with your astral marching bands,
A time is coming when Man packs his bags and gear,
Mad with his waking to it, for the Earth-Earthy Lands.

'He'd trusted the Ideal. Ah, stalls of such pinchbeck,
Bazaars of tawdry junk. If all were done again,
Dear madrepores, how we'd be upping sticks to trek
To you! Oh, even back towards the Ice Age, then . . .

'But there's Infinity, station of trains missed,
Where people, blind to signals, commiserate
With sobs of carriages and at their speediest,
Rush off at once – to snuff it crossing lines too late.

'– A fine smile (such as, on this sky's grey tones,
That triangle of exile birds) could cross my time;
I'll say: shift, oh, leave, don't turn a bag of bones
This way but quit this dwelling soonest, in your prime.'

For life is everywhere the same. Nothing you know!
Here's Action Station; some must be fired for promised
Future festivals, and some for so-called long ago.
Oh well, spin your wheel, and pray and stay honest.

XXV   IMPOSSIBILITÉ DE L'INFINI EN HOSTIES

Ô lait divin! potion assurément cordiale
À vomir les gamelles de nos aujourd'huis!
Quel bon docteur saura décrocher ta timbale
Pour la poser sur ma simple table de nuit,
      Un soir, sans bruit?

J'ai appris, et tout comme autant de riches langues
Les philosophies et les successives croix;
Mais pour mener ma vie au Saint-Graal sans gangue,
Nulle n'a su le mot, le Sésame-ouvre-toi,
      Clef de l'endroit.

Oui, dilapidé ma jeunesse et des bougies
À regalvaniser le fond si enfantin
De nos plus immémoriales liturgies,
Et perdu à ce jeu de purs et sûrs instincts,
      Tout mon latin.

L'Infini est à nos portes! à nos fenêtres!
Ouvre, et vois ces Nuits Loin, et tout le Temps avec!...
Qu'il nous étouffe donc! puisqu'il ne saurait être
En une hostie, une hostie pour nos sales becs,
      Ah! si à sec!...

XXV   IMPOSSIBILITY OF INFINITY IN WAFERS

O milk divine, undoubted cordial to make
Us vomit up our mess-tin days! What able
Doctor will know quite how to take your cake
And one night stick it on my bedside table
     Soundlessly, stable?

I've learnt, in tongues all equally rich,
Philosophies, successive cross on cross,
But none knew the Open-you-Sesame which
Would lead me to the Grail without the dross,
     Key to the gloss.

Yes, I have squandered youth and chandleries
Regalvanising the so child-like deeps
Of our more immemorial liturgies,
Lost in that pure sure instinct game for keeps
     My Latin, heaps.

It's at our windows, doors, Infinity!
Open, see Far those Nights, all Time beside!
May it choke us then, not deigning to be
In one wafer, one, for our foul gobs wide.
     Ah, but if dried! . . .

XXVI BALLADE

> OPHELIA: *You are merry, my lord.*
> HAMLET: *Who, I?*
> OPHELIA: *Ay, my lord.*
> HAMLET: *O God, your only jigmaker.* What
> should a man do but be merry?

Oyez, au physique comme au moral,
Ne suis qu'une colonie de cellules
De raccroc; et ce sieur que j'intitule
Moi, n'est, dit-on, qu'un polypier fatal!

De mon cœur un tel, à ma chair védique,
Comme de mes orteils à mes cheveux,
Va-et-vient de cellules sans aveu,
Rien de bien solvable et rien d'authentique.

Quand j'organise une descente en Moi,
J'en conviens, je trouve là, attablée,
Une société un peu bien mêlée,
Et que je n'ai point vue à mes octrois.

Une chair bêtement staminifère,
Un cœur illusoirement pistillé,
Sauf certains soirs, sans foi, ni loi, ni clé,
Où c'est précisément tout le contraire.

Allez, c'est bon. Mon fatal polypier
A distingué certaine polypière;
Son monde n'est pas trop mêlé, j'espère . . .
Deux yeux café, voilà tous ses papiers.

XXVI   BALLAD

> OPHELIA: *You are merry, my lord.*
> HAMLET: *Who, I?*
> OPHELIA: *Ay, my lord.*
> HAMLET: *O God, your only jigmaker. What should a man do but be merry?*

Oyez: alike, physical and moral spheres:
I'm just a flukish colony of cells;
And this liege lord I title Me, this swell's
Just a fatal polypary, it appears.

From So-and-So my heart to vedic tissue,
And likewise from my toes up to my hair,
Cells of no fixed address in thoroughfare,
Nothing authentic, no tenderable issue.

When I prepare for a descent in Me,
I convene them, find there at the table sat
A society, a trifle mixed at that,
I've not seen at my toll-gates pay their fee.

A body brutishly staminiferous,
A heart with pistils grown illusorily,
Save certain evenings: no faith, no law, no key,
Where it's precisely the contrarious.

Ah, now, that's good. My fatal polypary
Has noticed there a certain polyparess;
Her world, I hope, is not too mixed a mess.
Two coffee eyes, they're her passport to me.

XXVII   PETITES MISÈRES D'HIVER

Vers les libellules
D'un crêpe si blanc des baisers
Qui frémissent de se poser,
Venus de si loin, sur leurs bouts cicatrisés,
Ces seins, déjà fondants, ondulent
D'un air somnambule . . .

Et cet air enlise
Dans le défoncé des divans
Rembourrés d'eiders dissolvants
Le Cygne du Saint-Graal, qui rame en avant!
Mais plus pâle qu'une banquise
Qu'Avril dépayse . . .

Puis, ça vous réclame,
Avec des moues d'enfant goulu,
Du romanesque à l'absolu,
Mille Pôles plus loin que tout ce qu'on a lu! . . .
Laissez, laissez le Cygne, ô Femme!
Qu'il glisse, qu'il rame,

Oh! que, d'une haleine,
Il monte, séchant vos crachats,
Au Saint-Graal des blancs pachas,
Et n'en revienne qu'avec un plan de rachat
Pour sa petite sœur humaine
Qui fait tant de peine . . .

XXVII   PETTY MISERIES OF WINTER

To the dragonflies
Of a crape blank white of kisses
That are trembling to land their blisses,
Come from so far away, upon their cicatrices,
These breasts, softening in sighs,
Sway, sleepwalker-wise . . .

And this guise sinks low
In the cracking-up of settees,
Padded with eiderdowny ease,
The Grail Swan who rows ahead though he's
Paler than some stateless floe
In April overthrow . . .

Since he recalls you so
With childish greedy sulks to head
From romance to absolute instead,
Some thousand Poles off all that has been read! . . .
Oh, Woman, let the Swan now go,
Let him glide, let him row,

Oh, with a breath's disdain,
Soar away – and dry your spittle –
To the Grail of white pashas ripple,
Only to come back with a plan to save his little
Human sister once again
Who gives us so much pain . . .

XXVIII DIMANCHES

HAMLET: *Lady, shall I lie in your lap?*
(Il s'agenouille devant Ophélie.)
OPHELIA: *No, my lord.*
HAMLET: *I mean, my head in your lap?*
OPHELIA: *Ay, my lord.*
HAMLET: *Do you think I meant country matters?*
OPHELIA: *I think nothing, my lord.*
HAMLET: *That's a fair thought to lie between a maid's legs.*
OPHELIA: *What is, my lord?*
HAMLET: *Nothing.*

Les nasillardes cloches des dimanches
          À l'étranger,
Me font que j'ai de la vache enragée
Pour jusqu'à la nuit, sur la planche;
Je regarde passer des tas de robes blanches.

La jeune fille au joli paroissien
          Rentre au logis;
Son corps se sent l'âme fort reblanchie,
Et, raide, dit qu'il appartient
À une tout autre race que le mien!

Ma chair, ô Sœur, a bien mal à son âme.
          Oh! ton piano
Me recommence! et ton cœur s'y ânonne
          En ritournelles si infâmes,
Et ta chair, sur quoi j'ai des droits! s'y pâme . . .

Que je te les tordrais avec plaisir,
          Ce cœur, ce corps!
Et te dirais leur fait! et puis encore
          La manière de s'en servir!
Si tu voulais ensuite m'approfondir . . .

XXVIII   SUNDAYS

> HAMLET: *Lady, shall I lie in your lap?*
> (He kneels in front of Ophelia.)
> OPHELIA: *No, my lord.*
> HAMLET: *I mean, my head in your lap?*
> OPHELIA: *Ay, my lord.*
> HAMLET: *Do you think I meant country matters?*
> OPHELIA: *I think nothing, my lord.*
> HAMLET: *That's a fair thought to lie between a maid's legs.*
> OPHELIA: *What is, my lord?*
> HAMLET: *Nothing.*

The nasal bells of Sundays abroad
          Makes me rough it,
    On wild oats, cowed, and to stuff it,
Till night, bored stiff with my board;
I gaze at heaps of white gowns passing like a horde.

    That girl with pretty missal, see,
          Goes in, home reached,
    Her body smells her soul well bleached
And, starched, says it must clearly be
In quite another race than are the likes of me.

    My body, Sister, in soul is bilious.
          Oh, your piano
    Restarts on me; your heart, hesitando,
          Falters in ritournelles so infamous,
Your body – where I have some rights! – is rapturous . . .

    How I would twist for you with pleasure
          That body, that heart!
    Tell you their function, then impart
          Their manner of use at leisure!
If you then studied me the same good measure . . .

XXIX   LE BRAVE, BRAVE AUTOMNE!

Quand reviendra l'automne,
Cette saison si triste,
Je vais m' la passer bonne,
Au point de vue artiste.

Car le vent, je l' connais,
Il est de mes amis!
Depuis que je suis né
Il fait que j'en gémis . . .

Et je connais la neige,
Autant que ma chair même,
Son froment me protège
Contre les chairs que j'aime . . .

Et comme je comprends
Que l'automnal soleil
Ne m'a l'air si souffrant
Qu'à titre de conseil! . . .

Puis rien ne saurait faire
Que mon spleen ne chemine
Sous les spleens insulaires
Des petites pluies fines . . .

Ah! l'automne est à moi,
Et moi je suis à lui,
Comme tout à «pourquoi?»
Et ce monde à «et puis?»

Quand reviendra l'automne,
Cette saison si triste,
Je vais m' la passer bonne,
Au point de vue artiste.

XXIX   THE DANDY, DANDY AUTUMN!

When autumn comes around,
That season of sad hues,
I'll spend it fairly sound
About artistic views.

As for the wind, I know
He's just another friend.
Since I began to grow
He's made me groan no end.

I know the snow's complexion
Like hand inside my glove,
Her wheat is my protection
From the flesh-tones I love . . .

How well I know the sun
Of the autumnal season
Seems such a suffering one
Only to counsel reason! . . .

So nothing has the means
To stop my spleen again
Trudging through insular spleens
Of light and gentle rain . . .

Ah, autumn's mine, and I,
Well, I am hers again,
As all belongs to 'Why?'
And this world to 'What then?'

When autumn comes around,
That season of sad hues,
I'll spend it fairly sound
About artistic views.

XXX   DIMANCHES

C'est l'automne, l'automne, l'automne . . .
Le grand vent et toute sa séquelle!
Rideaux tirés, clôture annuelle!
Chute des feuilles, des Antigones,
      Des Philomèles,
Le fossoyeur les remue à la pelle . . .

(Mais, je me tourne vers la mer, les Éléments!
Et tout ce qui n'a plus que les noirs grognements!
Ainsi qu'un pauvre, un pâle, un piètre individu
Qui ne croit en son Moi qu'à ses moments perdus . . .)

Mariage, ô dansante bouée
Peinte d'azur, de lait doux, de rose,
Mon âme de corsaire morose,
Va, ne sera jamais renflouée! . . .
      Elle est la chose
Des coups de vent, des pluies, et des nuées . . .

(Un soir, je crus en Moi! J'en faillis me fiancer!
Est-ce possible . . . Où donc tout ça est-il passé! . . .
Chez moi, c'est Galathée aveuglant Pygmalion!
Ah! faudrait modifier cette situation . . .)

XXX SUNDAYS

Autumn, autumn, autumn, it is . . .
The high wind, its motley parade!
The curtains drawn, close-down of trade!
Fall of the leaves, of Antigones,
        Of Philomels, spade
On spadeful, the digger rakes in all he's made.

(But me, I turn towards the sea, the Elements!
And all that only has its pitch-black discontents!
Just like some poor, some paltry, some pallid geezer, I'm
One who believes in his I just in his spare time . . .)

Marriage, O life-buoy dance,
Painted sky-blue, fresh milk and pink;
Morose corsair, my soul must sink,
Never to be refloated, no chance! . . .
        Flotsam of ink-
Black clouds, of blasts of wind, the rain's advance . . .

(One night I believed in Me: I failed to get engaged for it!
Is that possible . . . Where's it all gone then, that bit!
With me, it's Galatea, blinding Pygmalion's stares!
Ah, it's high time to modify this state of affairs . . .)

XXXI   PETITES MISÈRES D'AOÛT

Oh! quelle nuit d'étoiles, quelles saturnales!
　　Oh! mais des galas inconnus
　　　　Dans les annales
　　　　　　Sidérales!
　　Bref, un Ciel absolument nu!

　　Ô Loi du Rythme sans appel!
　　Que le moindre Astre certifie
　　Par son humble chorégraphie
　　Mais nul spectateur éternel.

　　　　Ah! la Terre humanitaire
　　　　N'en est pas moins terre-à-terre!
　　　　　　Au contraire.

　　　　La Terre, elle est ronde
　　　　Comme un pot-au-feu,
　　　　C'est un bien pauv' monde
　　　　Dans l'Infini bleu.

Cinq sens seulement, cinq ressorts pour nos Essors . . .
　　　　Ah! ce n'est pas un sort!
Quand donc nos cœurs s'en iront-ils en huit-ressorts! . . .

　　　　Oh! le jour, quelle turne!
　　　　J'en suis tout taciturne.
　　　　Oh! ces nuits sur les toits!
　　Je finirai bien par y prendre froid.

　　　　　Tiens, la Terre,
　　　　　Va te faire
　　　　　Très-lan laire!

　　　　– Hé! pas choisi
　　　　D'y naître, et hommes!
　　　　Mais nous y sommes,
　　　　Tenons-nous y!

XXXI   PETTY MISERIES OF AUGUST

Oh, what a night of stars, what saturnalian stages!
 Oh, indeed, what galas never viewed
  In the pages
   Of sidereal ages!
 In brief, a sky that's absolutely nude!

  Oh, Law of Rhythm without appeal!
  That the least star attests to be
  Through its lowly choreography
  But no eternal watcher's real.

   Ah, Earth, human and worthy,
   Is no less of the earth earthy.
    On the contrary, turfy!

   The Earth is round in girth
   As a stockpot of stew,
   A really poor ol' earth
   In the Infinite blue.

Five senses solely, five springs for us to stretch our wings . . .
 Ah, not much of a lot that brings!
So when'll our hearts go off in eight-league boots with springs?

   Oh, dawn, what a tip!
   'S quite buttoned up my lip.
   These nights out on the tiles!
 I'll catch a right cold one of these whiles.

   Oh, Earth, get you
   To Timbuctoo,
   Shift yourself, shoo!

   – Hey! we didn't pick
   Being born and men!
   But here we are then,
   So here let us stick.

La pauvre Terre, elle est si bonne! . . .
Oh! désormais je m'y cramponne
De tous mes bonheurs d'autochtone.

Tu te pâmes, moi je me vautre.
Consolons-nous les uns les autres.

XXXII   SOIRS DE FÊTE

Je suis la Gondole enfant chérie
Qui arrive à la fin de la fête,
Pour je ne sais quoi, par bouderie,
(Un soir trop beau me monte à la tête!)

Me voici déjà près de la digue;
Mais la foule sotte et pavoisée,
Ah! n'accourt pas à l'Enfant Prodigue!
Et danse, sans perdre une fusée . . .

Ah! c'est comme ça, femmes volages!
C'est bien. Je m'exile en ma gondole
(Si frêle!) aux mouettes, aux orages,
Vers les malheurs qu'on voit au Pôle!

– Et puis, j'attends sous une arche noire . . .
Mais nul ne vient; les lampions s'éteignent;
Et je maudits la nuit et la gloire!
Et ce cœur qui veut qu'on me dédaigne!

Poor Earth, she's such a tonic! . . .
So, I'll cling on something chronic
With all my happiness autochthonic.

You get enrapt and me I'll revel.
Let's comfort each other on the level.

XXXII   FESTIVE EVENINGS

I am the Gondola Dear Child that skulks
In on the celebrations going dead,
Why I don't really know, perhaps the sulks,
(Too fine an evening gone straight to my head!)

And here I am already at the pier
And yet the multitude, decked out and blockhead,
Ah, doesn't mob the Child Prodigy here!
But dances on, not missing a single rocket . . .

That's how it is, the women flighty forms!
Well, good. I'll exile me by gondola, sole,
(So frail!) and with the seagulls and the storms,
Towards misfortunes seen around the Pole!

– And yet I lurk beneath a gloomy arch . . .
But no one comes; the coloured lights have waned;
And so I curse the night and glory's march!
And this heart, too, for wanting me disdained!

XXXIII   FIFRE

> OPHELIA: *You are keen, my lord, you are keen.*
> HAMLET: *It would cost you a groaning to take off my edge.*
> OPHELIA: *Still better and worse.*
> HAMLET: *So you must take your husbands.*

Pour un cœur authentique,
Me ferais des blessures!
Et ma Littérature
    Fermerait boutique.

Oh! qui me ravira!
C'est alors qu'on verra
Si je suis un ingrat!

Ô petite âme brave,
Ô chair fière et si droite!
C'est moi, que je convoite
    D'être votre esclave!

(Oui, mettons-nous en frais,
Et nous saurons après
Traiter de gré à gré.)

– «Acceptez, je vous prie,
Ô Chimère fugace
Au moins la dédicace
    De ma vague vie? . . .»

«Vous me dites avoir
Le culte du Devoir?
Et moi donc! venez voir . . .»

XXXIII FIFE

> OPHELIA: *You are keen, my lord, you are*
> *keen.*
>   HAMLET: *It would cost you a groaning to take*
> *off my edge.*
>   OPHELIA: *Still better and worse.*
>   HAMLET: *So you must take your husbands.*

For an authentic heart-swap
I'd bleed from wounds self-cut!
And my Scribblery shut
      Up shop.

Oh, who will ravish me!
It's then that they would see
If I'm some heartless he!

O little soul so brave,
Body so proud and straight!
It's me; how I lust to wait
      Upon you as your slave!

(Yes, let's take some trouble
Then we'll know how to couple
Pleasure to pleasure double.)

– 'Would you accept from me,
Oh, Fancy on the wing,
The dedication offering
      My vague biography? . . .'

'You bid me have the Duty
Cult for you, absolutely?
Me, too! Come, see, my beauty! . . .

XXXIV   DIMANCHES

> HAMLET: *I have heard of your paintings too,*
> *well enough.* God hath given you one face, and
> *you make yourselves another; you jig, you*
> *amble and you lisp, and nickname God's*
> *creatures, and make your wantonness your*
> *ignorance.* Go to; I'll no more on't; it hath
> *made me mad. To a nunnery, go.*

N'achevez pas la ritournelle,
En prêtant au piano vos ailes,
Ô mad'moiselle du premier.
Ça me rappelle l'Hippodrome,
Où cet air cinglait un pauvre homme
Déguisé en clown printanier.

Sa perruque arborait des roses,
Mais, en son masque de chlorose,
Le trèfle noir manquait de nez!
Il jonglait avec des cœurs rouges
Mais sa valse trinquait aux bouges
Où se font les enfants mort-nés.

Et cette valse, ô mad'moiselle,
Vous dit les Roland, les dentelles
Du bal qui vous attend ce soir!...
– Ah! te pousser par tes épaules
Décolletées, vers de durs pôles
Où je connais un abattoir!

Là, là, je te ferai la honte!
Et je te demanderai compte
De ce corset cambrant tes reins,
De ta tournure et des frisures
Achalandant contre-nature
Ton front et ton arrière-train.

XXXIV   SUNDAYS

> HAMLET: *I have heard of your paintings too,*
> *well enough. God hath given you one face, and*
> *you make yourselves another; you jig, you*
> *amble and you lisp, and nickname God's*
> *creatures, and make your wantonness your*
> *ignorance. Go to; I'll no more on't; it hath*
> *made me mad. To a nunnery, go.*

The ritournelle you mustn't cease;
The piano's soaring with your piece;
Young lady of the sixth form, play.
It brings to mind the Hippodrome
Where this tune stung a wretch's dome
Disguised as spring clown for a day.

His periwig was sporting roses
But on his mask, green with chlorosis,
The black clover failed as nose!
He juggled with red hearts in fives
But his waltz hobnobbed in low dives
Where still-born kids themselves compose.

That very waltz, young lady, trills
Of Rolands and the ball-gown frills
That wait for you this very night! . . .
To steer your shoulders, neck-line low,
Towards the sternest poles they'll go;
I know a shambles there all right.

There, there, I'll make you feel such shame!
I'll ask the cost of stays that frame
Your hollowed back, the bustle's bill,
The price of curls that tote for trade
Your brow and rump on this parade
Against the use of nature still.

Je te crierai: «Nous sommes frères!
Alors, vêts-toi à ma manière,
Ma manière ne trompe pas;
Et perds ce dandinement louche
D'animal lesté de ses couches,
Et galopons par les haras!»

Oh! vivre uniment autochtones
Sur cette terre (où nous cantonne
Après tout notre être tel quel!)
Et sans préférer, l'âme aigrie,
Aux vers luisants de nos prairies
Les lucioles des prés du ciel;

Et sans plus sangloter aux heures
De lendemains, vers des demeures
Dont nous nous sacrons les élus.
Ah! que je vous dis, autochtones!
Tant la vie à terre elle est bonne
Quand on n'en demande pas plus.

'We're brothers, girl,' I'll cry to you,
'So dress yourself the way I do.
My style does not deceive and faze.
And drop this crafty tittuping
Of beasts worn out with littering,
Let's gallop down the bridle-ways!'

Oh, live even stevens, autochthonous
On earth (where all there is of us,
Such as we are, is billeted.)
And not prefer, with soured soul,
To glow-worms where our prairies roll
The fireflies of heaven lea instead;

Without more sobbing in the days
After for dwelling place and ways
Where we ordain ourselves elect.
Ah, as I tell you, autochthonous,
Since life on earth is good to us
When that is all that you expect.

XXXV L'AURORE-PROMISE

Vois, les Steppes stellaires
Se dissolvent à l'aube . . .
La Lune est la dernière
À s'effacer, badaude.

Oh! que les cieux sont loin, et tout! Rien ne prévaut!
Contre cet infini; c'est toujours trop nouveau! . . .

Et vrai, c'est sans limites! . . .
T'en fais-tu une idée,
Ô jeune Sulamite
Vers l'aurore accoudée?

L'Infini à jamais! comprends-tu bien cela?
Et qu'autant que ta chair existe un au-delà?

Non; ce sujet t'assomme.
Ton Infini, ta sphère,
C'est le regard de l'Homme,
Patron de cette Terre.

Il est le Fécondeur, le Galant Chevalier
De tes couches, la Providence du Foyer!

Tes yeux baisent Sa Poigne,
Tu ne te sens pas seule!
Mais lui bat la campagne
Du ciel, où nul n'accueille! . . .

Nulle Poigne vers lui, il a tout sur le dos;
Il est seul; l'Infini reste sourde comme un pot.

Ô fille de la Terre,
Ton dieu est dans ta couche!
Mais lui a dû s'en faire,
Et si loin de sa bouche! . . .

XXXV   THE PROMISED DAWN

The stellar steppes, watch,
Dissolving into dawn . . .
The Moon's the last to scotch
Herself, the idle gawk.

Oh, how far away the skies, and total. Nothing will do
Against that infinity; it's always much too new.

It's limitless, all right! . . .
Have you guessed at its size,
O young Shulamite,
On elbows leant to the rise?

Infinity forever! D'you understand that ponder:
That there exists, as much as your flesh does, a yonder?

No; the topic bores you:
Your Infinite, your sphere,
The glance of Man absorbs you,
Boss of this Earth here.

He is the Fecundator, the Gallant Cavalier
Of all your labour, Providence of the Hearth, Good Cheer!

Your eyes kiss his Push,
You feel you're not alone!
– He beats about the bush
Of heaven where welcome's none! . . .

No Push helps him; everything on his back he's got;
He is alone; Infinity stays deaf as a pot.

O daughter of the Earth,
Your god is in your bed,
But he must prove his worth –
And so far from her head! . . .

Il s'est fait de bons dieux, consolateurs des morts.
Et supportait ainsi tant bien que mal son sort,

Mais bientôt, son idée,
Tu l'as prise, jalouse!
Et l'as accommodée
Au culte de l'Épouse!

Et le Déva d'antan, Bon Cœur de l'Infini
Est là . . . – pour que ton lit nuptial soit béni!

Avec tes accessoires,
Ce n'est plus qu'une annexe
Du Tout-Conservatoire
Où s'apprête Ton Sexe.

Et ces autels bâtis de nos terreurs des cieux
Sont des comptoirs où tu nous marchandes tes yeux!

Les dieux s'en vont. Leur père
S'en meurt. – Ô Jeune Femme,
Refais-nous une Terre
Selon ton corps sans âme!

Ouvre-nous tout Ton Sexe! et, sitôt, l'Au-delà
Nous est nul! Ouvre, dis? tu nous dois bien cela . . .

He's made himself good gods, consolers of the dead,
And thus supported, as best he can, his fate ahead.

> But envious, soon his idea
> You took to like a house
> And made it reappear
> As the Cult of the Spouse.

And the Deva of yesteryear, the Infinite's Kind Heart
Attends . . . so that your nuptial bed be blest to start.

> With all your props and gear
> There's only one green room
> In the All-Conservatory here
> Where your sex rigs the womb.

And these altars, built of our terrors of the skies,
Are the shop counters where you sell to us your eyes!

> The gods have gone. Their father
> Is dying of it. – Oh, young Woman,
> Remake us an Earth but after
> Your unsouled body, human!

Open all Your Sex to us, and instantly the Beyond
Is nothing. Didn't I say open? You owe us – respond!

XXXVI DIMANCHES

J'aurai passé ma vie à faillir m'embarquer
    Dans de bien funestes histoires,
    Pour l'amour de mon cœur de Gloire!...
– Oh! qu'ils sont chers les trains manqués
Où j'ai passé ma vie à faillir m'embarquer!...

Mon cœur est vieux d'un tas de lettres déchirées,
    Ô Répertoire en un cercueil
    Dont la Poste porte le deuil!...
– Oh! ces veilles d'échauffourées
Où mon cœur s'entraînait par lettres déchirées!...

Tout n'est pas dit encor, et mon sort est bien vert.
    Ô Poste, automatique Poste,
    Ô yeux passants fous d'holocaustes,
    Oh! qu'ils sont là, vos airs ouverts!...
Oh! comme vous guettez mon destin encor vert!

        (Une, pourtant, je me rappelle,
            Aux yeux grandioses
            Comme des roses,
            Et puis si belle!...
            Sans nulle pose.

Une voix me criait: «C'est elle! Je le sens;
Et puis, elle te trouve si intéressant!»
– Ah! que n'ai-je prêté l'oreille à ses accents!...)

XXXVI   SUNDAYS

I shall have spent my life failing to embark
    On quite baneful story after story
    For the love in my heart of Glory! . . .
    – Oh, how dear the missed trains are
Where I have spent my life in failing to embark! . . .

My heart's grown old with a heap of torn-up letters,
    Repertory in a winding-sheet, ghost man,
    And in the mourning comes the Postman! . . .
    – Oh, such vigils over frays, vendettas
My heart drags through in a train of torn-up letters! . . .

All's not yet said; my fate's still green and fair.
    Oh, Post, Post automatically sent,
    O passing eyes that holocausts dement,
    Oh that it's come to that, your frank air! . . .
Oh, how you look out for my destiny still fair!

    (One, however, memorable,
        And grand eyes those
        Just like the rose,
        And beautiful! . . .
        Never a pose.

A voice was calling, 'She's the one! I know. For you!
And, furthermore, she finds you interesting, too.'
– Ah, if only I had lent an ear to that view.)

XXXVII   LA VIE QU'ELLES ME FONT MENER

Pas moi, despotiques Vénus
Offrant sur fond d'or le Lotus
Du Mal, coiffées à la Titus!
Pas moi, Circées
Aux yeux en grand deuil violet comme des pensées!
Pas moi, binious
Des Papesses des blancs Champs-Élysées des fous,
Qui vous relayez de musiques
Par le calvaire de techniques
Des sacrilèges domestiques!

Le mal m'est trop! tant que l'Amour
S'échange par le temps qui court
Simple et sans foi comme un bonjour,
Des jamais franches
À celles dont le Sort vient le poing sur la hanche,
Et que s'éteint
La Rosace du Temple, à voir, dans le satin,
Ces sexes livrés à la grosse
Courir, en valsant, vers la Fosse
Commune des Modernes Noces.

Ô Rosace! leurs charmants yeux
C'est des vains cadrans d'émail bleu
Qui marquent l'heure que l'on veut,
Non des pétales,
De ton Soleil des Basiliques Nuptiales!
Au premier mot,
Peut-être (on est si distinguée à fleur de peau!)
Elles vont tomber en syncope
Avec des regards d'antilope –
Mais tout leur être est interlope!

Tu veux pas fleurir fraternel?
C'est bon, on te prendra tel quel,
Petit mammifère usuel!
Même la blague

XXXVII   THE LIFE THEY LEAD ME

Not me, Despot Venuses, coiffure
À la Titus, the Evil Lotus you proffer
On its golden ground, no offer.
        Not me, Circeans,
With mourning-violet eyes like pansies, no liens.
        Not me, bagpipes
Of Popettes of white Champs Élysées of foolish types
        Whose renderings rest you through
        The calvary of techniques that do
        Such sacrilege against a two.

        The harm's too much for me! as long as Love
        Varies these days, no turtle-dove,
        Simple and faithless as good day, guv,
                From devious lips,
To those whose Fate comes, fist on hips,
                Whose Temple's Rose
Window fades away, to see, in satin, those
        Two sexes, plain as beasts behave,
        Run waltzing to the common Grave
        Of Modern Marriage that they crave.

        O Rose Window! Their charming gaze
        Is two vain dials of blue glaze;
        Whatever time you want they raise;
                They're no flowers
Of your own Sun with its Basilican Nuptial hours!
                At the first word's peep,
Perhaps (one is so awfully refined skin-deep!)
        They'll drop in a syncopal attack
        With antelopan looks all quack.
        Their whole being's dodgy tack.

        You don't want brotherly to bloom?
        Right then. Be taken as you presume,
        Little normal mammalian womb.
                Even that hoax

Me chaut peu de te passer au doigt une bague.
                    – Oh! quel grand deuil,
Pourtant! leur ferait voir leur frère d'un autre œil!
            Voir un égal d'amour en l'homme
            Et non une bête de somme
            Là pour lui remuer des sommes!

            Quoi? vais-je prendre un air géant,
            Et faire appeler le Néant?
            Non, non; ce n'est pas bienséant.
                    Je me promène
Parmi les sommités des colonies humaines;
                Du bout du doigt
Je feuillette les versions de l'Unique Loi,
            Et je vivotte, et m'inocule
            Les grands airs gris du crépuscule,
            Et j'en garule! et j'en garule!

Putting the ring on your finger only nearly chokes.
What deep mourning, my!
It would bring them seeing their brother with another eye.
See man in love an equal yet,
And not a beast of burden set
To hump what they lay out to get!

What, shall I assume giant role,
Invoke the Void as final goal?
No, no, unseemly on the whole.
I'll stroll the heights
Among the human colonies' leading lights.
I'll leaf and paw
Through versions of the One, the Unique Law,
And run along, inoculate
Myself with dusk's airs, grey and great,
And garrulate on it, garrulate!

XXXVIII   DIMANCHES

Mon Sort est orphelin, les Vêpres ont tu leurs cloches . . .
Et ces pianos qui ritournellent, jamais las! . . .
Oh! monter, leur expliquer mon apostolat!
Oh! du moins, leur tourner les pages, être là,
Les consoler! (J'ai des consolations plein les poches) . . .

Les pianos se sont clos. Un seul, en grand deuil, s'obstine . . .
Oh! qui que tu sois, sœur! à genoux, à tâtons,
Baiser le bas de ta robe dans l'abandon! . . .
Pourvu qu'après, tu me chasses, disant: «Pardon!
Pardon, m'sieu! mais j'en aime un autre, et suis sa cousine!»

Oh! que je suis bien infortuné sur cette Terre! . . .
Et puis si malheureux de ne pas être Ailleurs!
Ailleurs, loin de ce savant siècle batailleur . . .
C'est là que je m' créerai un petit intérieur,
Avec Une dont, comme de Moi, Tout n'a que faire.

Une maigre qui me parlait,
Les yeux hallucinés de Gloires virginales,
De rendre l'âme, sans scandale,
Dans un flacon de sels anglais . . .

Une qui me fît oublier
Mon art et ses rançons d'absurdes saturnales,
En attisant, gauche vestale,
L'Aurore dans mes oreillers . . .

Et que son regard
Sublime
Comme ma rime
Ne permît pas le moindre doute à cet égard.

XXXVIII   SUNDAYS

My fate's an orphan; Vesper bells have stilled in their sockets . . .
    And those pianos ritournelle and won't abate! . . .
      Oh, to go up, explain to them my apostolate!
      Or. oh, at least to turn the pages for them, wait
To console them! (I have consolations in all pockets) . . .

The pianos shut. One, in deep mourning slogs on a dozen . . .
    Oh, sister, whoever you may be, groping, kneeling
      I'd kiss your skirt hem in abandonment of feeling! . . .
      Provided that you shoo me off and tell me, reeling:
'Excuse me, sir, excuse me. I love another. My cousin!'

Oh, such misfortunes on this Earth have I been through! . . .
    What's more, had rotten luck, not being Elsewhere!
      Elsewhere, far off this stroppy era's know-all air . . .
      That's where I will create a little snug to share
With One who just like Me, All only has to do.

        A slight one who talked to me,
     Eyes hallucinated with virginal Glory
        To give the soul, no scandal story,
        In a phial of Epsom salts, scot-free . . .

        One who drove from my head
   My art, its crazy ransoms, saturnalian-festal,
        In stirring, gawky vestal,
        The dawn amid my bed . . .

          And one whose glance
            Sublime
           As my rime,
Let not the slightest doubt of that advance.

XXXIX   PETITES MISÈRES DE MAI

On dit: l'Express
Pour Bénarès!

La Basilique
Des gens cosmiques!...

Allons, chantons
Le Grand Pardon!

Allons, Tityres
Des blancs martyres!

Chantons: Nenni!
À l'Infini,

Hors des clôtures
De la Nature!

(Nous louerons Dieu,
En temps et lieu.)

Oh! les beaux arbres
En candélabres!...

Oh! les refrains
Des Pèlerins!...

Oh! ces toquades
De Croisades!...

— Et puis, fourbu
Dès le début.

Et retour louche...
— Ah! tu découches!

XXXIX   PETTY MISERIES OF MAY

You say: Express
To Benares, yes!

Cathedral Steeple
Of cosmic people! . . .

Sing, as we throng,
Full Pardon's Song.

Tityruses, white,
Martyrs, step light!

Let's sing: Get stewed!
At Infinitude,

Outside enclosures
Of Nature's imposures!

(We'll praise God's face
In time and space.)

Oh, lovely arbours
Like candelabras! . . .

Oh, the refrains
Of Pilgrim trains! . . .

And oh, the mad
Crusading fad! . . .

– One foundered hack'd
Started knackered.

Sneaked home again . . .
– Oh, sleep out, then?

XL   PETITES MISÈRES D'AUTOMNE

> HAMLET: *Get thee to a nunnery; why wouldst*
> *thou be a breeder of sinners? I am myself*
> *indifferent honest; but yet I could accuse me*
> *of such things, that it were better, my mother*
> *had not borne me, I am very proud, revengeful,*
> *ambitious; with more offences at my beck, than*
> *I have thoughts to put them in etc . . . to a*
> *nunnery.*

Je me souviens – dis, rêvé ce bal blanc?
Une, en robe rose et les joues en feu,
M'a tout ce soir-là dévoré des yeux,
Des yeux impérieux et puis dolents,
    (Je vous demande un peu!)

Car vrai, fort peu sur moi d'un en vedette,
Ah! pas plus ce soir-là d'ailleurs que d'autres,
Peut-être un peu mon natif air d'apôtre,
Empêcheur de danser en rond sur cette
    Scandaleuse planète.

Et, tout un soir, ces grands yeux envahis
De moi! Moi, dos voûté sous l'À quoi Bon?
Puis, partis, comme à jamais vagabonds!
(Peut-être en ont-ils peu après failli? . . .)
    Moi quitté le pays.

Chez nous, aux primes salves d'un sublime,
Faut battre en retraite. C'est sans issue.
Toi, pauvre, et t'escomptant déjà déçue
Par ce cœur (qui même eût plaint ton estime)
    J'ai été en victime,

En victime après un joujou des nuits!
Ses boudoirs pluvieux mirent en sang
Mon inutile cœur d'adolescent . . .
Et j'en dormis. À l'aube je m'enfuis . . .
    Bien égal aujourd'hui.

XL PETTY MISERIES OF AUTUMN

> HAMLET: *Get thee to a nunnery; why wouldst*
> *thou be a breeder of sinners? I am myself*
> *indifferent honest; but yet I could accuse me*
> *of such things, that it were better, my mother*
> *had not borne me, I am very proud, revengeful,*
> *ambitious; with more offences at my beck, than*
> *I have thoughts to put them in etc . . . to a*
> *nunnery.*

I recall this white ball – dreamed, do you say? –
One, in pink gown and cheeks burning bright,
Had with her eyes devoured me all that night,
Eyes first imperious then wheedling their way,
      (That takes believing all right!)

Not much of me suggests a name in lights,
No more that evening than any time elsewhere,
Perhaps a touch of my born apostle's air,
Killjoy of dancing in the ring that excites
      These scandalous planetites.

And, a whole evening, these big eyes invaded
With me! Me, doubled up with What's the Use?
Then, gone, as if forever on the loose.
(Perhaps they've missed it a bit, being raided?)
      Me, quit the field, unaided.

With us, at the first shots of a sublime do,
It's beat retreat. There's no way out of this.
You, wretched, and already feeling dis-
Appointed by this heart (that pitied you
      For your regard, all through),

I've been victim, victim, night on toying night!
Her rainy boudoirs targeting in blood
My useless heart, adolescent, dud . . .
I slept on it. At dawn I took to flight . . .
      But today I'm all right.

XLI   SANCTA SIMPLICITAS

Passants, m'induisez point en beautés d'aventure,
　　Mon Destin n'en saurait avoir cure;
Je ne peux plus m'occuper que des Jeunes Filles,
　　Avec ou sans parfum de famille.

Pas non plus mon chez moi, ces précaires liaisons,
　　Où l'on s'aime en comptant par saisons;
L'Amour dit légitime est seul solvable! car
　　Il est sûr de demain, dans son art.

Il a le Temps, qu'un grand amour toujours convie;
　　C'est la table mise pour la vie;
Quand demain n'est pas sûr, chacun se gare vite!
　　Et même, autant en finir tout de suite.

Oh! adjugés à mort! comme qui concluraient:
　　«D'avance, tout de toi m'est sacré,
Et vieillesse à venir, et les maux hasardeux!
　　C'est dit! Et maintenant, à nous deux!»

Vaisseaux brûlés! et, à l'horizon, nul divorce!
　　C'est ça qui vous donne de la force!
Ô mon seul débouché! – Ô mon vatout nubile!
　　À nous nos deux vies! Voici notre île.

XLI   SANCTA SIMPLICITAS

Strollers, don't lead me astray to casual beauties.
    My Destiny wouldn't care for such cuties.
No longer can I pass my time on girls,
    With or without the whiff of family pearls.

No longer my cup of tea, such weak liaisons,
    Where you love as the season makes occasions.
Love called legit's the only solvent part!
    As it's sure of tomorrow in its art.

It has the Time great passions always need;
    It's the table that's laid for life indeed.
When tomorrow's doubtful you dock double quick!
    And equally finish in a nick.

Oh, sentenced to death, like those come to agree:
    'From the outset each bit of you's sacred to me;
Old age to come, and ills out of the blue.
    It's all said and done. And now to us two.'

Boats burnt; and in the offing no divorce!
    That's what gives you the strength and the force!
My one chance, nubile all or nothing stake!
    Our two lives ours! Our isle, our lake!

XLII   ESTHÉTIQUE

La Femme mûre ou jeune fille,
J'en ai frôlé toutes les sortes,
Des faciles, des difficiles;
Voici l'avis que j'en rapporte:

C'est des fleurs diversement mises,
Aux airs fiers ou seuls selon l'heure;
Nul cri sur elles n'a de prise;
Nous jouissons, Elle demeure.

Rien ne les tient, rien ne les fâche,
Elles veulent qu'on les trouve belles,
Qu'on le leur râle et leur rabâche,
Et qu'on les use comme telles;

Sans souci de serments, de bagues,
Suçons le peu qu'elles nous donnent,
Notre respect peut être vague,
Leurs yeux sont haut et monotones.

Cueillons sans espoirs et sans drames,
La chair vieillit après les roses;
Oh! parcourons le plus de gammes!
Car il n'y a pas autre chose.

XLII AESTHETIC

Ripe woman or young girl,
I've had a touch of every sort,
The hard to lay, the easy whirl,
Here's the advice all that has brought:

They're flowers diversely worn pro tem,
To suit occasion, lone or aloof;
No cry has leverage on them;
We may possess but She stays proof.

Nothing holds them, nothing heats.
Lovely they'd like us think they are,
To parrot back and gasp repeats,
And treat them so beyond all par.

Without the fag of rings and vows
Let's drain the little they offer us.
A vague respect we'd maybe rouse:
Their eyes aloft, monotonous.

Without a hope or scene let's pick.
For like the rose, flesh withers too;
Let's run through most the range and quick,
For there is nothing else to do.

XLIII L'ÎLE

C'est l'Île; Éden entouré d'eau de tous côtés! . . .
Je viens de galoper avec mon Astarté
À l'aube des mers; on fait sécher nos cavales.
Des veuves de Titans délacent nos sandales,
Éventent nos tresses rousses, et je reprends
Mon Sceptre tout écaillé d'émaux effarants!
On est gai, ce matin. Depuis une semaine
Ces lents brouillards plongeaient mes sujets dans la peine,
Tout soupirants après un beau jour de soleil
Pour qu'on prît la photographie de Mon Orteil . . .

Ah! non, c'est pas cela, mon Île, ma douce île . . .
Je ne suis pas encore un Néron si sénile . . .
Mon île pâle est au Pôle, mais au dernier
Des Pôles, inconnu des plus fols baleiniers!
Les Icebergs entrechoqués s'avançant pâles
Dans les brumes ainsi que d'albes cathédrales
M'ont cerné sur un bloc; et c'est là que, très-seul,
Je fleuris, doux lys de la zone des linceuls,
Avec ma mie!

   Ma mie a deux yeux diaphanes
Et viveurs! et, avec cela, l'arc de Diane
N'est pas plus fier et plus hautement en arrêt
Que sa bouche! (arrangez cela comme pourrez . . .)
Oh! ma mie . . . – Et sa chair affecte un caractère
Qui n'est assurément pas fait pour me déplaire:
Sa chair est lumineuse et sent la neige, exprès
Pour que mon front pesant y soit toujours au frais,
Mon Front Équatorial! Serre d'Anomalies! . . .
Bref, c'est, au bas mot, une femme accomplie.

Et puis, elle a des perles tristes dans la voix . . .
Et ses épaules sont aussi de premier choix.
Et nous vivons ainsi, subtils et transis, presque
Dans la simplicité des gens peints sur les fresques.

XLIII   THE ISLE

This is the Isle; Eden with the sea on every side! . . .
With my Astarte I've just galloped on a ride
To watch the dawn at sea; our horses someone handles,
Widows of Titans undo the latchets of our sandals,
Fan out our auburn tresses; once again I grasp
My Sceptre, studded with emeralds that make one gasp.
This morning one is light of spirit. This last week
Some slow mists plunged my subjects into pain and pique,
In longing for a fine and sunny day to show
So they could take a photo of my great Big Toe! . . .

Ah, no, it's not like that, my Isle, my gentle isle . . .
I'm not a Nero yet sufficiently senile . . .
My pale isle's at the Pole, last of the unknown poles
Where even the maddest whalers never chased their shoals!
Icebergs jostling together there, advancing pallid
In mists, like albescent cathedrals sallied,
Surround me on a floe: it's there, that, most alone,
I flourish, sweet lily of the winding-sheets' dead zone
With my dear one.

                    My dear one's eyes are lively, clear,
And, with all that, Diana's bow would not appear
Haughtier or more proud in speaking judgment than
Her mouth! (Arrange that in whatever way you can . . .)
Oh, my dear one . . . – And her body has a character
Assuredly not made to displease me in her.
Her skin is luminous and feels like snow, expressly
So that my heavy brow may always lie there, freshly,
My Equatorial Brow, my Hothouse of Anomalies! . . .
In brief, and truly, an accomplished woman she is.

And, more: she has the sadness of pearls in her voice . . .
And then, her shoulders are of the very first choice.
And so we live like this, subtle, frigid, rurals
With almost the simplicity of folk in murals.

Et c'est l'Île. Et voilà vers quel Eldorado
L'Exode nihiliste a poussé mon radeau.

Ô lendemains de noce où nos voix mal éteintes
Chantent aux échos blancs la si grêle complainte:

LE VAISSEAU FANTÔME

Il était un petit navire
Où Ugolin mena ses fils,
Sous prétexte, le vieux vampire!
De les fair' voyager gratis.

Au bout de cinq à six semaines,
Les vivres vinrent à manquer,
Il dit: «Vous mettez pas en peine,
Mes fils n' m'ont jamais dégoûté!»

On tira z' à la courte paille,
Formalité! raffinement!
Car cet homme il n'avait d'entrailles
Qu' pour en calmer les tiraill'ments,

Et donc, stoïque et légendaire,
Ugolin mangea ses enfants,
Afin d' leur conserver un père . . .
Oh! quand j'y song', mon cœur se fend!

Si cette histoire vous embête,
C'est que vous êtes un sans-cœur!
Ah! j'ai du cœur par d'ssus la tête,
Oh! rien partout que rir's moqueurs! . . .

And that's the Isle. To that Eldorado, thus staffed,
The Nihilistic Exodus has driven my raft.

O mornings after wedding-feasts our voices, hardly faint,
Sing to the blank-white echoes this high-pitched complaint:

THE GHOST SHIP (THE FLYING DUTCHMAN)

Now once there was a tiny lugger
Where Ugolino shipped his sons
Pretending, the old vampire bugger,
There was no charge for little ones.

And after five weeks passed, or six,
Supplies ran short far out to sea.
He said, 'Don't panic in this fix,
My sons, you've never disgusted me!'

They drew lots for the final meal.
Appearance sake! Sophistication!
For that man had no pangs to feel
Except for hunger's alleviation.

So, legendary and stoic, rather,
He ate his every single son
Just to ensure they'd have a father.
It breaks my heart to hear this one!

And if this tale makes you see red
It shows that you have little heart.
Myself, I've heart above my head.
Oh! only jeers from every part!

XLIV DIMANCHES

LAERTES to Ophelia:
The chariest maid is prodigal enough
If she unmask her beauty to the moon.

J'aime, j'aime de tout mon siècle! cette hostie
Féminine en si vierge et destructible chair
Qu'on voit, au point du jour, altièrement sertie
Dans de cendreuses toilettes déjà d'hiver,
Se fuir le long des cris surhumains de la mer!

(Des yeux dégustateurs âpres à la curée;
Une bouche à jamais cloîtrée!)

(– Voici qu'elle m'honore de ses confidences;
J'en souffre plus qu'elle ne pense!)

– Chère perdue, comment votre esprit éclairé,
Et ce stylet d'acier de vos regards bleuâtres
N'ont-ils pas su percer à jour la mise en frais
De cet économique et passager bellâtre? . . .
– Il vint le premier; j'étais seule devant l'âtre . . .

Hier l'orchestre attaqua
Sa dernière polka.

Oh! l'automne, l'automne!
Les casinos
Qu'on abandonne
Remisent leurs pianos! . . .

Phrases, verroteries,
Caillots de souvenirs.
Oh! comme elle est maigrie!
Que vais-je devenir . . .

Adieu! les files d'ifs dans les grisailles
Ont l'air de pleureuses de funérailles
Sous l'autan noir qui veut que tout s'en aille.

XLIV SUNDAYS

LAERTES to Ophelia:
The chariest maid is prodigal enough
If she unmask her beauty to the moon.

I love! I love with all my century this host,
Feminine, flesh so destructible, such chastity,
You see at daybreak, dodge each other on the coast –
Aloofly set in cindery garb for the winter to be –
Dashing beside the superhuman cries of the sea.

(Those eyes, samplers, gold-diggers after ore,
   Mouth cloistered for ever more.)

(– Here's one who honours me with confidences.
   I suffer for it more than she senses.)

– Dear lostling, why didn't your enlightened soul
And that steel stylet of your blue-grey eye
Know how to needle into open-work the whole
Expenditure of this miserly dandy fleeting by? . . .
– He came first; alone beside the hearth was I . . .

      The orchestra attacked yesterday
      The last polka it would play.

      Oh, autumn, autumn once more!
         The casinos lock
         Their pianos in store,
      Deserted round the clock! . . .

      Phrases, trinketry,
      Clots of memories,
      What's to become of me? . . .
      Oh, how slight she is!

Goodbye; the files of yews in their tints of grey
Appear to be the funeral mutes who mourn the day
Beneath the black south wind that wants it all away.

Assez, assez,
C'est toi qui as commencé.

Va, ce n'est plus l'odeur de tes fourrures.
Va, vos moindres clins d'yeux sont des parjures.
Tais-toi, avec vous autres rien ne dure.

Tais-toi, tais-toi.
On n'aime qu'une fois.

XLV   NOTRE PETITE COMPAGNE

Si mon Air vous dit quelque chose,
Vous auriez tort de vous gêner;
Je ne la fais pas à la pose;
Je suis La Femme, on me connaît.

Bandeaux plats ou crinière folle,
Dites? quel Front vous rendrait fou?
J'ai l'art de toutes les écoles,
J'ai des âmes pour tous les goûts.

Cueillez la fleur de mes visages,
Buvez ma bouche et non ma voix,
Et n'en cherchez pas davantage . . .
Nul n'y vit clair; pas même moi.

Nos armes ne sont pas égales,
Pour que je vous tende la main,
Vous n'êtes que de naïfs mâles,
Je suis l'Éternel Féminin!

Mon But se perd dans les Étoiles! . . .
C'est moi qui suis la Grande Isis!
Nul ne m'a retroussé mon voile.
Ne songez qu'à mes oasis . . .

Enough! Enough!
You started on this stuff.

Right then, it's no longer the scent of your furs.
Right, the least glints in your eyes are perjurers.
Shut up, nothing ever lasts with you characters.

Shut up. Shut up, do.
Once love comes to you.

XLV   OUR LITTLE COMPANION

And if my Bearing tells you a thing,
Any embarassment would be wrong;
I don't go in for posturing;
For I am Woman, known all along.

Broad bandeaux, wild mop or pile,
Say, which Forehead drives you mad?
I have the art for every style,
I've souls enough for every fad.

Gather the flower of my faces,
Thirst for my mouth, my voice leave be.
Never seek there a deeper basis . . .
None sees clear there, not even me.

Your arms aren't equal in the scales,
For me to give my hand, give in,
You're just a bunch of naive males,
I'm the Eternal Feminine!

My Aim is lost in Stellar Space! . . .
The Great Isis I am, supreme!
None lifts the veil to see my face.
Of my oases only dream . . .

Si mon Air vous dit quelque chose,
Vous auriez tort de vous gêner;
Je ne la fais pas à la pose:
Je suis La Femme! on me connaît.

XLVI COMPLAINTE DES CRÉPUSCULES CÉLIBATAIRES

C'est l'existence des passants . . .
Oh! tant d'histoires personnelles! . . .
Qu'amèrement intéressant
De se navrer de leur kyrielle!

Ils s'en vont flairés d'obscurs chiens,
Ou portent des paquets, ou flânent . . .
Ah! sont-ils assez quotidiens,
Tueurs de temps et monomanes,

Et lorgneurs d'or comme de strass
Aux quotidiennes devantures! . . .
La vitrine allume son gaz,
Toujours de nouvelles figures . . .

Oh! que tout m'est accidentel!
Oh! j'ai-t-y l'âme perpétuelle! . . .
Hélas, dans ce cas, rien de tel
Que de pleurer une infidèle! . . .

Mais qu'ai-je donc laissé là-bas,
Rien. Eh! voilà mon grand reproche!
Ô culte d'un Dieu qui n'est pas
Quand feras-tu taire tes cloches! . . .

And if my Bearing tells you a thing,
Any embarrassment would be wrong;
I don't go in for posturing;
For I am Woman, known all along.

XLVI COMPLAINT OF CELIBATE DUSKS

There's the existence of others passing . . .
So many personal histories! . . .
How bitterly interesting, asking
Yourself to suffer their litanies!

They go off scared by unseen dogs,
Carry their parcels, loaf and slack . . .
Ah, have they routine enough logs,
Killers of time, monomaniac,

Oglers equally of gold or strass
In quotidian shop-fronts arranged! . . .
The glass illuminates its gas,
The figures always chopped and changed.

Oh, to me, it's all peripheral!
That's the perpetual soul of me! . . .
Alas, then, nothing's comparable
To weeping an unfaithful she! . . .

But what have I left out there,
Nothing. Huh, that's my great rebuke!
Cult of a God who is nowhere
When will you hush your bells, you spook! . . .

Je vague depuis le matin,
En proie à des loisirs coupables,
Épiant quelque grand destin
Dans l'œil de mes douces semblables . . .

Oh! rien qu'un lâche point d'arrêt
Dans mon destin qui se dévide! . . .
Un amour pour moi tout exprès
En un chez nous de chrysalide! . . .

Un simple cœur, et des regards
Purs de tout esprit de conquête,
Je suis si exténué d'art!
Me répéter, oh! mal de tête! . . .

Va, et les gouttières de l'ennui!
Ça goutte, goutte sur ma nuque . . .
Ça claque, claque à petit bruit . . .
Oh! ça claquera jusque . . . jusque? . . .

Wandering since the morning, me,
A prey to guilty proclivities,
On watch for some great destiny
In eyes of my gentle resemblances . . .

Oh! just one coward stopping-point
In my destiny that unwinds! . . . This:
A love expressly mine, a joint
For two just like a chrysalis! . . .

A simple heart, looks that impart
No spirit of any conquest-making,
That's me, so bushed I am with art!
To repeat myself, my head, oh, aching! . . .

Sure, and the gutters of ennui chatter!
They drip and drip onto my neck . . .
It plips and plips its little patter . . .
Oh, it'll plip until . . . till next? . . .

XLVII   ÈVE, SANS TRÊVE

Et la Coiffure, l'Art du Front,
Cheveux massés à la Néron
Sur des yeux qui, du coup, fermentent;
Tresses, bandeaux, crinière ardente;
Madone ou caniche ou bacchante;
Mes frères, décoiffons d'abord! puis nous verrons.

Ah! les ensorcelants Protées!
Et suivez-les décolletées
Des épaules; comme, aussitôt,
Leurs yeux, les plus durs, les plus faux,
Se noient, l'air tendre et comme il faut,
Dans ce halo de chair en harmonies lactées! . . .

Et ce purgatif: Vierge hier,
Porter aujourd'hui dans sa chair,
Fixe, un Œil mâle, en fécondée!
L'âme doit être débordée!
Oh! nous n'en avons pas idée!
Leur air reste le même, avenant et désert . . .

Avenant, Promis et Joconde!
Et par les rues, et dans le monde
Qui saurait dire de ces yeux
Réfléchissant tout ce qu'on veut
Voici les vierges, voici ceux
Où la Foudre finale a bien jeté la sonde.

Ah! non, laissons, on n'y peut rien.
Suivons-les comme de bons chiens
Couvrons de baisers leurs visages
Du moment, faisons bon ménage
Avec leurs bleus, leurs noirs mirages
Cueillons-en, puis chantons: merci c'est bien, fort bien . . .

XLVII   EVE, NO REPRIEVE

And Hair-Styling, Art of the Brow,
Massed curls à la Nero now,
Over the eyes of instant smoulder,
Bands, ardent mop, or tress to shoulder,
Madonna, bitch, bacchante, hold her,
Brothers, let's first undo their hair; then we'll see somehow.

Ah, Proteans with their spell!
And follow them, the neckline's swell,
Off-shoulder, and how right on cue
Their eyes drown, hardest, most untrue,
Air tender, and quite proper, too,
In that halo of flesh where milky harmonies well! . . .

And that purgative: yesterday Chaste,
To bear today in her flesh, post-haste,
Fixed, a cock Eye – now fecund!
Her soul must overflow that second!
We'd no idea, oh, who'd have reckoned!
Their air is still the same, pleasing and vacant-faced . . .

– Pleasing, Promising and Giocond!
In any street, the world beyond,
Would know just how those eyes convey,
Reflecting all you want, and say:
Here come the virgins, here are they
The final Bolt has really plumbed to the last frond.

Ah, nothing we can do, let be.
Good dogs, let's follow faithfully
Cover the moment's face they wear
With kisses, set up house and share
Their black, their blue mirages there,
Let's pick some of them, sing: thanks, fine, that's fine by me . . .

XLVIII   DIMANCHES

Le Dimanche, on se plaît
À dire un chapelet
À ses frères de lait.

Orphée, ô jeune Orphée!
Sérails des coriphées
Aux soirs du fleuve Alphée . . .

Parcifal, Parcifal!
Étendard virginal
Sur les remparts du mal . . .

Prométhée, Prométhée!
Phrase répercutée
Par les siècles athées . . .

Nabuchodonosor!
Moloch des âges d'or
Régissez-nous encor? . . .

Et vous donc, filles d'Ève,
Sœurs de lait, sœurs de sève,
Des destins qu'on se rêve!

Salomé, Salomé!
Sarcophage embaumé
Où dort maint Bien-Aimé . . .

Ophélie toi surtout
Viens moi par ce soir d'août
Ce sera entre nous.

Salammbo, Salammbo!
Lune au chaste halo
Qui laves nos tombeaux . . .

XLVIII   SUNDAYS

Sundays, it's nice to say
A rosary and pray
For foster brothers away.

Orpheus, young Orpheus!
Chorus-girl harems loose,
Evenings by the Alpheus . . .

Parsifal, Parsifal!
Standard virginal
On evil's ramparts tall . . .

Prometheus, Prometheus!
Phrase ever in use
Atheist eras adduce . . .

Nebuchadnezzar, old
Moloch of ages of gold
Our realm d'you still hold? . . .

Eve's daughters, next: sisters
Fostered, and vimful trysters,
Dream-destinies to misters!

Salomé, Salomé! deep
Embalmed tomb-keep
Where many Loved Ones sleep . . .

Ophelia above all,
This August nightfall –
It'll just be us – call.

Salambo, Salambo!
Moon of virgin glow
Bathing our tombs below . . .

Grande sœur, Messaline!
Ô panthère câline
Griffant nos mousselines . . .

Oh! même Cendrillon
Reprisant ses haillons
Au foyer sans grillon . . .

Ou Paul et Virginie,
Ô vignette bénie
Des ciels des colonies . . .

– Psyché, folle Psyché,
Feu-follet du péché,
Vous vous ferez moucher! . . .

L   LA MÉLANCOLIE DE PIERROT

Le premier jour, je bois leurs yeux ennuyés . . .
        Je baiserais leurs pieds,
        À mort. Ah! qu'elles daignent
        Prendre mon cœur qui saigne!
Puis, on cause . . . – et ça devient de la Pitié;
Et enfin je leur offre mon amitié.

C'est de pitié, que je m'offre en frère, en guide;
        Elles, me croient timide,
        Et clignent d'un œil doux:
        «Un mot, je suis à vous!»
(Je te crois) Alors, moi, d'étaler les rides
De ce cœur, et de sourire dans le vide . . .

Messalina, big sister,
Pantherish persister,
Our muslin mauler, twister . . .

Oh, even Cinderellas, bending
Over your tatty mending,
Cricketless hearth attending . . .

Paul and Virginia, too;
O vignette blest of blue
Colonial skies' deep hue . . .

– Psyche, oh Psyche, you fool,
Sin's jill o' the wisp, oh you'll
Snuff it something cruel! . . .

L PIERROT'S MELANCHOLY

On the first day I drink their eyes that are bored stiff . . .
    I'd kiss their feet, to death. Ah, if
    They'd only deign to take my heart
    That's bleeding from some sort of dart!
But then we chat . . . That leads to Pity in a jiff.
And, last, I offer them my friendship, not a tiff.

It's out of pity I offer to be brother, guide.
    I'm timid, that's what they decide,
    And give a wink with kindly eye:
    'Speak up, I'm all yours!' (And my,
Do I believe you.) Then I'm to show where wrinkles hide
Within this heart, to smile into the void spread wide . . .

Et soudain j'abandonne la garnison,
      Feignant de trahisons!
      (Je l'ai échappé belle!)
      Au moins, m'écrira-t-elle?
Point. Et je la pleure toute la saison . . .
– Ah! j'en ai assez de ces combinaisons!

Qui m'apprivoisera le cœur! belle cure . . .
      Suis si vrai de nature
      Aie la douceur des sœurs!
      Oh viens! suis pas noceur,
Serait-ce donc une si grosse aventure
Sous le soleil? dans toute cette verdure . . .

LI   CAS RÉDHIBITOIRE

(MARIAGE)

Ah! mon âme a sept facultés!
Plus autant qu'il est de chefs-d'œuvre,
Plus mille microbes ratés
Qui m'ont pris pour champ de manœuvre.

Oh! le suffrage universel
Qui se bouscule et se chicane,
À chaque instant, au moindre appel,
Dans mes mille occultes organes! . . .

J'aurais voulu vivre à grands traits,
Le long d'un classique programme
Et m'associant en un congrès
Avec quelque classique femme.

Mais peut-il être question
D'aller tirer des exemplaires
De son individu si on
N'en a pas une idée plus claire? . . .

Abruptly I desert the garrison – action stations,
      Feigning there're treacherous machinations!
      (Phew! I escaped her pretty late!)
      At least she'll write, at any rate?
No. And I mourn for her that season . . . – Botherations!
I've had enough of all these combinations!

Who'll civilise my heart? A lovely ministry . . .
      By nature I'm all loyalty,
      And sisters' gentleness deserve!
      Come on, I'm not a rake or perv.
So would it be so gross an intrigue to see
Then, under the sun? In all this greenery . . .

LI   REDHIBITORY CASE

(MARRIAGE)

My soul has seven faculties!
More in that there are masterpieces,
A thousand more microbe failures seize
As training ground my folds and creases.

Oh, universal suffrage now for all
Who trip themselves, try trick on trick
At every moment, at the least call,
In my thousand hidden organs quick! . . .

I'd meant to live my boldest, strongest
The length of a classical programme, aim
To associate myself in a congress
With some or other classic dame.

But could it be a case of just
Going to pull some samples here
Of number one if one's nonplussed
With no idea of it that's clear? . . .

LII   ARABESQUES DE MALHEUR

Nous nous aimions comme deux fous;
On s'est quittés sans en parler.
(Un spleen me tenait exilé
Et ce spleen me venait de tout.)

Que ferons-nous, moi, de mon âme,
Elle de sa tendre jeunesse!
Ô vieillissante pécheresse,
Oh! que tu vas me rendre infâme!

Des ans vont passer là-dessus;
On durcira chacun pour soi;
Et plus d'une fois, je m'y vois,
On ragera: «Si j'avais su!» . . .

Oh! comme on fait claquer les portes,
Dans ce Grand Hôtel d'anonymes!
Touristes, couples légitimes,
Ma Destinée est demi-morte! . . .

– Ses yeux disaient: «Comprenez-vous!
Comment ne comprenez-vous pas!»
Et nul n'a pu le premier pas;
On s'est séparés d'un air fou.

Si on ne tombe pas d'un même
Ensemble à genoux, c'est factice,
C'est du toc. Voilà la justice
Selon moi, voilà comment j'aime.

LII   ARABESQUES OF UNHAPPINESS

We made love like a couple crazed;
And then both quit and no word said.
(A spleen put exile in my head,
A spleen that all there is had raised.)

What shall we do, me with my soul,
She with her youthful tenderness!
Oh, aging woman, sinneress,
How infamous you'll make my role!

Years'll pass picking that bone;
Each one will harden in a pair
And more than once I see me there,
You'll rage: 'If only I had known!' . . .

Oh, how you slam doors with a biff
In this Grand Hotel of the Anon!
Tourists, legal pairs and so on,
My Destiny's a half dead stiff! . . .

– 'Understand, you!' her eyes had blazed,
'You, how you never understand!'
Neither could've given on either hand;
We separated as if crazed.

If you don't fall without a shove,
Together on your knees, it's phoney;
It's fool's gold. That is the only
Justice to me. That's how I love.

LIII LES CHAUVES-SOURIS

C'est qu'elles m'ont l'air bien folles, ce soir,
Les cloches du couvent des carmélites!
Et je me demande au nom de quels rites . . .
    Allons, montons voir.

Oh! parmi les poussiéreuses poutrelles,
Ce sont de jeunes chauves-souris
Folles d'essayer enfin hors du nid
    Leurs vieillottes ailes!

– Elles s'en iront désormais aux soirs,
Chasser les moustiques sur la rivière,
À l'heure où les diurnes lavandières
    Ont tu leurs battoirs.

– Et ces couchants seront tout solitaires,
Tout quotidiens et tout supra-Védas,
Tout aussi vrais que si je n'étais pas,
    Tout à leur affaire.

Ah! ils seront tout aussi quotidiens
Qu'aux temps où la planète à la dérive
En ses langes de vapeurs primitives
    Ne savait rien d' rien.

Ils seront tout aussi à leur affaire
Quand je ne viendrai plus crier bravo!
Aux assortiments de mourants joyaux
    De leur éventaire,

Qu'aux jours où certain bohème filon
Du commun néant n'avait pas encore
Pris un accès d'existence pécore
    Sous mon pauvre nom.

LIII   THE BATS

It's just they sound quite mad tonight to me,
The bells of the convent of the Carmelites
And in the name, I wonder, of what rites . . .
        Come on, let's go and see.

Oh, in the dusty beams and moulderings,
There are some young bats huddled, mad to test
Themselves at last away beyond the nest
        On antiquated wings.

– They'll leave, in due course, in the evenings
To hunt the gnats along the river bank
When washerwomen cease to beat and spank
        Their daily launderings.

– And these settings will be quite alone,
Quite quotidian and quite beyond Vedantics;
As true as if I wasn't, in their antics,
        Their business, all their own.

Ah, they'll be just as quotidian a-wing
As in the days when, all adrift, the planet,
Swathed in the primitive vapours that began it,
        Knew nothing of anything.

They'll be about their business the same way
When I'll no longer come to cry: bravo!
To these assortments of dying gems on show
        In their hawker's tray,

Just as before some fluke bohemian stroke
Of common oblivion had not yet made
An opening in existence, cow-brain jade,
        Under my name, poor bloke.

LIV SIGNALEMENT

Chair de l'Autre Sexe! Élément non–moi!
Chair, vive de vingt ans poussés loin de ma bouche! . . .
L'air de sa chair m'ensorcelle en la foi
Aux abois
Que par Elle, ou jamais, Mon Destin fera souche . . .
Et, tout tremblant, je regarde, je touche . . .

Je me prouve qu'Elle est! – et puis, ne sais qu'en croire . . .
Et je revois mes chemins de Damas
Au bout desquels c'était encor les balançoires
Provisoires . . .
Et je me récuse, et je me débats!
Fou d'un art à nous deux! et fou de célibats . . .

Et toujours le même Air! me met en frais
De cœur, et me transit en ces conciliabules . . .
Deux grands yeux savants, fixes et sacrés
Tout exprès.
Là, pour garder leur sœur cadette, et si crédule,
Une bouche qui rit en campanule! . . .

(Ô yeux durs, bouche folle!) – ou bien Ah! le contraire:
Une bouche toute à ses grands ennuis,
Mais l'arc tendu! sachant ses yeux, ses petits frères
Tout à plaire,
Et capables de rendez-vous de nuit
Pour un rien, pour une larme qu'on leur essui'! . . .

Oui, sous ces airs supérieurs,
Le cœur me piaffe de génie
En labyrinthes d'insomnie! . . .
Et puis, et puis, c'est bien ailleurs,
Que je communie . . .

LIV SIGNALLY

Flesh of the Other Sex! Element non-me at all!
Flesh, live for twenty years grown far from my lips! . . .
　　Her flesh air binds me in the faith with back to wall,
　　　　　That in Her thrall
Or never My Destiny will make an old block's chips . . .
　　Trembling, I look, touch with fingertips . . .

I prove that She exists! – then don't know what to think . . . .
　　And see once more my roads to Damascus, at
Whose end there still remained the seesaws' rise and sink
　　　　　Brief high, low jink . . . .
　　And I decline to say, debate all that!
Crazed with a two-some's art, and crazed with celibate . . .

　　And always that same Air! causes me expense
Of heart and, in these conclaves, chills me through and through . . .
　　Two big and knowing eyes, holy, intense,
　　　　　Direct in sense.
There, to guard their little sister, and naive, too,
　　A mouth that laughs as the bellflowers do! . . .

(O stern eyes, mouth mad!) – or ah, well, contrariwise:
　　A mouth given to its great tediums outright
But how drawn! knowing her little brothers, her eyes'
　　　　　All pleasing guise,
　　And likely ones for rendezvous by night
For a nothing, a tear you wipe out of their sight . . .

　　　　　Yes, under this superior air,
　　　　　Genius paws my heart to flit
　　　　　In sleepless mazes in the pit! . . .
　　　　　Then, then, it is indeed elsewhere
　　　　　　　I commune a bit . . .

LV DIMANCHES

JAQUES: *Motley's the only wear.*

Ils enseignent
Que la nature se divise en trois règnes,
Et professent
Le perfectionnement de notre Espèce.

Ah! des canapés
Dans un val de Tempé!

Des contrées
Tempérées,
Et des gens
Indulgents
Qui pâturent
La Nature.
En janvier
Des terriers
Où l'on s'aime
Sans système,
Des bassins
Noirs d'essaims
D'acrobates
Disparates
Qui patinent
En sourdine . . .

Ah! vous savez ces choses
Tout aussi bien que moi;
Je ne vois pas pourquoi
On veut que j'en recause.

LV SUNDAYS

JAQUES: *Motley's the only wear.*

They teach
That nature is divided into three parts each.
Make theses
Concerning the perfecting of our Species.

Ah, the settees
In Tempe's vale of ease!

With countries warm,
Temperate norm,
With all the locals
Indulgent yokels
Who champ and top
Nature's crop.
Januaries where
Down in the lair
We love each other,
No systems smother,
With frozen pools
Blackened with schools
Of acrobat sports,
Of various sorts,
Who skate around
Without a sound . . .

Oh, you know it, too.
And just as well as me;
I find it hard to see
Why I'm retelling you.

LVI   AIR DE BINIOU

Non, non, ma pauvre cornemuse,
Ta complainte est pas si oiseuse;
Et Tout est bien une méprise,
Et l'on peut la trouver mauvaise;

Et la Nature est une épouse
Qui nous carambole d'extases,
Et puis, nous occit, peu courtoise,
Dès qu'on se permet une pause.

Eh bien! qu'elle en prenne à son aise,
Et que tout fonctionne à sa guise!
Nous, nous entretiendrons les Muses.
Les neuf immortelles Glaneuses!

(Oh! pourrions-nous pas, par nos phrases,
Si bien lui retourner les choses,
Que cette marâtre jalouse
N'ait plus sur nos rentes de prise?)

LVI   AIR ON BRETON PIPES

My poor old pipes, the plaint you noise
Is not the tedium you suppose.
The Whole's a blunder of some size
And you could reckon that bad news.

And Nature is a wife whose ploy's
To cannon us with ecstasies,
Then, without ceremony, slays
As soon as we relax or pause.

Well, let her take things at her ease
And may the lot work in her ways.
But we, the Muses we shall house,
The Nine Immortal Gleaners choose.

(Oh, couldn't we, in choicest phrase,
So well return her goods, supplies,
This envious stepma'am could impose
No claim upon our income, dues?)

Derniers vers

Last Poems

I have not art to reckon my groans . . .
Thine evermore, most dear lady, whilst this machine is to him.

J. L.

OPHELIA: He took me by the wrist, and held me hard:
Then goes he to the length of all his arm,
And, with his other hand thus o'er his brow,
He falls to such perusal of my face,
As he would draw it. Long stay'd he so:
At last, – a little shaking of mine arm,
And thrice his head thus waving up and down, –
He rais'd a sigh so piteous and profound,
That it did seem to shatter all his bulk,
And end his being. That done he lets me go,
And with his head over his shoulder turn'd
He seem'd to find his way without his eyes;
For out o'doors he went without their help,
And to the last bended their light on me.

POLONIUS: This is the very ecstasy of love.

I L'HIVER QUI VIENT

Blocus sentimental! Messageries du Levant!...
Oh, tombée de la pluie! Oh! tombée de la nuit,
Oh! le vent!... La Toussaint, la Noël et la Nouvelle Année,
Oh, dans les bruines, toutes mes cheminées!...
D'usines...

On ne peut plus s'asseoir, tous les bancs sont mouillés;
Crois-moi, c'est bien fini jusqu'à l'année prochaine,
Tant les bancs sont mouillés, tant les bois sont rouillés,
Et tant les cors ont fait ton ton, ont fait ton taine!...

Ah, nuées accourues des côtes de la Manche,
Vous nous avez gâté notre dernier dimanche.

Il bruine;
Dans la forêt mouillée, les toiles d'araignées
Ploient sous les gouttes d'eau, et c'est leur ruine.

Soleils plénipotentiaires des travaux en blonds Pactoles
Des spectacles agricoles,
Où êtes-vous ensevelis?
Ce soir un soleil fichu gît au haut du coteau,
Gît sur le flanc, dans les genêts, sur son manteau,
Un soleil blanc comme un crachet d'estaminet
Sur une litière de jaunes genêts,
De jaunes genêts d'automne.
Et les cors lui sonnent!
Qu'il revienne...
Qu'il revienne à lui!
Taïaut! Taïaut! et hallali!
Ô triste antienne, as-tu fini!...
Et font les fous!...
Et il gît là, comme une glande arrachée dans un cou,
Et il frissonne, sans personne!...

I THE COMING WINTER

Emoceanal blockade! Levantine packets!
Oh, rain falling, rain! Oh! night falling again,
Oh, the wind rackets! . . .
All Hallows, Christmas and the New Year,
Oh, in the drizzle, all my chimney-pieces appear –
Of factories . . .

You can no longer sit; all the benches soaked.
Believe me, it's all over again until next year.
Benches so thoroughly soaked, the woods so mildew-cloaked,
So well the horns have sounded halloo, sounded tally-ho here! . . .

Ah, clouds, come rushing from the Channel coasts,
You've ruined our last Sunday with your hosts.

It drizzles on;
And in the drenched forest, cobwebs, wrenched,
Give under drops of rain, and they are gone.

Suns plenipotent over the labours in those
Blond Pactoluses of country shows,
Where are you laid to rest?
Upon a hillock's crest, this evening, lies
An oddball sun, in the broom, cloak under thighs,
A white sun like a gob in a saloon,
Upon a litter of the yellow broom,
The yellow broom of Fall.
And for him the horns call,
For his return . . .
For his return to be himself anew!
Tally-ho! tally-ho! halloo!
O sorry antiphon, are you through? . . .
They play the fool! . . .
He lies there like a gland torn from the neck, in drool,
Shuddering, nobody there at all! . . .

Allons, allons, et hallali!
C'est l'Hiver bien connu qui s'amène;
Oh! les tournants des grandes routes,
Et sans petit Chaperon Rouge qui chemine!...
Oh! leurs ornières des chars de l'autre mois,
Montant en don quichottesques rails
Vers les patrouilles des nuées en déroute
Que le vent malmène vers les transatlantiques bercails!...
Accélérons, accélérons, c'est la saison bien connue, cette fois.

Et le vent, cette nuit, il en a fait de belles!
Ô dégâts, ô nids, ô modestes jardinets!
Mon cœur et mon sommeil: ô échos des cognées!...

Tous ces rameaux avaient encor leurs feuilles vertes,
Les sous-bois ne sont plus qu'un fumier de feuilles mortes;
Feuilles, folioles, qu'un bon vent vous emporte
Vers les étangs par ribambelles,
Ou pour le feu du garde-chasse,
Ou les sommiers des ambulances
Pour les soldats loin de la France.

C'est la saison, c'est la saison, la rouille envahit les masses,
La rouille ronge en leurs spleens kilométriques
Les fils télégraphiques des grandes routes où nul ne passe.

Les cors, les cors, les cors – mélancoliques!...
Mélancoliques!...
S'en vont, changeant de ton,
Changeant de ton et de musique,
Ton ton, ton taine, ton ton!...
Les cors, les cors, les cors!...
S'en sont allés au vent du Nord.

Je ne puis quitter ce ton: que d'échos!...
C'est la saison, c'est la saison, adieu vendanges!...
Voici venir les pluies d'une patience d'ange,
Adieu vendanges, et adieu tous les paniers,
Tous les paniers Watteau des bourrées sous les marronniers,
C'est la toux dans les dortoirs du lycée qui rentre,

Come on, come on, halloo the kill!
It's old well-known Winter who blows in;
Oh, the windings of the main roads,
And not a Little Red Riding-Hood trotting on . . .
Oh, wheel-ruts from their carts the other month that climb
Like quixotic rails and hold
Course for the flocks of routed clouds that the wind goads
And harries to the transatlantic fold! . . .
Let's hurry on, hurry up. The season's clearly here this time.

The wind last night has had a high old time, what style!
The havoc, the nests, the modest little garden rows!
My heart, my sleep: oh, echoes of the chopper blows! . . .

And all those boughs were green with leaves till then.
The undergrowth is just a mulch of dead leaves shed,
Leaves, folioles, may a fair wind carry you ahead
To ponds, in shoal and crocodile,
Or the gamekeeper's fire,
Or beds in ambulances that advance
For soldiers far away from France.

The season, the season's back. Rust invades the masses entire,
Along main roads where no one fares
Rust's gnawing at the kilometric spleens in lines of telegraphic wire.

Horn and horn and horn – melancholy airs! . . .
Melancholy airs! . . .
Are going, blown with changing tone,
Changing tone and tune – there's
Tally-ho, halloo, tally-ho blown! . . .
Horn, and horn, and horn! . . .
Are gone on the North wind borne.

I can't shake off that tone: what echoes crowd! . . .
The season's back, the season's back; and vintages goodbye! . . .
Here come the rains with patience of an angel on high.
Oh, vintages, goodbye, and goodbye all the panniers conveyed,
The Watteau panniers in bourrées beneath the chestnuts' shade.
Now it's the dormitory cough as boarding-school re-enters;

C'est la tisane sans le foyer,
La phtisie pulmonaire attristant le quartier,
Et toute la misère des grands centres.

Mais, lainages, caoutchoucs, pharmacie, rêve,
Rideaux écartés du haut des balcons des grèves
Devant l'océan de toitures des faubourgs,
Lampes, estampes, thé, petits-fours,
Serez-vous pas mes seules amours!...

(Oh! et puis, est-ce que tu connais, outre les pianos,
Le sobre et vespéral mystère hebdomadaire
Des statistiques sanitaires
Dans les journaux?)

Non, non! C'est la saison et la planète falote!
Que l'autan, que l'autan
Effiloche les savates que le Temps se tricote!
C'est la saison, oh déchirements! c'est la saison!
Tous les ans, tous les ans,
J'essaierai en chœur d'en donner la note.

It's herb tea without fireside chair,
Pulmonary t. b. saddening the district everywhere,
And all the misery of the great centres.

But woollens, medicine-chest, dreams, waterproofs,
Curtains open on balconies high on strands over roofs
Of suburbs looking like the sea,
Lamps, engravings, petit-fours and tea,
Won't you be the only loves for me?

(Oh, and then, beyond the pianos, don't you contemplate
The sober and vesperal mystery each week
The health figures speak
And papers tabulate?)

No! No! It's the season and the planet a nit-wit!
South-east blast, south-east blast
May that uncast the slippers Time has knit!
It's the season – oh heartbreak peeling-offs! – the season!
Every year passed, every year cast
I'll try in chorus to strike the right note out for it.

II LE MYSTÈRE DES TROIS CORS

Un cor dans la plaine
Souffle à perdre haleine,
Un autre, du fond des bois,
Lui répond;
L'un chante ton-taine
Aux forêts prochaines,
Et l'autre ton-ton
Aux échos des monts.

Celui de la plaine
Sent gonfler ses veines,
Ses veines du front;
Celui du bocage,
En vérité, ménage
Ses jolis poumons.

– Où donc tu te caches,
Mon beau cor de chasse?
Que tu es méchant!

– Je cherche ma belle,
Là-bas, qui m'appelle
Pour voir le Soleil couchant.

– Taïaut! Taïaut! Je t'aime!
Hallali! Roncevaux!

– Être aimé est bien doux;
Mais, le Soleil qui se meurt, avant tout!

Le Soleil dépose sa pontificale étole,
Lâche les écluses du Grand-Collecteur
En mille Pactoles
Que les plus artistes
De nos liquoristes
Attisent de cent fioles de vitriol oriental! . . .

II THE MYSTERY OF THE THREE HORNS

A horn upon the plain
Blows fit to burst a vein,
One brandished deep in woods
Answers it; and
One sings out ton-taine
To nearby forest terrain,
The other's ton-tons expand
To echoes in high land.

The one amid the plain
Feels its swelling vein,
Veins in its forehead stand;
The one back in the wood
Has lungs pretty good,
A pair just grand.

– My swell horn as you play
Where do you hide away?
How naughty you are getting!

– I'm after my girl, down there,
Who's calling me to share
The sight of the Sun setting.

– Tally-ho! Tally-ho! I love you.
Halloo! Roncevaux!

– To be loved's quite pleasant;
But suicidal Sun comes first at present!

The Sun takes off his pontiff's stole,
Opens the sluices of the Main Sewer;
A thousand Pactoluses roll
That our most artistic vintners
Stir up with tinctures
Of a hundred phials of oriental vitriol! . . .

Le sanglant étang, aussitôt s'étend, aussitôt s'étale,
Noyant les cavales du quadrige
Qui se cabre, et qui patauge, et puis se fige
Dans ces déluges de bengale et d'alcool! . . .

Mais les durs sables et les cendres de l'horizon
Ont vite bu tout cet étalage des poisons.

Ton-ton ton-taine, les gloires! . . .

Et les cors consternés
Se retrouvent nez à nez;
Ils sont trois;
Le vent se lève, il commence à faire froid.

Ton-ton ton-taine, les gloires! . . .

– «Bras-dessus, bras-dessous,
Avant de rentrer chacun chez nous,
Si nous allions boire
Un coup?»

Pauvres cors! pauvres cors!
Comme ils dirent cela avec un rire amer!
(Je les entends encor).

Le lendemain, l'hôtesse du *Grand-Saint-Hubert*
Les trouva tous trois morts.

On fut quérir les autorités
De la localité,

Qui dressèrent procès-verbal
De ce mystère très-immoral.

No sooner fallen headlong than sprawling out, the bloody pool,
Drowning the steeds as his quadriga wheels,
It rears, it plunges, then congeals
In these deluges of bengal lights and alcohol! . . .

But the hard sands and cinders on the horizon's line
Soon drank up all of this display of poisoned wine.

Ton-ton ton-taine, the glories! . . .

And the horns in consternation's throes
Meet up again and nose to nose;
They're three, all told;
The wind rises; it's getting cold.

Ton-ton ton-taine, the glories! . . .

– 'Well, arm in arm let's link,
Before we split for home, I think
What we might do surely's
Have a drink?'

Poor greenhorns! Poor greenhorns! They
Suggested that with such a bitter laugh!
(And still I hear them say it).

The hostess of The Great St Hubert the day after
Found where, all three dead, they lay.

The matter was pursued
With the local authorities who'd

Asked for a police report
On this mystery, most immoral sort!

III DIMANCHES

Bref, j'allais me donner d'un «Je vous aime»
Quand je m'avisai non sans peine
Que d'abord je ne me possédais pas bien moi-même.

(Mon Moi, c'est Galathée aveuglant Pygmalion!
Impossible de modifier cette situation.)

Ainsi donc, pauvre, pâle et piètre individu
Qui ne croit à son Moi qu'à ses moments perdus,
Je vis s'effacer ma fiancée
Emportée par le cours des choses,
Telle l'épine voit s'effeuiller,
Sous prétexte de soir sa meilleure rose.

Or, cette nuit anniversaire, toutes les Walkyries du vent
Sont revenues beugler par les fentes de ma porte:
Væ soli!
Mais, ah! qu'importe?
Il fallait m'en étourdir avant!
Trop tard! ma petite folie est morte!
Qu'importe *Væ soli!*
Je ne retrouverai plus ma petite folie.

Le grand vent bâillonné,
S'endimanche enfin le ciel du matin.
Et alors, eh! allez donc, carillonnez,
Toutes cloches des bons dimanches!
Et passez layettes et collerettes et robes blanches
Dans un frou-frou de lavande et de thym
Vers l'encens et les brioches!
Tout pour la famille, quoi! *Væ soli!* C'est certain.

La jeune demoiselle à l'ivoirin paroissien
Modestement rentre au logis.
On le voit, son petit corps bien reblanchi
Sait qu'il appartient
À un tout autre passé que le mien!

III   SUNDAYS

In short, I went to give myself with a 'Dear heart,
I love you' when, not without pain,
I thought I don't possess myself quite for a start.

(My Self, it's Galatea blinding Pygmalion's stares!
Impossible to modify this state of affairs.)

So, then, poor and pale and pitifully unsublime,
One who believes in his Self just in his spare time,
I watched my fiancee fade away,
Carried off by the way it goes,
As the briar sees the decay
And fall, the pretext evening, of its loveliest rose.

Now, this anniversary night, all Valkyries of the wind
Have come again to bellow through the cracks in my door:
Vae soli!
But ah, what good's that for?
Too late! It should have dinned
It into me before! My little folly is no more,
Dead! Ignore *Vae soli!*
Never again will I find my little folly.

Gagged, the great wind's tirade:
The morning sky puts on its Sunday best.
And, next, oh, come on then, carillonade,
All you good Sunday bells; give it socks!
And pass by, layettes and collarettes, white frocks,
In frou-frous of thyme and lavender dressed,
Towards incense and brioches!
All for the family good, eh? *Vae soli!* That's certainest!

The young lady, missal ivory-white
Primly goes in, her dwelling reached.
It's clear, her little body, well rebleached,
Knows it belongs to quite
Another past than mine all right!

Mon corps, ô ma sœur, a bien mal à sa belle âme . . .

Oh! voilà que ton piano
Me recommence, si natal maintenant!
Et ton cœur qui s'ignore s'y ânonne
En ritournelles de bastringues à tout venant,
Et ta pauvre chair s'y fait mal! . . .
À moi, Walkyries!
Walkyries des hypocondries et des tueries!

Ah! que je te les tordrais avec plaisir,
Ce corps bijou, ce cœur à ténor,
Et te dirais leur fait, et puis encore
La manière de s'en servir
De s'en servir à deux,
Si tu voulais seulement m'approfondir ensuite un peu!

Non, non! C'est sucer la chair d'un cœur élu,
Adorer d'incurables organes
S'entrevoir avant que les tissus se fanent
En monomanes, en reclus!

Et ce n'est pas sa chair qui me serait tout,
Et je ne serais pas qu'un grand cœur pour elle,
Mais quoi s'en aller faire les fous
Dans des histoires fraternelles!
L'âme et la chair, la chair et l'âme,
C'est l'Esprit édénique et fier
D'être un peu l'Homme avec la Femme.

En attendant, oh! garde-toi des coups de tête,
Oh! file ton rouet et prie et reste honnête.

– Allons, dernier des poètes,
Toujours enfermé tu te rendras malade!
Vois, il fait beau temps tout le monde est dehors,
Va donc acheter deux sous d'ellébore,
Ça te fera une petite promenade.

My body, O my sister, quite aches in its fine soul . . .

Oh, here we go again; your piano
Starts me off again, so natal now its calls!
And your self-ignorant heart stumbles in an
Unending string of ritournelles from dance-hall free-for-alls.
Your poor flesh makes itself ill there! . . .
Help me, Valkyries! Daughters
Of hypochondrias and slaughters!

Ah, how I'd twist them for you, and with pleasure,
That dainty body, that tenor's heart;
And tell you the truth about them, then impart
Their manner of use, at leisure,
The manner of use for two,
If only you would fathom me a bit after I do.

No, No! That's draining flesh of an elect heart,
The adoring of incurable organs; it's to aspire
To glimpse each other, before the tissues tire
In monomaniac desire, reclusives set apart!

To me her body wouldn't be just all there is,
To her I wouldn't only be just a big heart
But what would play fools in histories
Of brotherhood for a start;
Body and soul, soul and body knit,
That is the Spirit, proud in Eden-role,
To be Man with Woman for a bit.

Meanwhile, watch out for brainstorms, be on guard,
Oh, nose to the grindstone, stay straight and pray hard.

– Come on, you last of poets, last bard,
Always shut in, you'll make yourself quite ill.
Look, it's fine; the world is out once more.
Go on, you go and buy two penn'orth of hellebore.
That'll make you a nice little walk, that will.

IV   DIMANCHES

C'est l'automne, l'automne, l'automne,
Le grand vent et toute sa séquelle
De représailles! et de musiques!...
Rideaux tirés, clôture annuelle,
Chute des feuilles, des Antigones, des Philomèles:
Mon fossoyeur, *Alas poor Yorick!*
Les remue à la pelle!...

Vivent l'Amour et les feux de paille!...

Les Jeunes Filles inviolables et frêles
Descendent vers la petite chapelle
Dont les chimériques cloches
Du joli joli dimanche
Hygiéniquement et élégamment les appellent.

Comme tout se fait propre autour d'elles!
Comme tout en est dimanche!

Comme on se fait dur et boudeur à leur approche!...

Ah! moi, je demeure l'Ours Blanc!
Je suis venu par ces banquises
Plus pures que les communiantes en blanc...
Moi, je ne vais pas à l'église,
Moi, je suis le Grand Chancelier de l'Analyse,
Qu'on se le dise.

Pourtant, pourtant! Qu'est-ce que c'est que cette anémie?
Voyons, confiez vos chagrins à votre vieil ami...

Vraiment! Vraiment!
Ah! Je me tourne vers la mer, les éléments
Et tout ce qui n'a plus que les noirs grognements!

Oh! que c'est sacré!
Et qu'il y faut de grandes veillées!

IV   SUNDAYS

It's Fall, the Fall, the Fall comes on.
Wind, high with all its motley swell
Of full reprisals, rackets choric! . . .
The curtains fallen; annual closed spell;
Fall of leaflets, leaves, of Antigone, of Philomel:
My old digger, *Alas Poor Yorick*,
Rakes them in pell-mell! . . .

Long live Love and fires of straw as well! . . .

Towards the tiny chapel, frail,
Inviolable, the Young Girls trail,
Its chimeric bells, sounding
Of nice, nice Sunday,
Hygienically, elegantly giving them a hail.

How all about them turns proper, in the pale!
How all of it is Sunday!

How hard one turns and moody as they go down! . . .

Ah! me, I'm still the Polar Bear!
I have arrived here on this floe
Of purer white than these communicants wear . . .
Church? Not me, I don't go.
Me, I'm the Lord Chancellor of the Analysis; so:
Let's talk it to and fro.

And yet and yet! What is all this anaemia?
Come, confide your upsets in your old friend, see me a . . .

Indeed! Indeed! Well, me,
Ah, I turn towards the elements, the sea
And everything that only growls on black and grumpily!

Oh, what a blessed thing!
What great long vigils it must bring!

Pauvre, pauvre, sous couleur d'attraits! . . . .

Et nous, et nous,
Ivres, ivres, avant qu'émerveillés . . .
Qu'émerveillés et à genoux! . . .

Et voyez comme on tremble
Au premier grand soir
Que tout pousse au désespoir
D'en mourir ensemble!

Ô merveille qu'on n'a su que cacher!
Si pauvre et si brûlante et si martyre!
Et qu'on n'ose toucher
Qu'à l'aveugle, en divin délire!

Ô merveille,
Reste cachée idéale violette,
L'Univers te veille,
Les générations de planètes te tettent
De funérailles en relevailles! . . .

Oh, que c'est plus haut
Que ce Dieu et que la Pensée!
Et rien qu'avec ces chers yeux en haut,
Tout inconscients et couleurs de pensée! . . .
Si frêle, si frêle!
Et tout le mortel foyer
Tout, tout ce foyer en elle! . . .

Oh, pardonnez-lui si, malgré elle,
Et cela tant lui sied,
Parfois ses prunelles clignent un peu
Pour vous demander un peu
De vous apitoyer un peu!

Ô frêle, frêle et toujours prête
Pour ces messes dont on a fait un jeu
Penche, penche ta chère tête, va,
Regarde les grappes des premiers lilas,

Wretched, wretched, in attractive colouring! . . .

And we, and we
Drunk, drunk, before, amazed . . . we fling
Ourselves, amazed, to our knee! . . .

Look how you tremble whether,
On the first great evening there,
That all is driving to the despair
Of dying for it together!

O marvel you've known only to hide!
So wretched, yearning, such a martyrdom!
A touch is only to be tried
Blind, in divine delirium!

O marvel, do
Stay hidden, ideal violet,
The Universe takes care of you;
Generations of wet-nurse planets pet you yet,
Lurching from funeral to churching! . . .

Oh, how much more high
Than this God is, or Thought's vast book!
And nothing doing but with these dear eyes on high
Quite inconscient, pensive pansies' look! . . .
So frail, so frail!
And all that mortal inglenook,
All, all in her, the nook female! . . .

Oh, pardon her, if in spite of her –
And well that suits her bent –
Sometimes her pupils stir and flutter a bit
To ask that you should take a bit
Of pity for her sake a bit!

O frail, frail, and, for those masses here
That have been made a game, always ready for it,
Bow, bow down your head so dear and fond,
Look at the earliest lilac sprays; respond.

Il ne s'agit pas de conquêtes, avec moi,
Mais d'au-delà!

Oh! puissions-nous quitter la vie
Ensemble dès cette Grand'Messe,
Écœurés de notre espèce
Qui bâille assouvie
Dès le parvis! . . .

V   PÉTITION

Amour absolu, carrefour sans fontaine;
Mais, à tous les bouts, d'étourdissantes fêtes foraines.

Jamais franches,
Ou le poing sur la hanche:
Avec toutes, l'amour s'échange
Simple et sans foi comme un bonjour.

Ô bouquets d'oranger cuirassés de satin,
Elle s'éteint, elle s'éteint,
La divine Rosace
À voir vos noces de sexes livrés à la grosse,
Courir en valsant vers la fosse
Commune! . . . Pauvre race!

Pas d'absolu; des compromis;
Tout est pas plus, tout est permis.

Et cependant, ô des nuits, laissez moi, Circés,
Sombrement coiffées à la Titus,
Et les yeux en grand deuil comme des pensées!
Et passez,
Béatifiques Vénus
Étalées et découvrant vos gencives comme un régal,

No question of conquests clearly with me,
But of beyond!

Oh, couldn't we desert this life, the pair
Of us, just as the Great Mass ceases,
Utterly sickened by our species
That, bloated, stare
From church square! . . .

V   PETITION

Absolute Love, cross-roads without a fountain there;
But in all four directions a mind-numbing travelling fair.

Never frank,
Or fist on flank:
With all of them love swaps round, bland
And faithless as a 'Good day!'

O sprays of orange-blossom armoured in satin,
She's setting, she's setting,
The divine Rosace,
To watch your marriage-feast of sexes, free as a beast,
Run waltzing to the common grave. Deceased! . . .
Poor wretched race!

No absolutes; compromises now;
The whole no longer; anything, anyhow.

And yet, O nights, Circeans, lay off me,
Hair in the sombre style like Titus's,
Your eyes in full mourning like pansies. Let me be,
And leave me free,
Beatific Venuses
Displayed and showing gums off such a treat,

Et bâillant des aisselles au soleil
Dans l'assourdissement des cigales!
Ou, droites, tenant sur fond violet le lotus
Des sacrilèges domestiques,
En faisant de l'index: *motus!*

Passez, passez, bien que les yeux vierges
Ne soient que cadrans d'émail bleu,
Marquant telle heure que l'on veut,
Sauf à garder pour eux, pour Elle,
Leur heure immortelle.
Sans doute au premier mot,
On va baisser ces yeux,
Et peut-être choir en syncope,
On est si vierge à fleur de robe
Peut-être même à fleur de peau,
Mais leur destinée est bien interlope, au nom de Dieu!

Ô historiques esclaves!
Oh! leur petite chambre!
Qu'on peut les en faire descendre
Vers d'autres étages,
Vers les plus frelatées des caves,
Vers les moins ange-gardien des ménages!

Et alors, le grand Suicide, à froid,
Et leur *Amen* d'une voix sans Elle,
Tout en vaquant aux petits soins secrets,
Et puis leur éternel air distrait
Leur grand air de dire: «De quoi?»
«Ah! de quoi, au fond, s'il vous plaît?»

Mon Dieu, que l'Idéal
La dépouillât de ce rôle d'ange!
Qu'elle adoptât l'Homme comme égal!
Oh, que ses yeux ne parlent plus d'Idéal,
Mais simplement d'humains échanges!
En frère et sœur par le cœur,
Et fiancés par le passé,

Gaping your oxters at the sun
In the deafening chirr the cicadas repeat!
Or, standing, holding, on violet ground, the mark
Of the home-profaning lotus,
Miming with index: *Keep it dark!*

Pass by, pass by, although your two virgin eyes
Are just enamelled dials of blue
Telling whatever time one wants them to,
But saving as their due, for She,
Their hour of immortality.
Doubtless, at the first peep
They'll lower those eyes too,
Maybe have a syncopal episode,
One's such a virgin down to the coat –
Perhaps it even goes skin-deep –
But, in God's name, their destiny's an interloping parvenue!

O historic slaves!
Oh, their little room!
How they can be brought down soon
Towards other floors,
Towards the most sophisticated caves,
Towards the least guardian-angel household chores!

And then the noble suicide, icy,
And their *Amen*, in a She-less voice,
Absorbed in secret little attentions, cares,
Next their eternally vacant airs,
Their grand manner of saying 'What, precisely?'
That 'Now what, basically, please?' of theirs.

My God, if the Ideal
Had stripped her of that angel mask!
If she'd adopted Man as peer for real!
Oh, that her eyes no longer speak of the Ideal,
But simply human interchanges ask!
As brother and sister in the heart's vista,
Engaged at last by ages past,

Et puis unis par l'Infini!
Oh, simplement d'infinis échanges
À la fin de journées
À quatre bras moissonnées,
Quand les tambours, quand les trompettes,
Ils s'en vont sonnant la retraite,
Et qu'on prend le frais sur le pas des portes,
En vidant les pots de grès
À la santé des années mortes
Qui n'ont pas laissé de regrets,
Au su de tout le canton
Que depuis toujours nous habitons,
Ton ton, ton taine, ton ton.

United then by the infinite!
Oh, simply infinite interchanges told!
In the dim of day
With four arms making hay
When the trumpet blare and the drumbeat
March away and play retreat,
And you take the air at the door
Draining pots of earthenware
To the health of the dead years of yore
That shed no regrets there
As far as the whole ward can con
Where we reside forever on,
Ton ton, ton taine, ton ton.

VI SIMPLE AGONIE

Ô paria! – Et revoici les sympathies de mai.
Mais tu ne peux que te répéter, ô honte!
Et tu te gonfles et ne crèves jamais.
Et tu sais fort bien, ô paria,
Que ce n'est pas du tout ça.

Oh! que
Devinant l'instant le plus seul de la nature,
Ma mélodie, toute et unique, monte,
Dans le soir et redouble, et fasse tout ce qu'elle peut
Et dise la chose qu'est la chose,
Et retombe, et reprenne,
Et fasse de la peine,
Ô solo de sanglots,
Et reprenne et retombe
Selon la tâche qui lui incombe.
Oh! que ma musique
Se crucifie,
Selon sa photographie
Accoudée et mélancolique!...

Il faut trouver d'autres thèmes,
Plus mortels et plus suprêmes.
Oh! bien, avec le monde tel quel,
Je vais me faire un monde plus mortel!

Les âmes y seront à musique,
Et tous les intérêts puérilement charnels,
Ô fanfares dans les soirs,
Ce sera barbare,
Ce sera sans espoir.

Enquêtes, enquêtes,
Seront l'unique fête!
Qui m'en défie?
J'entasse sur mon lit, les journaux, linge sale,
Dessins de mode, photographies quelconques,

VI SIMPLE DEATH-PANGS

O pariah! – They're here again, the sympathies of May.
But, shame, you can only repeat yourself once more!
Swell yourself up and never snuff it, no way,
And, pariah, you know quite pat
It's nothing at all to do with that.

Oh, would –
Guessing that most lonely second of nature –
Would that my music, unique and total, soar
At evening, and redouble, doing all it could,
And speak the case that is the case,
And lapse and recover again,
And give a bit of pain,
O solo throbs of sobs,
And recover again and lapse anew,
To match the task that it must do.
Oh would my melody
Mortify its craft,
To match her, photographed,
Resting on elbows, melancholy! . . .

I have to find some other theme,
More mortal and much more supreme.
Well, with the world such as it is,
I'll make me a world more mortal than this!

Souls will be to music there,
All all the interests childish sensualities,
Oh fanfares varying, every evening,
It will be barbarian,
No hope will it be leaving.

Inquests, inquests will be
The single festivity!
Who defies me over it?
I'll heap on my bed: newspapers, dirty linen stacked,
Fashion sketches, sundry photographs,

Toute la capitale,
Matrice sociale.

Que nul n'intercède,
Ce ne sera jamais assez,
Il n'y a qu'un remède,
C'est de tout casser.

Ô fanfares dans les soirs!
Ce sera barbare,
Ce sera sans espoir.
Et nous aurons beau la piétiner à l'envi,
Nous ne serons jamais plus cruels que la vie,
Qui fait qu'il est des animaux injustement rossés,
Et des femmes à jamais laides . . .
Que nul n'intercède,
Il faut tout casser.

Alléluia, Terre paria,
Ce sera sans espoir,
De l'aurore au soir,
Quand il n'y en aura plus il y en aura encore,
Du soir à l'aurore.
Alléluia, Terre paria!
Les hommes de l'art
Ont dit: «Vrai, c'est trop tard.»
Pas de raison,
Pour ne pas activer sa crevaison.

Aux armes, citoyens! Il n'y a plus de RAISON:

Il prit froid l'autre automne,
S'étant attardé vers les peines des cors,
Sur la fin d'un beau jour.
Oh! ce fut pour vos cors, et ce fut pour l'automne,
Qu'il nous montra qu' «on meurt d'amour»!
On ne le verra plus aux fêtes nationales,
S'enfermer dans l'Histoire et tirer les verrous,
Il vint trop tôt, il est reparti sans scandale;
Ô vous qui m'écoutez, rentrez chacun chez vous.

The capital intact,
The social pact.

Let no one intercede
It'll never be enough,
Just one cure guaranteed:
To smash up all this stuff.

Oh fanfares varying, every evening,
It will be barbarian,
No hope will it be leaving.
For us to vie in trampling it will be in vain,
We'll never be more cruel than life in giving pain.
That acts so some beasts are unfairly thrashed,
Some women ugly indeed . . . .
Let no one intercede,
All must be smashed.

Hallelujah, you Pariah Earth.
There'll be no hope, first light
Till come the night,
When there is nothing left of it there'll yet be some,
From night till light come.
Hallelujah, you Pariah Earth!
Men of the art have stated:
'In fact, it's too belated.'
No reason
Not to buck up and slit its weasan.

To arms, citizens! There's no more REASON:

He caught cold the other autumn,
Loitering to the miseries of horns
Towards the end of a fine day.
Oh, it was for your horns and it was for autumn
He'd shown us how one 'dies for love' that way!
On national holidays you won't see him from hence
Slide the bolt and lock himself in History's tomes.
He came too soon and went back, giving no offence.
Oh you who hear me speak, go back to your own homes.

VII SOLO DE LUNE

Je fume, étalé face au ciel,
Sur l'impériale de la diligence,
Ma carcasse est cahotée, mon âme danse
Comme un Ariel;
Sans miel, sans fiel, ma belle âme danse,
Ô routes, coteaux, ô fumées, ô vallons,
Ma belle âme, ah, récapitulons.

Nous nous aimions comme deux fous,
On s'est quitté sans en parler,
Un spleen me tenait exilé,
Et ce spleen me venait de tout. Bon.

Ses yeux disaient: «Comprenez-vous?
Pourquoi ne comprenez-vous pas?»
Mais nul n'a voulu faire le premier pas,
Voulant trop tomber *ensemble* à genoux.
(Comprenez-vous?)

Où est-elle à cette heure?
Peut-être qu'elle pleure . . .
Où est-elle à cette heure?
Oh! du moins, soigne-toi, je t'en conjure!

Ô fraîcheur des bois le long de la route,
Ô châle de mélancolie, toute âme est un peu aux écoutes,
Que ma vie
Fait envie!
Cette impériale de diligence tient de la magie.

Accumulons l'irréparable!
Renchérissons sur notre sort!
Les étoiles sont plus nombreuses que le sable
Des mers où d'autres ont vu se baigner son corps;
Tout n'en va pas moins à la Mort,
Y a pas de port.

VII   MOON SOLO

On top of the diligence I smoke awhile,
Paraded, face turned upward to the sky;
My carcass shaken, my soul is dancing high
In Ariel style;
No bile, no guile, mobile, my fine soul dancing by;
O mountain slopes, O valleys, smoke, O highways straight,
My fine soul, ah, let's recapitulate.

Like two fools we loved each other, crazed.
Then, no word said, one upped and went;
A spleen held me in banishment,
Spleen that all had raised. Good.

Her eyes blazed: 'Understand or not?
Why don't you ever understand?'
But neither wished to yield on either hand,
Hoping too much to kneel *together* on the spot.
(Understand or not?)

Where at this hour is she?
And she's in tears maybe . . .
Where at this hour is she?
Oh, at least, take care, I beg you, please!

O, on the road the freshness of the woods we skirt,
O shawl of melancholy, every soul's a bit alert,
How the life of me
Stirs jealousy!
This top-deck of the diligence is wizardry.

Let's gather in the irretrievable whole!
Our fate outdo, outbrave!
The stars outnumber all the sands that shoal
In seas where others watched her body bathe;
All goes no less to the grave;
There's no haven.

Des ans vont passer là-dessus,
On s'endurcira chacun pour soi,
Et bien souvent et déjà je m'y vois,
On se dira: «Si j'avais su . . .»
Mais mariés de même, ne se fût-on pas dit:
«Si j'avais su, si j'avais su! . . .»?
Ah! rendez-vous maudit!
Ah! mon cœur sans issue! . . .
Je me suis mal conduit.

Maniaques de bonheur,
Donc, que ferons-nous? Moi de mon âme,
Elle de sa faillible jeunesse?
Ô vieillissante pécheresse,
Oh! que de soirs je vais me rendre infâme
En ton honneur!

Ses yeux clignaient: «Comprenez-vous?
Pourquoi ne comprenez-vous pas?»
Mais nul n'a fait le premier pas
Pour tomber ensemble à genoux. Ah! . . .

La Lune se lève,
Ô route en grand rêve! . . .

On a dépassé les filatures, les scieries,
Plus que les bornes kilométriques,
De petits nuages d'un rose de confiserie,
Cependant qu'un fin croissant de lune se lève,
Ô route de rêve, ô nulle musique . . .
Dans ces bois de pins où depuis
Le commencement du monde
Il fait toujours nuit,
Que de chambres propres et profondes!
Oh! pour un soir d'enlèvement!
Et je les peuple et je m'y vois,
Et c'est un beau couple d'amants,
Qui gesticulent hors la loi.

Years will pass picking that bone;
Both harden for their own good care,
Often already I see myself there:
One tell the other: 'If only I'd known . . .'
But wouldn't both have said, if married too:
'If only I'd known; if only I'd known! . . .'?
Ah, cursèd rendezvous!
And heart no-exit zone! . . .
I've misbehaved, too true.

Faddists for happiness, us two,
So, what shall we do? With my soul, me;
She with her fallible youth?
O sinner woman growing long in the tooth,
Oh, the evenings I'll bring myself notoriety
In honour of you!

Her eyes were fluttering: 'Understand or not?
Why don't you ever understand?'
But neither'd yielded first on either hand
To kneel as one upon the spot. Ah! . . .

Moon's rising beam;
O road in full dream! . . .

The cotton-mills have passed, and sawmills those,
Then nothing more than milestones on and on,
Little clouds of confectioner's rose,
While a slender crescent moon raises its beam;
O dream road, O music gone! . . .
In these pine woods where, right
From the beginnings of the earth,
It was always night,
What rooms profound and decent in its girth!
Oh, for an evening of elopement there!
I people them; and see myself there straight,
And it's a noble loving pair
Of outlaws that gesticulate.

Et je passe et les abandonne,
Et me recouche face au ciel,
La route tourne, je suis Ariel,
Nul ne m'attend, je ne vais chez personne,
Je n'ai que l'amitié des chambres d'hôtel.

La lune se lève,
Ô route en grand rêve!
Ô route sans terme,
Voici le relais,
Où l'on allume les lanternes,
Où l'on boit un verre de lait,
Et fouette postillon,
Dans le chant des grillons,
Sous les étoiles de juillet.

Ô clair de Lune,
Noce de feux de Bengale noyant mon infortune,
Les ombres des peupliers sur la route . . .
Le gave qui s'écoute . . .
Qui s'écoute chanter . . .
Dans ces inondations du fleuve du Léthé . . .

Ô Solo de lune,
Vous défiez ma plume,
Oh! cette nuit sur la route;
Ô Étoiles, vous êtes à faire peur,
Vous y êtes toutes! toutes!
Ô fugacité de cette heure . . .
Oh! qu'il y eût moyen
De m'en garder l'âme pour l'automne qui vient! . . .

Voici qu'il fait très très-frais,
Oh! si à la même heure,
Elle va de même le long des forêts,
Noyer son infortune
Dans les noces du clair de lune! . . .
(Elle aime tant errer tard!)
Elle aura oublié son foulard,
Elle va prendre mal, vu la beauté de l'heure!

I pass on, leaving them to roam,
Lie back and face the empyreal;
The road winds on; I'm Ariel.
No one expects me; bound for no one's home;
For me, only the amity of rooms in some hotel!

Moon's rising beam,
O road in full dream!
O road without end,
The coach-inn's nearby,
Where lanterns light again,
A glass of milk's drunk dry;
Then postilion whip astir
In the crickets' chirr,
Under the stars of July.

O the Moonlight,
Wedding of Bengal flares drowning my plight;
The poplar shadows on the way we're bound . . .
Torrent that likes the sound . . .
The sound of its own song . . . beneath these
Inundations of the river Lethe's . . .

O moon Solo, soar;
My pen, you floor,
Oh! this night upon the road,
O Stars, you instil fear,
You're all there! The whole load!
O the fleeting of the moment here . . .
Oh! for some way
For me to keep the soul of it for autumn's day! . . .

It's so fresh here, so fresh the air;
Oh, and if at this very time,
She, too, is strolling by the woods somewhere
To drown her plight
In the wedding of the lunar light! . . .
(She so likes a late stroll!)
She'll have forgotten her stole;
She'll take sick, seeing the beauty of the time!

Oh! soigne-toi, je t'en conjure!
Oh! je ne veux plus entendre cette toux!

Ah! que ne suis-je tombé à tes genoux!
Ah! que n'as-tu défailli à mes genoux!
J'eusse été le modèle des époux!
Comme le frou-frou de ta robe est le modèle des frou-frou.

VIII   LÉGENDE

Armorial d'anémie!
Psautier d'automne!
Offertoire de tout mon ciboire de bonheur et de génie
À cette hostie si féminine,
Et si petite toux sèche maligne,
Qu'on voit aux jours déserts, en inconnue,
Sertie en de cendreuses toilettes qui sentent déjà l'hiver,
Se fuir le long des cris surhumains de la Mer.

Grandes amours, oh! qu'est-ce encor? . . .

En tout cas, des lèvres sans façon,
Des lèvres déflorées,
Et quoique mortes aux chansons,
Âpres encore à la curée.
Mais les yeux d'une âme qui s'est bel et bien cloîtrée.

Enfin; voici qu'elle m'honore de ses confidences.
J'en souffre plus qu'elle ne pense.

– «Mais, chère perdue, comment votre esprit éclairé
Et le stylet d'acier de vos yeux infaillibles,
N'ont-ils pas su percer à jour la mise en frais
De cet économique et passager bellâtre?»

Oh, I don't want to hear that cough from you!
Oh! I beg you, take care of yourself, please!

Ah, if only I'd fallen at your knees!
Ah, if only you'd fainted at my knees!
I would've been the model spouse of hes!
Just as the frou-frou of your gown's the model frou-frou for shes!

VIII   LEGEND

Armorial of anaemias!
Autumnal psalterion,
Offertory of all my cibory of happiness and genius,
To this host so feminine,
So little cough, malignant dry, mean,
Seen on desolate days like nobodies,
Set in cindery garb aware already of the winter to be,
Dodging along the superhuman cries of the Sea.

Grand passions, oh, not on that still? . . .

In any case, lips uninhibited,
Deflowered lips, and they,
Although to serenades long dead,
Still eager for prey,
But eyes of a soul that's well and truly cloistered away.

At last: here's one that honours me with confidences.
I suffer more from them than she senses.

– 'But, dear lostling, how come the infallible look
Of your eyes with its steel stylet, and your knowing spirit,
Have failed to pierce to open-work the pocket-book
Of this economical dandy coming across your path?'

– «Il vint le premier; j'étais seule près de l'âtre;
Son cheval attaché à la grille
Hénnissait en désespéré . . .»

– «C'est touchant (pauvre fille)
Et puis après?
Oh! regardez, là-bas, cet épilogue sous couleur de couchant!
Et puis, vrai,
Remarquez que dès l'automne, l'automne!
Les casinos,
Qu'on abandonne
Remisent leur piano;
Hier l'orchestre attaqua
Sa dernière polka,
Hier, la dernière fanfare
Sanglotait vers les gares . . .»

(Oh! comme elle est maigrie!
Que va-t-elle devenir?
Durcissez, durcissez,
Vous, caillots de souvenir!)

– «Allons, les poteaux télégraphiques
Dans les grisailles de l'exil
Vous serviront de pleureuses de funérailles;
Moi, c'est la saison qui veut que je m'en aille,
Voici l'hiver qui vient.
Ainsi soit-il.
Ah! soignez-vous! Portez-vous bien.

«Assez! assez!
C'est toi qui as commencé!

«Tais-toi! Vos moindres clins d'yeux sont des parjures.
Laisse! Avec vous autres rien ne dure.
Va, je te l'assure,
Si je t'aimais, ce serait par gageure.

«Tais-toi! tais-toi!
On n'aime qu'une fois!»

– 'He came first; I was alone beside the hearth;
His horse hitched to the railings neighed,
Like a desperate thing shook . . . .'

– 'Touching do (poor maid)
And what then?
Oh, look, over there, that epilogue under colour of a sunset view!
And, true, again,
Notice, now it's autumn, autumn once more!,
The casinos,
Deserted, store
Their pianos;
Yesterday, the orchestra attacked
Its last polka in fact;
Yesterday, towards the trains,
The last fanfare sobbed its strains . . .'

(Oh, how emaciated she is!
What will become of her?
Clots of memories,
Inure yourselves, inure!)

– 'And now then: telegraph poles,
In banishment's network knit,
Will serve as your women weeping funeral woe;
As for me, it's the season that means I go,
Here comes winter's spell.
So be it.
Ah! look after yourself. Keep well.

'Enough! Enough!
You started on this stuff!

'Shut up. The slightest lights in your eye are perjuries.
Give over! With your sort nothing lasts as it is.
So now. Let me assure you of this:
If I loved you it would be for a bet, miss.

'Shut up! Shut up, do!
Love comes once to you!'

Ah! voici que l'on compte enfin avec Moi!

Ah! ce n'est plus l'automne, alors
Ce n'est plus l'exil.
C'est la douceur des légendes, de l'âge d'or,
Des légendes des Antigones,
Douceur qui fait qu'on se demande:
«Quand donc cela se passait-il?»

C'est des légendes, c'est des gammes perlées,
Qu'on m'a tout enfant enseignées,
Oh! rien, vous dis-je, des estampes,
Les bêtes de la terre et les oiseaux du ciel
Enguirlandant les majuscules d'un Missel,
Il n'y a pas là tant de quoi saigner?

Saigner? moi pétri du plus pur limon de Cybèle!
Moi qui lui eusse été dans tout l'art des Adams
Des Édens aussi hyperboliquement fidèle
Que l'est le Soleil chaque soir envers l'Occident!...

IX

Oh! qu'une, d'Elle-même, un beau soir, sût venir
Ne voyant plus que boire à mes lèvres, ou mourir!...

Oh! Baptême!
Oh! baptême de ma Raison d'être!
Faire naître un «Je t'aime!»
Et qu'il vienne à travers les hommes et les dieux,
Sous ma fenêtre,
Baissant les yeux!

Qu'il vienne, comme à l'aimant la foudre,
Et dans mon ciel d'orage qui craque et qui s'ouvre,

Ah! At last someone's reckoned with Me, too!

Ah, autumn it no longer is, then the old
Banishment no more.
It's the gentleness of legends, of the age of gold,
Of legends of Antigones,
Gentleness that makes one register:
'When then did this happen before?'

It's of legends, its tints perfectly caught,
That, all child, I was taught,
Oh, nothing, let me tell you, like prints,
The beasts of the field and the fowls of the air
Engarlanding the majuscules of a missal's prayer,
Nothing so much there as to bleed, no mort?

Bleed? Me, from Cybele's purest oil of lemon pressed!
Me, who might have been for her in all Adamic arts
Of Edens as hyperbolically the loyalest
As is the Sun each evening to its western parts! . . .

IX

If of her own accord one had thought to drop by
Intending nothing more than taste my lips or die! . . .

Oh! Baptism!
Oh! baptism of my Reason for being here!
To steer an 'I love you!' to birth, to the chrism,
And that, through men and gods, he'd come,
Beneath my window appear,
Eyes lowered, dumb!

Oh, may he come, as love at first sight's lightning dart,
And in my stormy sky which cracks and spreads apart,

Et alors, les averses lustrales jusqu'au matin,
Le grand clapissement des averses toute la nuit! Enfin!

Qu'Elle vienne! et, baissant les yeux
Et s'essuyant les pieds
Au seuil de notre église, ô mes aïeux,
Ministres de la Pitié,
Elle dise:

«Pour moi, tu n'es pas comme les autres hommes,
Ils sont ces messieurs, toi tu viens des cieux.
«Ta bouche me fait baisser les yeux
Et ton port me transporte
Et je m'en découvre des trésors!
Et je sais parfaitement que ma destinée se borne
(Oh, j'y suis déjà bien habituée!)
À te suivre jusqu'à ce que tu te retournes,
Et alors t'exprimer comment tu es!

«Vraiment je ne songe pas au reste; j'attendrai
Dans l'attendrissement de ma vie faite exprès.

«Que je te dise seulement que depuis des nuits je pleure,
Et que mes sœurs ont bien peur que je n'en meure.

«Je pleure dans les coins, je n'ai plus goût à rien;
Oh, j'ai tant pleuré dimanche dans mon paroissien!

«Tu me demandes pourquoi toi et non un autre,
Ah, laisse, c'est bien toi et non un autre.

«J'en suis sûre comme du vide insensé de mon cœur
Et comme de votre air mortellement moqueur.»

Ainsi, elle viendrait, évadée, demi-morte,
Se rouler sur le paillasson que j'ai mis à cet effet devant ma porte.
Ainsi, elle viendrait à Moi avec des yeux absolument fous,
Et elle me suivrait avec ces yeux-là partout, partout!

And, then, the lustral deluges, not till morning past,
The great squeal of deluges all night long! At last!

Oh may She come! lowering those eyes of hers
And wiping her shoes
On the threshold of our shrine, O Ministers
Of Pity, O my forbears in queues,
She'd opine:

'For me, you're not like all those other men;
They're just those misters; you, you come down from the skies.
Your mouth makes me lower my eyes,
And your deportment's my transport
And I lay bare for it treasures of every sort
And I know perfectly where my destiny's bound
(Oh, to me it's already quite familiar)
Following you till the point you turn around,
And then to get out how you are!

'Indeed, I never think of anything else; I'll wait to tend
You in the tenderness of my life that's found its end.

'And may I just tell you the frights of nights I cry,
How my dear sisters really fear that I shall die?

'No taste for anything here; I weep in any old nook.
Sundays, how much I've wept in my prayer-book.

'You ask me why yourself and not another,
Ah, skip all that, it's clearly you and not another.

'I'm sure of that as of the numb void in my heart,
And of that air of deadly mockery on your part.'

– So she would come, a runaway and half-dead,
Rolling on the straw mat placed on purpose at the entrance to
        my homestead.
So she would come to Me with eyes in an absolute mad stare,
And she would follow me with those same eyes everywhere,
        everywhere!

X

Ô géraniums diaphanes, guerroyeurs sortilèges,
Sacrilèges monomanes!
Emballages, dévergondages, douches! Ô pressoirs
Des vendanges des grands soirs!
Layettes aux abois,
Thyrses au fond des bois!
Transfusions, représailles,
Relevailles, compresses et l'éternelle potion,
Angélus! n'en pouvoir plus
De débâcles nuptiales! de débâcles nuptiales!...

Et puis, ô mes amours,
À moi, son tous les jours,
Ô ma petite mienne, ô ma quotidienne,
Dans mon petit intérieur,
C'est-à-dire plus jamais ailleurs!

Ô ma petite quotidienne!...

Et quoi encore? Oh, du génie,
Improvisations aux insomnies!

Et puis? L'observer dans le monde,
Et songer dans les coins:
«Oh, qu'elle est loin! Oh, qu'elle est belle!
Oh! qui est-elle? À qui est-elle?
Oh, quelle inconnue! Oh, lui parler! Oh, l'emmener!»
(Et, en effet, à la fin du bal,
Elle me suivrait d'un air tout simplement fatal.)

Et puis, l'éviter des semaines
Après lui avoir fait de la peine,
Et lui donner des rendez-vous
Et nous refaire un chez nous.

Et puis, la perdre des mois et des mois,
À ne plus reconnaître sa voix!...

X

Oh, diaphanic geraniums, war-locked sortileges,
Sacrileges monomanic!
Enthusiasms, promiscuous spasms, douches! Oh, presses
Of vintages of the great evenings' successes!
Layettes at bay,
Thyrsi in woods hidden away!
Transfusions, reprisals,
Churchings, compresses and the eternal potion,
Angelus! To be worn out
With nuptial debacles! Nuptial debacles! . . .

And then, O my loves and lays,
All mine, her all-the-days,
O my unique one, my week-to-week-one,
In my little interior there,
That is to say: never more elsewhere!

O my little week-to-week one! . . .

And what else? Oh, a bit of genius,
Improvisations in nights insomnious.

And then? To watch her in the world,
And muse in odd nooks:
'How beautiful she looks! How far off, too!
Oh, who is she? Oh whose is she?
Coo, such a strange one! Oh, to talk to her! Oh, to walk her off!'
(And, in effect, at the end of the dance,
She'd follow me with an air of simply fatal chance.)

And then, to avoid her, weeks of it,
After upsetting her a bit,
And give her times to rendezvous
And make again a place for two.

And then for months and months to lose her track
Till not even her tone of voice comes back! . . .

Oui, le Temps salit tout,
Mais, hélas! sans en venir à bout.

Hélas! hélas! et plus la faculté d'errer,
Hypocondrie et pluie,
Et seul sous les vieux cieux,
De me faire le fou,
Le fou sans feux ni lieux
(Le pauvre, pauvre fou sans amours!)
Pour, alors, tomber bien bas
À me purifier la chair,
Et exulter au petit jour
En me fuyant en chemin de fer,
Ô Belles-Lettres, ô Beaux-Arts
Ainsi qu'un Ange à part!

J'aurai passé ma vie le long des quais
À faillir m'embarquer
Dans de bien funestes histoires,
Tout cela pour l'amour
De mon cœur fou de la gloire d'amour.

Oh, qu'ils sont pittoresques les trains manqués!...

Oh, qu'ils sont «À bientôt! à bientôt!»
Les bateaux
Du bout de la jetée!...

De la jetée bien charpentée
Contre la mer,
Comme ma chair
Contre l'amour.

Yes, Time soils everything
But, alas, never finishing.

Alas, alas! the aptitude for straying,
Hypochondriac pain and rain,
Loner who'll jaunt the old haunts
And prove myself the fool,
The fool without hearth or bath
(Wretched, wretched fool, amourless!)
For, then, sinking so low
To purify my flesh again,
Exulting, in the dawn chorus,
To avoid myself by train.
O Belles-Lettres, O Fine Art
Like an Angel set apart!

I shall have passed my life, daylight and dark,
On platforms failing to embark
On some pretty dreadful stories –
And all that for the love
Of my heart, mad for the glories of love.

Oh, how picturesque the missed trains look! . . .

Oh how 'So long! So long!' they are,
Boats from the far
End of the pier! . . . the sound

Pier, founded good and sound
Against the waves
As my body staves
Off love's.

XI   SUR UNE DÉFUNTE

Vous ne m'aimeriez pas, voyons,
Vous ne m'aimeriez pas plus,
Pas plus, entre nous,
Qu'une fraternelle Occasion? . . .
– Ah! elle ne m'aime pas!
Ah! elle ne ferait pas le premier pas
Pour que nous tombions ensemble à genoux!

Si elle avait rencontré seulement
A, B, C, ou D, au lieu de Moi,
Elle les eût aimés uniquement!

Je les vois, je les vois . . .

Attendez! Je la vois,
Avec les nobles A, B, C, ou D.
Elle était née pour chacun d'eux.
C'est lui, Lui, quel qu'il soit,
Elle le reflète;
D'un air parfait, elle secoue la tête
Et dit que rien, rien ne peut lui déraciner
Cette étonnante destinée.

C'est Lui; elle lui dit:
«Oh, tes yeux, ta démarche!
Oh, le son fatal de ta voix!
Voilà si longtemps que je te cherche!
Oh, c'est bien Toi, cette fois . . .»

Il baisse un peu sa bonne lampe,
Il la ploie, Elle, vers son cœur,
Il la baise à la tempe
Et à la place de son orphelin cœur.

Il l'endort avec des caresses tristes,
Il l'apitoie avec de petites plaintes,

XI ON A DEAD WOMAN

Come off it, you'd not be loving me,
Would you?, not loving me much more,
Much longer – between ourselves – than for
Some fraternal Opportunity? . . .
– Ah, she's not in love with me!
Ah, she wouldn't take the first step, not she,
For us to kneel together on the floor!

If she'd initially met, some week,
A, B, C, or D, instead of Me
Her love for each had been unique!

It's them I see, it's them I see . . .

Hang on! Now I can see her,
With the noble A, B, C, or D.
Oh, born for each of them was she.
It's him, Him, whatever character,
It's him she reflects;
She shakes her head with perfect pose, effects,
And says that nothing, nothing can extirpate
From her this astounding fate.

He's the One; she tells him:
'Oh your eyes, your bearing, too!
Oh, your voice's fatal chime!
Oh ages, I've been looking out for you!
Oh, You're exactly it, this time! . . .'

He turns her splendid lamp down now;
Against his heart he folds her, She;
He kisses her on the brow
And where her orphan heart must be.

With sad embraces he makes her sleep;
He stirs her pity with little plaintive things;

Il a des considérations fatalistes,
Il prend à témoin tout ce qui existe,
Et puis, voici que l'heure tinte.

Pendant que je suis dehors
À errer avec elle au cœur,
À m'étonner peut-être
De l'obscurité de sa fenêtre.

Elle est chez lui, et s'y sent chez elle,
Et comme on vient de le voir,
Elle l'aime, éperdûment fidèle,
Dans toute sa beauté des soirs!...

Je les ai vus! Oh, ce fut trop complet!
Elle avait l'air trop trop fidèle
Avec ses grands yeux tout en reflets
Dans sa figure toute nouvelle!

Et je ne serais qu'un pis-aller,

Et je ne serais qu'un pis-aller,
Comme l'est mon jour dans le Temps,
Comme l'est ma place dans l'Espace;
Et l'on ne voudrait pas que j'accommodasse
De ce sort vraiment dégoûtant!...

Non, non! pour Elle, tout ou rien!
Et je m'en irai donc comme un fou,
À travers l'automne qui vient,
Dans le grand vent où il y a tout!

Je me dirai: Oh! à cette heure,
Elle est bien loin, elle pleure,
Le grand vent se lamente aussi,
Et moi je suis seul dans ma demeure,
Avec mon noble cœur tout transi,
Et sans amour et sans personne,

He has deliberations fatalist and deep;
Witness he bids whatever is to keep;
When, there and then, his time rings.

Meanwhile I'm outside in the dark
To wander round with her at heart,
And wondering perhaps, to see
Her window dark as dark may be.

She's home with him, and feels at home,
And as one's just observed it, yes,
She loves him, wildly faithful grown,
In all her evening loveliness! . . .

I've seen them both. Oh, too much perfection!
That far too faithful air she'd shown,
Those big eyes giving full reflection
In that new face that's all her own!

And I would only be a stop-gap,

And I would only be a stop-gap,
As is my place in Space,
As is in Time my date;
And nobody would want me to accommodate
To such a fate, truly disgusting, base! . . .

No, no! For Her, all or nothing's the case!
I will arise and go, then, like a fool, in Fall
That's drawing on now at a pace,
In the high wind where there is all!

I'll tell myself: Oh, at this time of day
She's weeping, she's so far away,
And the high wind begins its crying,
Me, by myself, indoors, I stay,
Apart, my fine heart faint, and sighing,
No loved one, no one there at all,

Car tout est misère, tout est automne,
Tout est endurci et sans merci.

Et, si je t'avais aimée ainsi,
Tu l'aurais trouvée trop bien bonne! Merci!

XII

> *Get thee to a nunnery; why wouldst thou be*
> *a breeder of sinners? I am myself indifferent*
> *honest; but yet I could accuse me of such things,*
> *that it were better my mother had not borne*
> *me. We are arrant knaves, all; believe none of*
> *us. Go thy ways to a nunnery.*
>
> HAMLET

Noire bise, averse glapissante,
Et fleuve noir, et maisons closes,
Et quartiers sinistres comme des Morgues,
Et l'Attardé qui à la remorque traîne
Toute la misère du cœur et des choses,
Et la souillure des innocentes qui traînent,
Et crie à l'averse: «Oh! arrose, arrose
Mon cœur si brûlant, ma chair si intéressante!»

Oh, elle, mon cœur et ma chair, que fait-elle?...

Oh! si elle est dehors par ce vilain temps,
De quelles histoires trop humaines rentre-t-elle?
Et si elle est dedans,
À ne pas pouvoir dormir par ce grand vent,
Pense-t-elle au Bonheur,
Au bonheur à tout prix,
Disant: tout plutôt que mon cœur reste ainsi incompris?

Soigne-toi, soigne-toi! pauvre cœur aux abois.

For all is misery, all is Fall,
All's merciless and calcifying.

And, if I'd loved you just like this,
You'd have found it too much of a good one! Thank you, miss!

XII

> *Get thee to a nunnery; why wouldst thou be*
> *a breeder of sinners? I am myself indifferent*
> *honest; but yet I could accuse me of such things,*
> *that it were better my mother had not borne*
> *me. We are arrant knaves, all; believe none of*
> *us. Go thy ways to a nunnery.*
>
> HAMLET

Wind black; downpour's yelp and thresh;
River black; and licensed brothels enough;
And districts all as sinister as Morgues,
And this Guy Late who's dragging on the trace
All the misery of heart and stuff,
The soiling of naive girls who swan around the place,
And cries, 'Water, water,' in the downpour's face,
My ardent heart so parched, my so interesting flesh!'

Oh, she, my heart and soul, now what's she doing? . . .

Oh, if she's out in all this awful weather,
What all too human affairs was she pursuing?
And, if indoors, altogether
Unable to sleep in this high wind at the end of its tether,
Does she keep thinking of Happiness,
Happiness at all cost, and say:
Anything rather than my heart's misjudged this way?

Take care, take care of yourself! Poor cornered heart.

(Langueurs, débilité, palpitations, larmes,
Oh, cette misère de vouloir être notre femme!)

Ô pays, ô famille!
Et l'âme toute tournée
D'héroïques destinées
Au-delà des saintes vieilles filles,
Et pour cette année!

Nuit noire, maisons closes, grand vent,
Oh! dans un couvent, dans un couvent!

Un couvent dans ma ville natale
Douce de vingt mille âmes à peine,
Entre le lycée et la préfecture
Et vis-à-vis la cathédrale,
Avec ces anonymes en robes grises,
Dans la prière, le ménage, les travaux de couture;
Et que cela suffise . . .
Et méprise sans envie
Tout ce qui n'est pas cette vie de Vestale
Provinciale,
Et marche à jamais glacée,
Les yeux baissés.

Oh! je ne puis voir ta petite scène fatale à vif,
Et ton pauvre air dans ce huis-clos,
Et tes tristes petits gestes instinctifs,
Et peut-être incapable de sanglots!

Oh! ce ne fut pas et ce ne peut être,
Oh! tu n'es pas comme les autres,
Crispées aux rideaux de leur fenêtre
Devant le soleil couchant qui dans son sang se vautre!
Oh! tu n'as pas l'âge,
Oh, dis, tu n'auras jamais l'âge,
Oh, tu me promets de rester sage comme une image? . . .

(Listlessness, weakness, palpitations, tears,
Oh the misery that wanting to be our wife endures!)

O family, O native land!
And the soul quite bent
On heroic destinies that went
Beyond the holy old maids' – and
On this year intent!

Night black, licensed houses, wind high,
Oh, in a convent, in a convent try!

A convent in my birth-place, say,
Town cushy with twenty thousand souls near on,
Between the prefecture and the high school,
Facing the cathedral, with those grey
Habited anonymities comply
In prayer, in chores, in sewing tasks, the rule,
And may it satisfy . . .
And may you despise without desire
Whatever's not entirely this provincial Vestal's way
Of life, and may
You always frigidly tread,
Eyes lowered, bowed head.

Oh, I can't picture your little scene fatal to the quick,
And your air of wretchedness in that closed keep,
And your sad little instinctive gestures don't click,
And perhaps unable to sob and weep.

Oh! It wasn't and it cannot be like that,
Oh you are not like all of those,
Shrivelled behind their curtained window gazing at
The setting sun that flounders in its gory throes!
Oh, you're not that old,
Oh, say you'll never be that old,
Oh, you promise me you'll be as good as gold? . . .

La nuit est à jamais noire,
Le vent est grandement triste,
Tout dit la vieille histoire
Qu'il faut être deux au coin du feu,
Tout bâcle un hymne fataliste,
Mais toi, il ne faut pas que tu t'abandonnes,
À ces vilains jeux!...

À ces grandes pitiés du mois de novembre!
Reste dans ta petite chambre,
Passe, à jamais glacée,
Tes beaux yeux irréconciliablement baissés.

Oh, qu'elle est là-bas, que la nuit est noire!
Que la vie est une étourdissante foire!
Que toutes sont créature, et que tout est routine!

Oh, que nous mourrons!

Eh bien, pour aimer ce qu'il y a d'histoires
Derrière ces beaux yeux d'orpheline héroïne,
Ô Nature, donne-moi la force et le courage
De me croire en âge,
Ô Nature, relève-moi le front!
Puisque, tôt ou tard, nous mourrons...

The night's forever black,
The wind is highly sad,
All brings the old tale back:
It must be two in fireside chairs,
All bodges up a fatalistic hymniad,
But you, you don't have to let yourself in for this,
These shabby games for pairs! . . .

In these great pities of November gloom!
Stay in your little room,
Get by forever frigidly,
Your lovely eyes lowered irreconcilably, rigidly.

Oh, how black's the night! And she's out there in this!
What a bewildering fairground racket life is!
How creaturish they all are, and everything routine!

Oh, and we will die!

Ah well, to love whatever histories
Lie unseen behind those lovely eyes, orphan, heroine,
O Nature, give me courage and strength
To think myself of age at length,
O Nature, raise my confidence high!
Since, sooner or later, we'll die . . .

Poèmes divers

Other Poems

BALLADE DE RETOUR

Le Temps met Septembre en sa hotte,
Adieu, les clairs matins d'été!
Là-bas, l'Hiver tousse et grelotte
En son ulster de neige ouaté.
Quand les casinos ont jeté
Leurs dernières tyroliennes,
La plage est triste en vérité!
Revenez-nous, Parisiennes!

Toujours l'océan qui sanglote
Contre les brisants irrités,
Le vent d'automne qui marmotte
Sa complainte à satiété,
Un ciel gris à perpétuité,
Des averses diluviennes,
Cela doit manquer de gaieté!
Revenez-nous, Parisiennes!

Hop! le train siffle et vous cahote!
Là-bas, c'est Paris enchanté,
Où tout l'hiver on se dorlote:
C'est l'Opéra, les fleurs, le thé,
Ô folles de mondanité
Allons! Rouvrez les persiennes
De l'hôtel morne et déserté!
Revenez-nous, Parisiennes!

ENVOI

Reines de grâce et de beauté,
Venez, frêles magiciennes,
Reprendre votre Royauté:
Revenez-nous, Parisiennes!

BALLADE OF RETURNING

September's stolen in Time's swag.
Goodbye! Clear summer mornings go.
Here's Winter, cough and moan and gag,
Wearing his ulster of watered snow.
When the casinos close the show
With their last Tyrolean whirls,
The beach is sad, and truly so!
Return to us, Parisian girls!

Always, on reefs that lose their rag,
The ocean sobbing out its woe;
The autumn wind having its nag,
Its full complaint, and blow by blow.
A sky that's grey, forever low,
Diluvian cloudbursts, downpours, swirls.
This sort of thing lacks zip, you know.
Return to us, Parisian girls!

The train whistles, jolts you and bag!
You're off. Enchanted Paris ho,
Which coddles you through winter's drag:
The Opera, flowers, tea, to go,
Frivolities of worldly show,
Come! Reopen the shutters, churls,
On the glum hotel's deserted row.
Return to us, Parisian girls!

ENVOY

Queens of grace and beauty, oh,
Frail sorceresses, sling your pearls.
Resume your royal status quo.
Return to us, Parisian girls!

NOCTURNE

Je songe au vieux Soleil un jour agonisant,
Je halète, j'ai peur, pressant du doigt ma tempe,

En face, pourtant trois jeunes filles, causant,
Brodent à la clarté paisible de la lampe.

[J'ÉCOUTE DANS LA NUIT RAGER
LE VENT D'AUTOMNE]

J'écoute dans la nuit rager le vent d'automne,
Sous les toits gémissants combien de galetas
Où des mourants songeurs que n'assiste personne
Se retournant sans fin sur de vieux matelas
Écoutent au dehors rager le vent d'automne.

Sonne, sonne pour eux, vent éternel, ton glas!
Au plus chaud de mon lit moi je me pelotonne
Oui! je ferme les yeux, je veux rêver, si las,
Que je suis dans l'azur, au haut d'une colonne
Seul, dans un blanc déluge éternel de lilas.

Mais zut! j'entends encor rager ce vent d'automne.
Messaline géante, oh! ne viendras-tu pas
M'endormir sur tes seins d'un ron-ron monotone
Pour m'emporter, bien loin, sur des grèves, là-bas
Où l'on n'entend jamais jamais le vent d'automne.

NOCTURNE

I dream of the old Sun in its death throes one day;
I'm panting, fearful, a finger to my temple, right.

Opposite, though, three young girls, chattering away,
Embroider in the lamp's clear and peaceful light.

[ALL NIGHT I HEAR THE WIND OF AUTUMN ROAR]

All night I hear the wind of autumn roar.
Beneath the groaning roofs how many a glory-hole –
Where dying dreamers no one tends any more
On old mattresses endlessly twist and roll –
Can hear outside the wind of autumn roar.

Eternal wind, toll your knell for them, toll.
I curl myself up deep in the bed's warm core.
Yes, shut my eyes; I want, sick and tired of soul,
To dream that white eternal lilac showers pour
Through azure on me, lone upon my stylite pole.

But, dash it, still I hear the wind of autumn roar.
Giant Messalina, won't you come and let me loll
To sleep upon your steady purring breasts and soar
Away on them with you to some gold beach or mole
Where never, never to hear the wind of autumn roar?

LES BOULEVARDS

Sur le trottoir flambant d'étalages criards,
Midi lâchait l'essaim des pâles ouvrières,
Qui trottaient, en cheveux, par bandes familières,
Sondant les messieurs bien de leurs luisants regards.

J'allais, au spleen lointain de quelque orgue pleurard,
Le long des arbres nus aux langueurs printanières,
Cherchant un sonnet faux et banal où des bières
Causaient, lorsque je vis passer un corbillard.

Un frisson me secoua. – Certes, j'ai du génie,
Car j'ai trop épuisé l'angoisse de la vie!
Mais, si je meurs ce soir, demain, qui le saura?

Des passants salueront mon cercueil, c'est l'usage;
Quelque voyou criera peut-être: «Eh! bon voyage!»
Et tout, ici-bas comme aux cieux, continuera.

THE BOULEVARDS

On pavements loud with gaudy wares to buy
Noon freed from work the pale shop-girls and hands
To trot bareheaded, in the usual bands,
Sounding the men out well with the glad eye.

I went, to some far organ's grizzling cry,
Past trees, bare in the languor of vernal glands,
Seeking a fake, hack sonnet's opening strands,
Where beers were talking – when a hearse went by.

A shudder shook me. I've genius, not a doubt,
For I've zonked the agony of living out!
But if I die tonight who'll know I've gone?

People will respect my bier – that's what's done;
Some lout exclaim, perhaps: 'Good trip, my son!'
And all, here on earth as in heaven, carry on.

DANS LA RUE

C'est le trottoir avec ses arbres rabougris.
Des mâles égrillards, des femelles enceintes,
Un orgue inconsolable ululant ses complaintes,
Les fiacres, les journaux, la réclame et les cris.

Et devant les cafés où des hommes flétris
D'un œil vide et muet contemplaient leurs absinthes
Le troupeau des catins défile lèvres peintes
Tarifant leurs appas de macabres houris.

Et la Terre toujours s'enfonce aux steppes vastes,
Toujours, et dans mille ans Paris ne sera plus
Qu'un désert où viendront des troupeaux inconnus.

Pourtant vous rêverez toujours, étoiles chastes,
Et toi tu seras loin alors, terrestre îlot
Toujours roulant, toujours poussant ton vieux sanglot.

IN THE STREET

The pavement with its trees stunted and thin;
The pregnant women and the bawdy males;
Complaints an inconsolable organ wails;
The cabs, the dailies, adverts, all the din.

Past café fronts where gaunt men ponder in
Their absinthe, gaze blank and mute as veils,
File herds of whores with painted lips and nails,
Hiking up dismal houri tits and skin.

And Earth in vast steppes forever mired,
Forever, and when a thousand years have flown
Paris will be a waste of herds unknown.

And still you'll muse, oh chaste stars, untired:
And island Earth, be gone with a far lob,
Forever rolling, heaving your old sob.

[N'ALLEZ PAS DEVANT CES VERS-CI]

N'allez pas devant ces vers-ci,
Ô spécimen du faible sexe
En un accent très circonflexe
Courber votre divin sourcil.

Vous habitez une âpre rue
Vouée à Denfert-Rochereau
Mais d'ignorer quel numéro
Toute mon âme est fort férue.

Vous chantez comme un bengali
Un bengali bien égoïste
Qui ne veut plus qu'être un artiste

Et tenir le reste en oubli,
Ah! Triste, triste, triste, triste,
Oh! Sandâ, Sandâ Mahâli!

[DON'T COME ACROSS THESE LINES OF MINE]

Don't come across these lines of mine,
O sample of the weaker sex,
And raise up in a circumflex
Your eyebrows so divine.

In a harsh-sounding street you live
Honouring Denfert-Rochereau.
But to forget the number which I know
My soul is smitten with a sieve.

You sing like a Bengali – man –
Bengali most egotistic who
Would be the artist through and through

And keep all else from mind and scan.
Oh dismal, dismal, dismal, you;
Oh, Sanda, Sanda Mahali, oh, San.

Notes

Reference numbers to pages are given in roman type, followed (where necessary) by a colon and line numbers for the poem in question in italic. The notes are mainly concerned with the exigencies of translation, although some of the more obscure references are glossed.

The Complaints

TO PAUL BOURGET

27   Bourget was a minor novelist and poet who befriended and encouraged Laforgue. He was one of those who recommended Laforgue for the post of French reader in the Empress Augusta's court.

27:*3*   The reference to Laforgue's age as twenty perhaps shows this to be as early as the 'Autobiographical Preludes', though such literal readings are notoriously dubious.

27:*6*   Armida is the heroine of *Jerusalem Delivered* by Tasso. She charmed Rinaldo in a garden and kept him from the Crusades.

27:*14*   A reference to the Lac de Bourget.

27:*17*   *Les Aveux* ('The Vows') was the title of Bourget's book of poems published in 1882.

AUTOBIOGRAPHICAL PRELUDES

29   It is perhaps unfortunate that Laforgue insisted on the appropriateness of opening *The Complaints* with this long 'philosophical' and rather juvenile piece. On the other hand it does serve as a handy guide to the basic ideas which recur in his work. These are not difficult nor very original; the originality is in the variety of treatments that they receive. He could no longer believe in religion – he had been a strong Catholic – nor in personal freedom, seeing all existence as unconsciously driven by laws outside itself, just as were the stars and galaxies. His physiological studies sometimes made him see the body itself as a colony of various cells and organisms. (see 'Ballad' in *Flowers of Good Will*, p. 315). Later, in his poems of sexual encounters his attitude to women as agents of the law to go forth and multiply makes him regard their approach as a threat to his

independent intelligence. He also frequently blames their attitude on upbringing and has been seen as an early women's liberationist in his appeals to them to be more like brothers and peers than generative machines. Some commentators suggest this attitude to generation was influenced by his mother's life bearing a large family and dying shortly after a childbirth. His basic reaction to all this was to try to maintain an intellectual aloofness from the mechanical processes of the universe, an aloofness protected by irony, buffoonery and a pyrotechnic style. A second reaction was to simplify and, in Buddhist fashion, try to accept the system, switching off the abstracting intelligence, and going along with the unconscious flow of the universe. These ideas are a good rule-of-thumb guide through *The Complaints*. Three habitual words may as well be defined here.

The Inconscient: Laforgue's word for the process of the universe that pays no heed to the living or conscious. (A word which, incidentally, connects him to Hardy, a curious but instructive parallel.) This term as noun and adjective has been retained wherever possible in these versions to prevent confusion with Freudian and other usages of the term 'unconscious'.

The Ideal: a somewhat ironic term for the undetectable purpose the laws of the universe pursue.

The Unique: often used to represent private and personal experience and values. The Moon represents the detached ironic intellectual attitude. The Sun, and sunset, which in French can pun with bed/bedding, is used to represent the generative drive, and is frequently telescoped with rose windows of cathedrals, the sky and women's eyes which have immense forces of attraction and repulsion for him.

28:*3*   There's a sort of pun here where he telescopes 'Mardi gras' with 'Noël gras'. Not much can be done about that in translation.

28:*17*   The cathedral must be Notre Dame.

28:*18*   *Jourdain*: this is a punning reference to Molière's M. Jourdain and the Biblical River Jordan, presumably suggested by the Seine.

28:*25*   Laforgue was a Norman. It's a mystery why he calls himself a Breton. Probably he wished to play down autobiography or make some in-joke with friends. It might be a glancing reference to Corbière but he usually tried to play down any poetic connection in that direction.

30:*24*   *Galatea*: the name later given to the statue which Pygmalion made and then fell in love with. Laforgue telescopes her with Eve here. The name recurs quite often in his poems.

30:*30*   A parody of the *Ubi Sunt* tradition in poetry which might best be represented in Britain by Dunbar's 'Lament for the Makers'.

32:*15*   *Who loves me, follow me!*: a war-cry attributed to Philippe VI of Valois. He was apparently followed into battle by only one of his barons.

32:*21*   The Latin phrase means 'I am a worm and you are dust'. It is a mixture of quotations from the Bible.

34:*1*   *Errabundancy*: invented to match a neologism of Laforgue's from the same Latin root.

PROPITIATORY COMPLAINT TO THE INCONSCIENT

37   *Aditi*: mother of the twelve gods in Vedic mythology, representing Nature's generative powers.

The short verses parody the Lord's Prayer. Laforgue has a now rather dated and juvenile love of blasphemy which frequently recurs in *The Complaints* and less so afterwards.

39:*3*   The raft mentioned here may be a reference to a famous picture, 'Le Radeau de la Méduse' (The Raft of the Medusa) by Géricault, painted in 1819. On this raft, shipwrecked sailors were reported to have turned to cannibalism to survive.

PETITIONARY COMPLAINT OF FAUST JUNIOR

39   Guichard, as J. A. Hiddleston records, has suggested that this poem may be a parody of 'La Prière' by Sully Prudhomme:

> Ah! si vous saviez comme on pleure
> De vivre seul et sans foyers,
> Quelquefois devant ma demeure
>   Vous passeriez . . .
>
> (If you could know how the tears flow
> Living alone, no fireside yours,
> You'd sometimes find your walk would go
>   Past my doors . . .)

Indeed, the poem expresses a mood which Laforgue often felt and deflated ironically in his own poems.

39:*6*   *Your suns of Panurge*: a variant of the expression 'the sheep of Panurge', meaning 'followers of the general drift'. This reflects Laforgue's regular association of the sun with the blind forces of generation and his cosmic application of evolutionary ideas.

39:*15*   *your Double*: the French word is 'Sosie', from Molière's *Amphitryon*.

COMPLAINT TO OUR LADY OF EVENTIDE

41   The poem is a neat example of Laforgue's love of using religious imagery in a blasphemous way.

41:2   This introduces an abiding image of Laforgue's of a mechanistic evolutionary Nature as a factory of generation. In fact, he advised artist friends to look at industrial landscapes as a source for pictures – an attitude not shared by some of those he influenced.

41:12   *Crucigeals* attempts to create one of Laforgue's neologisms.

41:18   *Resexprocated* is an attempt at another of his rather awful inventions.

COMPLAINT OF VOICES UNDER THE BUDDHIST FIG TREE

42   Some editions claim that Laforgue omitted a 'd' from the word *bouddhique* ('Buddhist'). Misprint or not, it seems irrelevant, and it is therefore spelt normally here.

46:16   In the original text Laforgue appears to have made a dreadful pun by turning a word *sensuelles* (sensual) into *sangsuelles* (bloodsual – or some such). There is an erratum correcting the pun, though some say this is the printer's. To follow the printer makes things easier.

49:6   In the last line of the last speech of The Young People, the tight rhyme-scheme has required the use of the word 'plugged' in the sense of 'commercially promoted'.

49:22   It is some relief that the eastern context allowed the use of the word 'nautch' to solve a desperate rhyme problem.

COMPLAINT OF THIS GOOD MOON

51   Gradually the moon comes to represent for Laforgue the attitude of intellectual detachment from blind generative forces. Here, in this slight but amusing piece, she seems to represent a kind of human attachment versus the immensity of the universe. The opening and closing verses are a parody in the rhythm of the popular song 'Sur le pont d'Avignon', difficult to reproduce here.

COMPLAINT OF PIANOS HEARD IN THE PLUSHY QUARTERS

53   This finely wrought poem introduces Laforgue's obsession with the sound of piano practices. They seem to suggest to him the innocence of girls about to be swept involuntarily into the romantic/domestic image of woman.

55:2   *Rolands*: representing versions of the chivalrous knight as in *The Song of Roland*.

COMPLAINT OF THE WOMAN GOOD AND DEAD

57   This witty little poem is a sort of pantoum in form, an example
      of Laforgue's metrical skill and invention in creating a pattern
      of repeating lines. Only two rhymes are available in this form.
      A more lyrical example of a true pantoum is Baudelaire's
      'Harmonie du soir'.

57:9 The word translated 'carnation' is a crux that recurs in trans-
      lating Laforgue. The French word *œillet* means 'carnation',
      'eyelet' and, in Laforgue, 'little eye'. It thus has overtones for
      him of weddings, marriage and the generative forces. (He was
      very clothes-conscious and fascinated by women's dress – much
      eyeleted in those days.) The adjective *blanc*, describing it,
      means according to context 'white', 'blank', 'pure', in its dom-
      inant mode. Not much can be done about this in translation.
      'Iris' might suggest eyes and flowers but of the wrong connota-
      tions as would the 'whites' of the eyes.

COMPLAINT OF THE BARREL-ORGAN

59   Named in French after its inventor Barbarie, the organ suggests
      to Laforgue the idea of barbarian. (The adjectival form is used
      to name the dark ages.) The poem intercuts different stanza
      forms and voices as does 'Complaint of Pianos heard in the
      Plushy Quarters', a favourite device of Laforgue's.

61:7 *Corrosive ballets*: an image of the sexual dance or game.

COMPLAINT OF A CERTAIN SUNDAY

63   This poem, one of Laforgue's most moving and least ironic, has
      long been associated with his affair with the mysterious R, who
      appears cryptically in his agenda. Arkell's biography of
      Laforgue calls this in question, suggesting a more fleeting can-
      didate and proposing a solution to the mystery of R.

COMPLAINT OF ANOTHER SUNDAY

65   Some suggest the very odd syntax of the opening is a
      Laforguian glance at German syntax.

65:8 *Val-de-Grâce*: Laforgue lived in a flat opposite this view for
      some time.

COMPLAINT OF DIFFICULT PUBERTIES

69:9 *carnation eye*: an expansion to deal with the 'œillet' problem (see
      note on 'Complaint of the Woman Good and Dead' above).

COMPLAINT OF THE END OF DAYS

70:25 The French refers in its word for orphan (*orpheline*) to a Biblical text for which the Authorised Version gives 'comfortless'.

COMPLAINT OF THE POOR KNIGHT ERRANT

93   A bravura piece of exceeding vigour and boisterous rhymes, some difficult to render.

COMPLAINT OF NUPTIAL FORMALITIES

97   Laforgue is dealing cynically with French Romantic love poetry with its ubiquitous hexameters. For once, there seems a degree more sympathy for the woman. The hunting horn comes eventually to represent the sexual chase in his later poetry and seems here to suggest that the woman likes the chase but not the mort.

COMPLAINT OF THE BLACKBALLED

103   Some commentators regard this poem as a nasty piece of work. It is – but we now have only the poem to judge, not the woman it was a response to. Charenton was a mental hospital in Paris. The poem was originally called 'Complaint of a Sleepless Night' and might be more excusable with that title.

COMPLAINT OF CONSOLATIONS

107:*14*   *the all-weather business* is a quibble on costermongering and prostitution.

107:*23*   *thing*: some say Laforgue overlooked a misprint of *chose* for *choisi*, the standard French for 'chosen'. It seems to me one of his neologisms to emphasise that man is made of material stuff driven by the need to generate but in this instance the author himself is detached enough to be inanimate as an object.

107:*21*   *Whole* is capitalised here and in line 24 because it represents Laforgue's use of *Tout*, which has been used very positively in French verse to represent the Unity of the Universe. Laforgue's more negative approach is perhaps well served by the English homophone 'hole'. 'Whole' has been used as the standard translation wherever possible.

COMPLAINT OF GOOD COUPLES

109   Some critics have bridled at what they regard as the male chauvinism of this piece. The last verse, however, seems to suggest a relaxation of all such roles. And Laforgue might have retorted that he would expect a woman-artist to write in much the same vein, provided she had talent. (He was not so sure of Sanda Mahali in one of his uncollected poems. See p. 452.)

109:*7*   *skeye-blue pink* in verse 2 is a version of *œillet* again. This time the English jocularism has encouraged this eccentric one-off.

He might mean, though, the eye of the spout or a decoration on the pot or be glancing at the woman pouring the tea, possibly also a glance at the generative sun.

COMPLAINT OF LORD PIERROT

111   This poem and several following in *The Complaints* anticipate the clown/pierrot theme of the next book *The Imitation of Our Lady the Moon*. The opening parodies the famous French song 'Au Clair de la Lune'. I've done what I could to replicate the rhythm. The word 'lord' is used in the French also.

COMPLAINT OF THE WIND BORED AT NIGHT

121   The wind in Laforgue usually represents the passion of love – often when thwarted. The lover has spent one evening in nothing further than contemplation of the sexual encounter and imagines himself trapped by thwarted passion like an animal trapped in the wind outside the loved one's tower. In the last large verse he imagines his mausoleum in the form of a bathroom.

COMPLAINT OF THE POOR HUMAN BODY

125   The chorus of this poem uses a colloquial pronunciation of *belle* ('beautiful') for which the Australianism is the neatest answer.

COMPLAINT OF THE KING OF THULE

127   One of Laforgue's frequently anthologised poems, this shows what a range he was developing. His habitual theme of the sexual drive being a part of the deterministic universe is treated here with a lightness of touch. Irony is never entirely absent however.

COMPLAINT OF GREAT PINES IN A DESERTED VILLA

137   A finely wrought poem with the rhymes of the two-lined stanza consistent throughout. His parents were not buried in Alsace, a licence that has bothered some literal-minded commentators, as has the reference to Montmartre – which might conceivably be a self-mocking reference to his status as poet.

COMPLAINT OF THE POOR YOUNG MAN

147   This and the next poem show Laforgue's fascination with popular song, whose rhythms he likes to adapt. The original idea of the complaints came to him from hearing such a song. This one is difficult to render since it has one almost totally consistent set of rhymes throughout and a noisy near-meaningless refrain here left in the original sounds.

COMPLAINT VARIATIONS ON THE WORDS 'LIGHT BEAM, BEAM LIGHT'

155   Another light poem, playing with the word *falot* and the adjective *falotte*. The words mean: 'a ship's light', 'a beam', 'something trivial'. This has been impossible to match as neatly in English. The problem is exacerbated by the use of a running rhyme.

GRAND COMPLAINT OF THE CITY OF PARIS

161   The word translated 'white' in the sub-heading may quibble on 'sleepless'.

COMPLAINT OF THE SAGE OF PARIS

179   This is an early poem and one has the same reservations about it as expressed in the note to 'Autobiographical Preludes' (see above).

COMPLAINT OF COMPLAINTS

185   It became a habit of Laforgue's to end a collection with a self-disparaging poem. This is one of the neatest in form.

COMPLAINT-EPITAPH

187:6   *weal* might be taken as a pun extending both meanings of 'mortal'.

The Imitation of Our Lady the Moon

A WORD TO THE SUN FOR STARTERS

191   In verses 5 and 8, the word 'Phœbus' in French can be used to label an inflated euphuistic style of writing as well as the sun.

193:4   Hence the use of italics in my '*Sol*ecism' and the crazy pun *Phoebal / feeble*.

OPEN SEA

196:2   *mettre en rubriques* ('to put in rubrics') is a French idiom for 'to publish'; but the idea of cramming so much into an exam rubric in English seemed very Laforguian in spirit.

MOONSHINE

197   The scholars are opposed on the opening line. Anne Holmes has remarked of it: 'the meaning surely is "To think that I will ever live on that planet"'. But Hiddleston remarks of the line: '*Ne* is missing before *vivra*: a popular form.' This view would support

the translation 'never' rather than 'ever' – a reading, it seems to me, more consonant with Laforgue's habitual ideas when you consider the next line.

The poem is one of several in which Laforgue bends French prosodic principles by ending every line with the muted final *-e* which is normally alternated with other rhymes. In English this would give double rhymes throughout – which become rather clanging, not too witlessly so, I hope, here. Such rhymes also give an uneven syllable-count with which the standard English iambic measures are uneasy. I have tried to keep the count here also, and in one or two other poems where the French rhyme is disregarded in favour of standard English rhymes.

CLIMATE, FLORA AND FAUNA OF THE MOON

199   This sometimes witty but too often totally subjective catalogue is the sort of poem Laforgue could do in his sleep and it has helped to give him the reputation of being a purely verbal poet.

ONE-STRING GUITAR

203   Laforgue was fond enough of the somewhat tangential last word in this title to use it more than once. In colloquial French it occurs in a phrase for harping on and on; hence the added epithet to indicate a degree of tedium.

PIERROTS

205   Wherever possible 'Pierrot' is used as a translation of the identical French to avoid the connotation of clownishness in the more common English term. Sometimes metrical considerations have prevented consistency.

PIERROTS (*One has principles*)

213:*1*   The French idiom of doing things *pour des prunes* ('for prunes') means 'a waste of effort'. It has been retained here because of its British association with school dinners and their consequences.

PIERROTS (*Scene short but typecast*)

214:*5*   The French noun *agitation* has five syllables pronounced deliberately as an ironic reference to classical French prosody. Not much one can do about this.

ASIDES OF PIERROTS, IV

218:*9*   This line uses Laforgue's favourite *œillet* as a vocative. 'Pink' with its suggestion of naive youthful skin, seemed the best choice of translation here.

ASIDES OF PIERROTS, V

221:*12* Some commentators suggest that 'holocausts' might be Laforgue's oblique way of referring to abortion and its risks, then social, as well as medical.

ASIDES OF PIERROTS, XI

227:*4* The Latin refers to the Catholic liturgy *Ave maris stella* ('Hail, star of the sea').

ASIDES OF PIERROTS, XV

231 Laforgue rhymes single and muted final -*e* rhymes together here, sharing the same first vowel sound. I hope to suggest this by assonating the rhymes while slightly altering the final consonant sounds.

MOONS IN DISTRESS

235 Here Laforgue more or less anticipates Wilfred Owen by ending all the *a*-rhymes with the same consonant cluster. The *b*-rhyme is consistent throughout.

NIGHTLY

239 This is the sort of poem that Laforgue could write with the slightest glance at the moon. Verbal, again, but so much more amusing when he keeps it brief. The same is true of the next poem 'States', though, except for one crazy rhyme indicated by 'romantic/rum antic', it is by no means as neat.

THE MOON IS STERILE

243:*14* The French for 'Do', here, a variant spelling of the *Doh, re, mi*, is *Ut* which in several poems Laforgue uses to suggest 'uterus', it seems. This English slang is used as a nearly equivalent suggestion, hence the preference for the rarer spelling.

STERILITIES

247 This is no more than a crazy rhyming game with internal and running rhymes which are more or less indicated in this version. Line 3 is a reference to menses – which shows Laforgue's daring, and may partly explain his abiding moon image as the monthly guarantor that birth or abortion would not be required. The reference to Ophelia is another indication of Laforgue's growing obsession with *Hamlet* that dominates much of his later work.

LINEN, SWAN

249 This poem, virtually a diatribe against some woman, takes off as

yet another catalogue of enthusiastic disgust and fury at all
whitish materials associated with virginity, childbirth, hospi-
tals, perhaps influenced by his mother's death. Laforgue, the
clothes-conscious, is said by some commentators to have been a
bit of a voyeur. (Strange irony of fate that he married the
daughter of a man who dealt in corsetry.)

GAMES
257 In this poem Laforgue keeps an even syllable count if the muted
final *-e* of the rhyming is counted. I have used double rhyme but
kept the syllable count to nine to be a bit odd in English. I have
also used a four-stress line according to English practice. The
italic in the penultimate verse is a desperate measure at what
may well be a Laforguian pun on the German *lied*.

ADVISE, I BEG YOU
261 It was Laforgue's habit to close each book with a self-deprecat-
ing ironic poem; compare this one with 'Complaint of
Complaint' and 'Complaint-Epitaph' in *The Complaints*.
Lines 1–2: the poet voices the reader's complaint of all these
poems repeatedly about the moon.
Lines 5–10: he voices objections to his questioning of sexual
relationships, his obsession with the nothingness of death.
261:*17* Possibly a reference to his incipient tuberculosis.

Flowers of Good Will

Many of these poems seem to be about Laforgue's obsessive indecision
over whether he should marry Leah Lee, the woman he did eventually
marry. Poems XLI and XLII are perhaps clearest on this.

IV MANIAC
269:*1* *simples* (both in French and English) are herbs. The archaism is
retained since there could be a quibble in French on simpletons.
In a letter by T. S. Eliot to Conrad Aiken, 25 July 1914, occur
some lines which may have been suggested by this poem and
pianos elsewhere in Laforgue:

> The married girl who lives across the street
> Wraps her soul in orange-coloured robes of Chopinese.

VI RIGOURS LIKE NO OTHER

273   Laforgue is mocking love-souvenirs by making them speak as his version of masculine and feminine attitudes. The clipped form seems a mockery in itself.

X AESTHETIC

282:*14*   In French *faire l'ange* ('to make an angel') may mean to perform an abortion. Laforgue also plays on the nineteenth-century cliché of the 'angelic' woman.

XIV THE ETERNAL QUIDPROQUO

291   Mademoiselle Aïssé, according to Pascal Pia's researches, was a Circassian orphan brought to Paris, at the age of four, by a French diplomat. She described the brilliant society she joined, was much courted but the constant mistress of the Chevalier d'Aydie. She died in 1733 at the age of forty. Mondor was a foreign merchant who sold drugs and ointments in Paris a hundred and more years earlier. Laforgue ignores this anachronism.

XXII THE GOOD APOSTLE

307   In French colloquial speech a 'good apostle' can also be a sanctimonious old rogue.

XXVII PETTY MISERIES OF WINTER

317   This carefully wrought poem strikes many as obscure. It seems to mean something like this: there is no spontaneity or sincerity in the woman's expectation of love-making as she waits with all her finery ready. This puts off the Swan – white for detachment here – one of Laforgue's personas. He in turn has put her off by recalling her to the biological determinism of it all. The Swan pleads to escape this so that he may eventually return to save the woman also.

XLVII COMPLAINT OF CELIBATE DUSKS

363:*9*   *Strass* was a special glass invented by a German of this name for producing imitation gems for jewellery. It was apparently quite effective.

LI REDHIBITORY CASE (Marriage)

373   *Redhibitory*, a legal word, describes a purchase defective in such a way that it may be returned to the seller and restitution may be required.

LVI AIR ON BRETON PIPES

383   In this typically Laforguian signing-off poem, he uses a sort of

half rhyme in which the last consonant of the rhyme word is the only exact match and a match with all the other rhymes. It's not so marked in English without the muted final -*e* sounds.

Last Poems

These notes are mainly concerned with listing the sources of these free-verse poems in the formal first versions in *The Flowers of Good Will*.

I THE COMING WINTER

387   This poem as with most of the *Last Poems* is in free verse but heavily rhymed medially and finally. Again the sunset symbolises the routine dying of the generative powers. The horns represent the sexual chase and also the sounding of the mort at the death of the sun.

II THE MYSTERY OF THE THREE HORNS

395:7   The implications, ironic and otherwise, of the abrupt use of the word *gloires* ('glories') in the free-standing chorus lines may be more easily understood if one bears in mind what Hiddleston points out. When poems IX and X were first published in *La Vogue* as a single poem, they were given as epigraph a line of Petrarch's in a French version which may be translated as: 'Let's pause, love, and ponder on (or contemplate) our glory'. Laforgue uses the word in several of his poems, I think, with the Petrarch in mind.

III SUNDAYS

397   Elements of this poem derive from 'The Truth of the Matter' (p. 271), 'Celibate, Celibate, All's only Celibate' (p. 303), 'Station Beside the Sea' (p. 311), 'XXVIII: Sundays', (p. 319) and 'XXX: Sundays', (p. 323).

IV SUNDAYS

401   Elements derive from parts of 'XXX: Sundays' (p. 322).

V PETITION

405   Elements derive from 'The Life they Lead Me' (p. 341).

VII MOON SOLO

415   Elements derive from 'Arabesques of Unhappiness' (p. 375).

VIII LEGEND

421   Elements largely from 'XLIV: Sundays' (p. 358).

IX (*'If of her own accord one had thought to drop by'*)
425   Elements derive from 'Imagine a Bit' (p. 265). Almost the whole text is used with variations to rhythm and phrasing.

X (*'Oh, diaphanic geraniums, war-locked sortileges'*)
429   Elements derive from 'XXXVI: Sundays' (p. 338) but the image of sea departures is added.

XI ON A DEAD WOMAN
433   Elements derive from the last verse of 'Arabesques of Unhappiness' (p. 375).

Other Poems

BALLADE OF RETURNING
445   A ballade is a very formal poem with only one set of rhymes repeated in each verse. I am afraid 'churls' in the penultimate verse is a desperate rhyming addition. Laforgue maybe sometimes thought other people churlish but seldom said it as bluntly as this. An amusing poem introducing the autumn-winter motif which became almost habitual to him. It was first published in *L'Art et la Mode*, 1881, as Pia records.

NOCTURNE
447   Again the brevity and succinctness make rhyming difficulties. Laforgue himself did not specify the side of the temple in question. The poem exists as a single undated ms., published first, it appears, in Pia's edition.

[ALL NIGHT I HEAR THE WIND OF AUTUMN ROAR]
447   Again, autumn and one set of rhymes. The poem exists as a single undated ms., again appearing first in Pia's edition.

[DON'T COME ACROSS THESE LINES OF MINE]
453   First published in *La Revue Blanche*, 1 April 1895. An amusing story is thought to lie behind this poem. Laforgue had promised to visit the woman mentioned on one of his visits back to Paris. The flirtatiousness had got more serious than he needed and he chickened out of the encounter. His hotel, though, was in the street mentioned and he was probably seen going in and out with all the time in the world to drop by. The word 'smitten' represents a French word used almost equally exclusively for being overcome by love.

Notes on the Text

As with the notes on the text, reference numbers to pages are given in roman type, followed (where necessary) by a colon and line numbers for the relevant poem in italic.

Les Complaintes

PRÉLUDES AUTOBIOGRAPHIQUES
32:*26* *L'être est forme* . . .: Pia reads 'en' for 'est'. Collie and Hiddleston as here.

COMPLAINTE DES VOIX SOUS LE FIGUIER BOUDDHIQUE
For this title, see the note on the translation of the poem.
42:*00* Here and in Hiddleston the accent Laforgue or printer omitted from 'Alléluia' is restored.
44:*17* *Tièdes, je* . . .: Laforgue printed a capital J here, or at least the printer did. It hardly makes an emphasis.
46:*16* *sangsuelles*: arguably, an erratum corrected this awful pun.

COMPLAINTE DE CETTE BONNE LUNE
50 Here the verses have been indented to show the voices more clearly.

COMPLAINTE DES PRINTEMPS
76:*6* M. Debauve acquired proofs which, among other variants, read 'éternel' for 'impudent'. The latter seems more Laforguian.
78:*11* In the penultimate couplet-stanza the comma ending line 1 has been added here. Also added is the accent in the final word of the last couplet-stanza.

COMPLAINTE DES FORMALITÉS NUPTIALES
96:*12* The accent on 'Alléluia' has been restored.

COMPLAINTE DES CONSOLATIONS
106 In stanza 2, a comma has been inserted after 'Les Landes'.

COMPLAINTE DU VENT QUI S'ENNUIE LA NUIT
120–2 The chorus lines have been realigned to reflect the rhyme-scheme.

120:*8* Here Pia reads 'la' for 'ta'. He records no variant reading in his notes but both Hiddleston and Collie read 'ta' which seems preferable.

COMPLAINTE DU ROI DE THULÉ
128:*1* In the opening line of the third verse, 'Voile' has been capitalised to match the other occurrences in the poem. A comma has been inserted to end the penultimate line of the penultimate verse.

COMPLAINTE DES CLOCHES
134:*5* In verse 5, an exclamation mark has been omitted after 'lys' as being supernumerary.

COMPLAINTE DE L'OUBLI DES MORTS
144–6 The lines of the chorus verses have been aligned to reflect the rhyme scheme.

COMPLAINTE DU PAUVRE JEUNE HOMME
146–50 The second line of each verse is ended here with a comma throughout for reasons of syntax and consistency, whereas Laforgue ended only verse 2 in this way, using semi-colons in the other verses. In verse 4 a comma has been inserted before the footnote reference number, to match the punctuational point before the refrain as in the other verses.

COMPLAINTE VARIATIONS SUR LE MOT «FALOT, FALOTTE»
156:*18* In verse 6, a comma has been inserted at the end of line 4 to mark off the following parenthesis. In this verse also a small 'j' replaces the capital originally used for 'janviers' – which was more likely to be the printer's than Laforgue's.

COMPLAINTE D'UNE CONVALESCENCE EN MAI
174:*15* Several editions print 'Qui m'a jamais rêvé?' here. It seems a possible Laforguianism. However, Collie thinks it should be 'Qui n'a . . .', the reading followed here.

L'Imitation de Notre-Dame la Lune

UN MOT AU SOLEIL POUR COMMENCER
190:*8* A comma, nowadays supernumerary, has been removed from before the dash.

CLIMAT, FAUNE ET FLORE DE LA LUNE

200:*1*   Pia prints a comma after 'par caravanes' and before the dash.

202:*4*   In the penultimate verse Laforgue's odd spelling of 'Éginètes' has been retained.

PIERROTS, IV

208   The speech-marks in the second verse of part IV are an addition for the sake of clarity.

PIERROTS (*On a des principes*)

212   A text of this poem, published in 1892, differing from this one, has a most Laforguian opening line: 'Elle disait de son air blond fondamental'. One is tempted to regard it as a splendid after-thought. The internal chiming is suggestive of the internal rhymes of *Derniers Vers*.

STÉRILITÉS

246:*6*   Hiddleston ends the opening word of verse 2 without an 's'; Pia ends it with one.

Des Fleurs de Bonne Volonté

II FIGUREZ-VOUS UN PEU

264   The bracket Laforgue opens at verse 3 has been closed at the end of the same verse, though he did not. It does not make much sense for it to close at the same point as the second set at the end of line 10 where, in any case two closing brackets would then be required.

IX PETITES MISÈRES DE JUILLET

281   In the penultimate stanza a capital J has been removed from 'Janvier' as more likely the printer's than Laforgue's.

XVI DIMANCHES

294:*16*   Pia retains a fairly useless full stop, discarded here, after the bracket in the penultimate verse.

XVII CYTHÈRE

296   An exclamation mark has been inserted after 'ah' in line 2. A comma has been removed from the end of the first line of verse 3.

XVIII DIMANCHES

298   In the opening line of the last verse Laforgue's question-mark has been moved outside the closing speechmarks. That seems to be the logic of the sentence.

XIX ALBUMS

300:27 The English spelling of 'comfort' is actually what Laforgue used.

XXIV GARE AU BORD DE LA MER

310   Speechmarks have been removed from the start of lines 2 to 4 in verses 3 to 6.

XXIX LE BRAVE, BRAVE AUTOMNE

320   A comma has been added at the end of the third line of the last verse, which is in all other respects identical to the first stanza.

XXXIII FIFRE

328   A full stop has been added before the closing bracket of verse 4. In verses 5 and 6 the repeated speechmarks have been removed from lines 2, 3 and 4, and 1, 2, and 3, respectively.

XXXVII LA VIE QU'ELLES ME FONT MENER

340   In verse 3 a fairly meaningless semi-colon has been removed before the dash in the penultimate line.

XXXIX PETITES MISÈRES D'AUTOMNE

348:1 A comma before the dash has been removed as unnecessary.

XLIV DIMANCHES

358:25 A comma has been removed from the end of the line, after 'grisaillent'.

L LA MÉLANCOLIE DE PIERROT

370   A poem 'XLIX Rouages' is indicated in Laforgue's manuscript but has not been found. Hence the gap in numbering.

Derniers vers

385   The epigraphic material from *Hamlet* is somewhat eccentric in Laforgue's use. He has signed Hamlet's letter to Ophelia as his own, for example. The wording of the verse is correct but Polonius's speech is not presented as the next in Shakespeare.

I L'HIVER QUI VIENT
386:*19* A comma has been added to close line 4 of the fifth stanza.

VII SOLO DE LUNE
418   In the stanza opening 'Ô clair de Lune', Laforgue precedes each
       set of omission marks closing the last four lines with commas.
       Hiddleston removes the first and last. But it seems all are
       unnecessary.
420:*1* In the 6th line from the end a comma has been inserted after
       'toi'.

IX *('Oh! qu'une, d'Elle-même, un beau soir, sût venir')*
426:*5* In stanza 4 a comma has been added after 'aïeux' to close line 3.

XII *('Noire bise, averse glapissante')*
436:*15* A comma has been added after 'prix'.

Brief Bibliography

Poésies complètes, ed. Pascal Pia (Gallimard, Paris, 1970)

Les Complaintes et les premiers poèmes, ed. Pascal Pia, (Gallimard, Paris, 1979)

L'Imitation de Notre-Dame la Lune; Des Fleurs de bonne volonté, ed. Pascal Pia (Gallimard, Paris, 1979)

Les Complaintes, ed. Michael Collie (Athlone Press, London, 1977)

Poems: Jules Laforgue, ed. J. A. Hiddleston (Blackwell, Oxford, 1975)

Looking for Laforgue (an informal biography), David Arkell (Carcanet Press, Manchester, 1979)

Selected Writings of Jules Laforgue, ed. and translated by William Jay Smith (Grove Press, New York, 1956)

Moral Tales, translated with an introduction by William Jay Smith (New Directions, New York, 1985)

Martin Bell: Complete Poems, ed. Peter Porter, page 58 (Bloodaxe, Newcastle upon Tyne, 1988)

Hart Crane: Complete Poems, ed. Brom Weber, pages 33–34, 132–34 (Bloodaxe, Newcastle upon Tyne, 1984)

Index of French Titles

Index of English Titles